The Essence *of* Style

How the French Invented High Fashion, Fine Food, Chic Cafés, Style, Sophistication, and Glamour

JOAN DeJEAN

FREE PRESS
NEW YORK   LONDON   TORONTO   SYDNEY

FREE PRESS
A Division of Simon & Schuster, Inc.
1230 Avenue of the Americas
New York, NY 10020

First Free Press paperback edition 2006

FREE PRESS and colophon are trademarks
of Simon & Schuster, Inc.

For information about special discounts for bulk purchases,
please contact Simon & Schuster Special Sales:
1-800-456-6798 or business@simonandschuster.com.

Designed by Dana Sloan

Manufactured in the United States of America

3   5   7   9   10   8   6   4

The Library of Congress has cataloged the hardcover edition as follows:

DeJean, Joan E.
The essence of style : how the French invented high fashion, fine food, chic cafés,
style, sophistication, and glamour / Joan DeJean.
p. cm.
Includes bibliographical references and index.
1. France—Social life and customs—17th century. 2. Louis XIV, King of France,
1638–1715—Influence. 3. Fashion—France—History—17th century. 4. Cookery,
French—History—17th century. I. Title.

DC128.D454 2005

391'.00944'09032—dc22   2005040019

ISBN-13: 978-0-7432-6413-6
ISBN-10:   0-7432-6413-4
ISBN-13: 978-0-7432-6414-3 (Pbk)
ISBN-10:   0-7432-6414-2 (Pbk)

Contents

The
Essence
of Style

INTRODUCTION

Living Luxe

Why is it that people all over the world share the conviction that a special occasion becomes really special only when a champagne cork pops? And why is that occasion so much more special when the sparkling wine being poured is French? Why are diamonds the status symbol gemstone, instantly signifying wealth, power, and even emotional commitment? What makes fashionistas so sure that a particular designer accessory—a luxe handbag, for instance—will be the ultimate proof of their fashion sense that they are willing to search high and low for it and, if necessary, wait for months for the privilege of paying a small fortune to acquire it? Why is having a haircut from the one-and-only stylist, and that stylist alone, so essential to the psychic well-being of so many that it seems they would do almost anything to make sure that less magic scissors never come near their hair?

All these dilemmas, and many other mysteries of the fashionable life as well, first became what we now call issues at the same period—what may well be the most crucial period ever in the history of elegance, élan, and luxury goods. At that moment, Louis XIV, a handsome and charismatic young king with a great sense of style and an even greater sense of history, decided to make both himself and his country legendary. When his reign began, his nation in no way exercised dominion over the realm of fashion. By its end, his subjects had become accepted all over the Western world as the absolute arbiters in matters of style and taste, and his nation had found an economic mission: it ruled over the sectors of the luxury trade that have dominated that commerce ever since.

This book chronicles the origins of fashion and gastronomy and the process that brought luxury goods and luxurious experiences into the lives of people all over the Western world. It tells how the young King succeeded in giving his nation's culture a unique definition. It also describes how he accomplished something far more impressive: he set new standards for food, fashion, and interior decoration, standards that still provide the framework for our definitions of style.

Experiences that range from dining out in a fashionable spot to shopping in a chic boutique for a must-have fashion accessory or a diamond ring; luxury products such as champagne, as well as some of the dishes we most love to savor while we sip it (crème brûlée, for instance)—all of them came into being at the same moment. The extraordinary wave of creativity that swept over France under Louis XIV's patronage unleashed desires that now seem fundamental. Without the Sun King's program for redefining France as the land of luxury and glamour, there would never have been a Stork Club, a Bergdorf Goodman, a Chez Panisse, or a Cristophe of Beverly Hills (and President Clinton would never have dreamed of holding Air Force One on the runway of LAX for an hour while Cristophe worked his styling magic on his hair).

The story of Louis XIV and of France at the defining moment of its history, the half century between 1660 and Louis XIV's death in 1715, is a saga that forces us to ask ourselves just how it is that countries and cities acquire a personality or a sense of definition. In most cases, no one person can be said to be responsible for these national images. The characteristics on which they are based—Dutch cleanliness, German precision—are the product of the shared sociopsychological makeup of a people.

But in the case of France, a national personality was the product of the type of elaborate and deliberate image making of which Hollywood or Madison Avenue would be proud. In the sixteenth century, the French were not thought of as the most elegant or the most sophisticated European nation. By the early eighteenth century, however, people all over Europe declared that "the French are stylish" or "the French know good food," just as they said, "the Dutch are clean." France had acquired a sort of monopoly on culture, style, and luxury living, a position that it has occupied ever since. At the same time, Paris had won out over all its obvious contemporary rivals—Venice, London, Amsterdam—and had become universally recognized as *the* place to find elegance, glamour, even romance. Beginning in the late seventeenth century, travelers were saying what novelists and filmmakers are still repeating: travel to Paris was guaranteed to add a touch of magic to every life.

Most remarkable of all is the fact that, from this moment on, that touch of magic became widely desired: elegance, luxury, and sophistication became factors to be reckoned with, to an extent never before conceivable. Within restricted, elite circles, sophisticated food and elegant dress had always been aspired to. Some of the trends described here had precedent, for example, in ancient Rome. At different moments, certain nations had been widely thought to be more knowledgeable about the luxurious life than others: during the Renaissance, for example, Italy set the standards for fine dining and dress.

All these earlier incarnations of the good life are, however, different in three essential ways from what was put into place in seventeenth-century France. First, their impact was always extremely limited: very few people outside of Italy ever dressed or ate in the Italian manner; even within Italy, the new luxury rarely touched the lives of those outside court circles. Second, even though we would surely agree that what was then considered a fabulous feast or a sumptuous outfit was indeed extraordinary, none of those fashions are still being copied. Finally, never before had a city ruled over the empire of style and sophistication for more than a brief period. In the 1660s, Paris began a reign over luxury living that still endures, three and a half centuries later. This happened because the French understood the importance of marketing: thus, when fashion became French, the fashion industry began, along with concepts such as the fashion season that continue to be essential to that industry's functioning.

The institutions, the values, and the commodities that came into existence under Louis XIV's patronage marked a radically new departure for the realm of luxury. For the first time, new standards for elegant living transcended all the barriers, both geographic and social, that had previously limited their influence. A French shopgirl would certainly not have been able to afford an entire outfit in the latest fashion. Even if she got only one new accessory, however, she wanted to get it just right—the right cut, the right color, to be worn the right way—and she wanted it to be beautiful. Indeed, one late-seventeenth-century commentator prepared foreigners planning a trip to Paris for a new experience: "Every ordinary woman there will be more magnificently dressed than the finest ladies in their home nations."

People in cities all over Europe became slaves to French food, fashion, and design, and to food, fashion, and design that imitated as closely as possible what was being created in Paris. As the German lawyer and philosopher Christian Thomasius announced in 1687: "Today we want everything to be French. French clothes, French dishes, French furniture." And even before the United States was a nation—as soon as the new cities in North America had populations large enough to constitute a market—we became a society of consumers: in matters of taste and style, many of the original American conspicuous consumers began to dream of dancing to the French drummer, too.

The refashioning of France did not take place because the French had somehow become inherently more elegant or had suddenly been genetically endowed with the most refined palates in the world. Today at least, the French do share characteristics that support their national image—they like to talk about food, particularly while putting away prodigious repasts, far more than, say, the English; an abnormally high percentage of French women have the fabulous bodies that make fashion into a statement without ever having sweated through a step class. It's not important that we'll never know whether any of this was already true in the seventeenth century, for one thing at least is clear: the transformation of the French into gourmets and fashion queens was a matter of much more than shared national propensities. It was truly an affair of state.

During the summer of 1676, Louis XIV came up with what some saw as one of the more eccentric of his many plans for the beautification of Paris. He imported hundreds of wildly expensive white swans to add a touch of elegance to the Seine. He ordered a colony established on a small island directly opposite the capital's favorite promenade, the Cours-la-Reine; Parisians and visitors could thus take a stroll, display their latest finery, and observe the exotic birds, all at the same time. The birds were also perfectly positioned so that anyone traveling from Paris to Versailles would have a view of them along the way. Critics pointed out that the noble birds were not cut out for the polluted and congested waters of a river that then bustled with the transport of merchandise to and from the French capital. The King would have none of it. It was style he was after, and style he was determined to get. It is hardly surprising that—despite the numerous laws that were passed to protect their nests—many of the King's exotic birds died. What is amazing is that so many of them survived that, more than half a century later, the head of the Parisian police was still personally looking out for their well-being.

From the beginning, it was always thus. Louis XIV seems to have known exactly the image he wanted conveyed when anyone thought of Paris or of France, an image of graceful elegance and tasteful opulence. In order to achieve this goal, every detail received his personal attention—from swans to streetlights for his capital city to the heels for men's shoes. "Louis XIV thought of everything," remarked one of his greatest admirers, Voltaire; "not only did great things happen during his reign, but he made them happen." In almost all cases, he not only succeeded in achieving his goals; those goals, once achieved, have since become synonymous with what we now think of both as a quintessentially French look and as the essence of style.

Even his methods are still our methods. Ours is an age in which everything from supermarkets to drugstores to cafés can increasingly be found open, as we now say, 24/7. The frontier between day and night is constantly being eroded because we refuse to wait for what we want. As long as the asparagus are tasty and the blooms beautiful, we don't care where they were grown. Critics may rail against our desire to dominate nature, but it has become a fact of life. And it means that Louis XIV is someone our instant-gratification society can understand. Like us, he wanted what he wanted when he wanted it: baby peas, bright lights, more diamonds than anyone had ever seen. When nature was against him, he had the technology invented that would make it bow to his desires. His life and his person were an advertisement for the passion for aesthetic perfection. The first customers for the fabulous new French fashions and cuisine and design also wanted a piece of the Sun King's very own style.

In 1660, Paris was poised to leave its mark on the Western world. In the course of the seventeenth century, and particularly during the century's final decades, Paris more than doubled in size. By 1700, Paris and London were about the same size (roughly 550,000 inhabitants), the largest cities in Europe, and virtually tied for the position of fourth-largest city in the world—after Constantinople, Edo (today's Tokyo), and Beijing. They had left far behind the many European cities—Venice, Prague, Naples,

Rome—that had been only slightly smaller at the beginning of the century. Amsterdam had also known a growth spurt during the same period, but it never rivaled the two leaders. During the eighteenth century, London would continue its remarkable growth, whereas Paris remained stationary. But when Louis XIV began his reign, France's capital was on the move, undergoing one of the most spectacular periods of expansion in its history.

Louis XIV is remembered as the most powerful monarch in French history, the king who transformed France into a modern nation. In the early 1660s, at the beginning of his personal reign, he consciously set out to make France different from all its European rivals. In particular, he wanted to overshadow the country he contemptuously referred to as "that nation of shopkeepers," the Dutch, then Europe's greatest mercantile and shipping power. (He put England, Holland's foremost rival in these domains, in the same category.) The King resolved that France would become a mercantile superpower and that it would achieve this status fully on its own terms. With the help of his *contrôleur général des finances*, or minister of finance, Jean-Baptiste Colbert—the man who wrote the modern book on economic protectionism and trade wars—he was determined to corner for his country a hugely lucrative market: the luxury trade.

The partnership between the style-obsessed monarch and the hard-nosed businessman was a marriage made in heaven that was the guiding force during the key decades (1661–1683) for the invention of France's new national image. Together, they invented in particular the perfect partnership between art and merchandising: the King always required absolute stylistic perfection; Colbert kept his eye resolutely on the bottom line. Together, they created the first economy driven by fashion and taste. Because of their partnership, luxury commerce was, well, made commercial to a previously unheard-of degree. Colbert worked closely with the country's business elite; he made sure that every aspect of high-end merchandising—from trade regulations to import duties—was tailored to favor his nation's business community.

The foundation of the economic policy that Colbert imposed on France was simple: a nation's prosperity and strength were directly tied to the quantity of gold and silver it held in reserve. In order to increase this supply, imports had to be kept as low as possible, exports as high as possible. Those decades during which Colbert was in office were also the moment at which France knew its most acute monetary crisis of the seventeenth and eighteenth centuries. For centuries after the conquest of the New World, precious metal had entered into circulation in France via Spain: just after the mid-seventeenth century, this source suddenly dried up.

In such an economic climate, Colbert's bottom line was plain: first, to make sure that all the goods Louis XIV considered essential to the promotion of his image as the wealthiest, the most sophisticated, and the most powerful monarch in Europe would be produced in France and by French workers; and second, to make certain that as many people as possible would be slavishly following the Sun King's dictates and buying only the same French-made luxury goods that the King featured at Versailles. Colbert accomplished his mission so successfully that one of his eighteenth-century successors, the Genevan banker Jacques Necker, who was among the last finance ministers to serve the French state before the Revolution of 1789, paid him the ultimate compliment, businessman to businessman: "For the French, taste is the most fruitful of businesses." The King created new standards for luxury that were accepted as inherently French, and Colbert saw to it that every product that could be linked to that look had been marketed as widely as possible. And we think that Hollywood and Madison Avenue are only now inventing tie-ins.

Thus, virtually under royal decree, France embarked upon the most extraordinary age of creativity in its history. By the end of the seventeenth century, the two concepts that have ever since been most essential to both the country's fame and its trade balance had been invented and had immediately become inextricable from France's national image: haute cuisine and haute couture. At the same time, a number of professions were created that even today remain essential to the self-image of the nation that rein-vented elegance and style: the world was introduced to the first celebrity chefs, celebrity couturieres—and even the first celebrity hairdressers. Institutions that have remained central to the experi-ence of Paris had come into existence: among them, the first ele-gant cafés anywhere; the prototype for today's most famous flea market, Paris's marché aux puces; the original restaurant scene; and an amazing variety of upscale boutiques—for instance, the concentration of fancy gem stores and jewelry merchants near the Place Vendôme that tourists still ogle today.

France's national image was the product of a collaboration between a king with a vision and some of the most brilliant artists, artisans, and craftspeople of all time—men and women who were the founding geniuses in domains as disparate as wine making, fashion accessorizing, jewelry design, cabinetry, codifica-tion of culinary technique, and hairstyling. There was a second collaboration: between Louis XIV and a series of brilliant inven-tors, the creators of everything from a revolutionary technology for glassmaking to a visionary pair of boots. Each of these areas seems modest enough in and of itself. All together, however, they added up to an amazingly powerful new entity. Thanks to Louis XIV, France had acquired a reputation as the country that had written the book on elegant living.

No one could argue that royal patronage alone made possible the extraordinary burst of creativity that characterized Louis XIV's reign. It is, however, certain that the Sun King's wild cravings sharpened the entrepreneurial instincts of those who, at virtually the same moment, revolutionized fields ranging from jewelry design to menu design to interior design. Such a range of talent could never have flourished without the omnipresent devotion to stylistic and aesthetic perfection that reigned over the French court. Once again according to Voltaire: "Almost everything was either reinvented or created in [Louis XIV's] time."

In matters of style and fashion, just as Louis XIV had wanted, the French did it first; they did it best—and they did it most luxuriously. They produced the Vuitton bags, the Hermès scarves, the Chanel suits, the Lalique glass, the Dom Pérignon champagne of the day (and in the case of the champagne, the real Dom Pérignon was actually making it), always the most deliriously dear consumer goods and never, never the less expensive knockoffs (*that* was always England's preserve). France had become a mercantile power to be reckoned with, and no one would ever have called it a nation of shopkeepers.

Louis XIV also fostered the first culture to recognize the full potential of décor. By the end of the seventeenth century, France had become known as the world center for interior decoration—indeed, the modern concept of interior decoration may be said to have been created during the Versailles era. Décor functioned as an essential part of the new art of living then being established, as the necessary backdrop to a life of quality. During the seventeenth century's closing decades, French architects and designers put together the first coffee table books on interior decoration: they collected lavish engravings of, say, the new ways in which mirrors were being used to add dazzle to a room. These books circulated all over Europe, introducing the look designers quickly named "the royal style" or "the French look."

The story of how Paris became what we now think of when someone says "Paris" is the story of men and women who were able to reinvent the wheel in many different domains because they understood the fundamental importance of these two concepts: *Stick to the high-end and forget the low. Never underestimate the importance of décor and ambiance.* Take, for example, the café. The coffeehouse became an institution in England, the Netherlands, and Germany in the 1650s and 1660s. The original coffeehouses were fairly modest affairs; men frequented them to drink coffee and beer and to smoke. This concept had no appeal in France. And then, in 1675, the humble English coffeehouse was reinvented and quickly became an essential part of the new capital Paris was then becoming.

Francesco Procopio transformed the coffeehouse; he made it exquisite. His peers referred to him as an "artist": he had, after all, created the formula that made the café a way of life in Paris. Elsewhere, cafés featured nothing worthy of the name décor, whereas, at the Café Procope, the tables were made of marble, crystal chandeliers hung from the ceiling, the walls were decorated with elegant mirrors, and coffee was served from silver pots. Beer was banished from these elegant surroundings; patrons sipped exotic cocktails instead. And they could snack on delicate pastries and sorbets in flavors such as amber and musk. The Procope was, in short, the original chic café.

Its example was quickly emulated: by the turn of the eighteenth century, the world's first café scene had been created in the newly fashionable Saint-Germain-des-Prés neighborhood. Parisian cafés attracted a very different clientele than their counterparts elsewhere in Europe—elegant women, who would never have set foot in a coffeehouse, frequented cafés to see and show off all the latest fashions.

The same ground rules—make it chic and make it *cher*—launched what was soon considered a quintessentially French profession, hairdresser to the rich and famous. One man created the new profession—the word *coiffeur* was invented to describe his work. The first coiffeur was known to all simply as "le sieur [Monsieur] Champagne." Champagne instilled new beliefs in his clients: the right hairdresser could work miracles; hair could be styled in more ways than anyone had ever thought possible; a fashionable woman simply had to change her style to follow current trends. Because of Champagne, hairdos began to change with the fashion seasons, and women began to panic whenever they had a bad hair day—in fact, hairstyles became so complicated that, for the first time ever, they had good reason to panic.

Champagne, like many mythic coiffeurs since then, tyrannized his clientele: otherwise all-powerful princesses trembled, terrified that he might drop them from his A-list; they begged him to accompany him on their travels. Champagne's success launched the hair salon. By the century's end, the best-known coiffeurs and coiffeuses still made house calls for their favorite clients, but they also had shops, conveniently clustered near the Louvre, where well-heeled tourists could have their hair styled in the latest Paris fashion in order to dazzle those back home.

The original hair salons were only one example of how the new emphasis on style changed the way the city looked and functioned. The wave of creativity that swept over France reinvented shopping. Prior to the age of Louis XIV, fashion was most often negotiated in private: merchants visited clients in their homes, bringing with them samples of their wares. And when people did shop in public, they did so under conditions that were hardly designed to encourage them to linger over their purchases. Before Louis XIV's reign, shops were mere storehouses for merchandise, so no attention was paid to their décor. The bottom half of a shop's shutters folded down to make a table on which goods were displayed; the top half folded up, forming a protective awning. Customers remained in the street and never went inside. Those who made fashion into an industry also thought up a revolutionary way of showing off their ever-expanding range of offerings. They invented both the modern shop and the modern experience of shopping.

During the last two decades of the seventeenth century, for the first time ever, customers began to go inside to make their purchases (Figure I). The earliest modern shops were the precursors of our chic boutiques; they displayed the glorious fabrics and designer accessories that quickly made Paris the fashion capital of the Western world. And they displayed the new luxury goods in surroundings that were worthy of them, the first interiors designed to make people want to make purchases. In his account of his 1698 visit to Paris, the English physician Martin Lister called attention to the new kind of shop he had discovered there, shops so "finely adorned" that they had "an air of greatness." He also remarked on another innovation—the original shopwindows, which had niches designed to show off samples of the wares available inside. These were still another milestone in the history of shopping, the earliest eye-catching façades.

The experience of boutique shopping began when the first

fashionistas were enticed into these original high-end shops, which, by the century's end, had begun to cluster near a street that continues even now to feature cutting-edge boutiques, the rue Saint-Honoré. In those boutiques, the fashion queens of Versailles learned such new pleasures as the joy of displaying their most perfect outfits to an insider audience and the thrill of observing a particularly perfect new accessory that someone else had found before them and that they now just had to have.

At the same moment, a second category of merchants was also transforming shopping into an activity so glam that an elite clientele would want to indulge in it in public. We would now call them antique dealers, but in the seventeenth century theirs was a

FIGURE I. This engraving, from January 1678, is the earliest depiction of customers inside a shop. It shows two fashion trendsetters viewing the wide array of luxury goods—fabulous fabrics, shoes and boots, gloves—displayed in the posh interior of the original upscale boutique.

profession so new that it did not yet have a name. Their shops featured what could be called couture for the home, a range of objects—from high-end furniture to old master paintings and exotic wares from the Orient—that until then had been of interest only to a small audience of collectors, who had displayed them in their private museums. Suddenly they were being acquired by the beautiful people as decoration for their elegant interiors. To attract this new type of buyer, merchants created an equally well turned out shopping experience. Customers shopped in elegantly decorated interiors in which a dazzling selection of goods was artfully arranged. And they were waited on by attractive shopgirls dressed in the latest fashions. This was an idea so unique to the Parisian scene that well over a century later, an American journalist visiting Paris was still startled by this aspect of shopping in Paris: "In France there are no shop-*men*. No matter what is the article of trade . . . you are waited upon by girls, always handsome, and always dressed in the height of the mode."

And Louis XIV presided over all these transformations like a master choreographer. As the Italian diplomat Giovanni Battista Primi Visconti concluded after a lengthy sojourn at the court of Versailles: "He [Louis XIV] knew how to play the king perfectly on all occasions." During the final decades of his reign, he became a sort of one-man stylistic police, obsessively checking to make sure everything around him constantly lived up to his aesthetic standards. When all was just right, he took great pleasure in the conspicuous display of gorgeousness. For example, on December 7, 1697, the King—he was then fifty-nine—hosted some of the grandest festivities of the age to celebrate the marriage of his eldest grandson, the Duc de Bourgogne. For one evening reception, Versailles' Hall of Mirrors was lit with four thousand candles, transforming it into a vast arcade of flickering light.

In his memoirs, Versailles insider the Duc de Saint-Simon gave the celebration coverage worthy of Tom Wolfe. He portrayed the King "tak[ing] great pleasure in examining everyone's outfits. The air of contentment with which he savored the profusion of materi-

als and the brilliant inventiveness was evident, as well as the satisfaction with which he praised . . . the most superb and ingeniously designed outfits." Saint-Simon went on to deride the wave
of moderation-is-so-very-overrated consumerism unleashed by
the monarch's personal pleasure in a job well done: "People were
trying to outdo each other to find the most sumptuous clothing.
All Paris's shops were stripped bare in a few days. The entire town
was in the grips of frenetic opulence." Two duchesses were even
rumored to have kidnapped their favorite couturiere, in order to
guarantee that they would get just the outfits they wanted for the
festivities—and that no one else would be able to avail themselves
of her services. (Can you imagine two starlets bundling Donatella
Versace off to a hideaway so that no one could outshine them on
the red carpet on Oscar night?) As Saint-Simon concluded, "There
was no way to restrain oneself in the midst of so much madness.
It was essential to have several complete new outfits; between
Madame de Saint-Simon and myself, it cost us 20,000 livres"—
roughly $1 million in today's terms.* Luxe indeed.

On some level, the King knew that he had created a monster:
in this case, he wondered how it was "that there were so many
husbands crazy enough to let themselves be ruined so that their
wives could own fancy dresses." And the royal wedding was, of
course, only a drop in the bucket of the wildly conspicuous con-

---

*The basic currency of seventeenth-century France was the livre, or pound (not to
be confused with the pound already used in England at that time). A livre contained twenty sous. The French currency system has gone through so many radical
realignments since Louis XIV's day that it is theoretically impossible to do what I
have just done, convert a sum given in livres into U.S. dollars. The conversion—
20,000 livres = roughly $1 million—is based on the only possible point of com-
parison: the value of labor. The average daily wage for an unskilled worker in Paris
from 1690 to 1695 was 15 sous. The price of Saint-Simon's clothing (20,000 livres)
was thus the equivalent of 25,000 workdays for a late-seventeenth-century worker
on minimum wage. In the United States today, an eight-hour day at the federal
minimum wage would yield $41.20, and 25,000 workdays would be worth
$1,030,000. The equation—20,000 livres = $1 million—will be the basis for any
conversions I make in the following pages.

sumption characteristic of the Versailles era. Louis XIV's critics decried his free spending and said that he would bankrupt his country. At some moments, it certainly seemed that they would be proven right. The following pages will be full of the fabulous things that the King's passion for style inspired his subjects to create and rarely discuss the husbands who were ruined when their wives got in over their heads in the whirl of luxury. Was it all worth it? The King might have said that without his extravagant spending, the luxurious experiences for which his country is still celebrated would not have come into existence. The businessman might have added that without it, tourism would not be France's number-one industry today.

In fact, the modern tourist industry began the minute the new French style was in place: it was as if Louis XIV had given it a raison d'être. One of the earliest appearances of "tourism" listed by the *Oxford English Dictionary,* from 1872, sums it up perfectly: "Tourism was born in the seventeenth century, and Englishmen were the first to practice it." The young English nobles who were the original modern tourists attracted a great deal of attention because they were such high livers. Gregorio Leti, an Italian historian writing in the 1690s, noted that they traveled "with beautiful style" and that they "spent magnificently." He added that far and away the favored destination for all their magnificent spending was Paris. The English visitors to Paris were soon joined by the first hordes of German, Dutch, and Scandinavian tourists; Italians and Spanish in smaller numbers met up with them in Paris— thus, the kind of free-spending café society now known as Eurotrash first came to be. To accommodate it, a tourist infrastructure quickly sprang up.

To introduce foreign visitors to the wonders of the French capital and to its new infrastructure, between 1690 and 1720 the first modern guidebooks were published. There had been earlier guides to major cities; they discussed only their principal monuments. Never before had such volumes included, in addition to the information about must-see sites, the kind of advice we now expect to find: where to stay, what to eat, and what to do. Most of the first guidebooks to Paris suggested walks along planned itineraries through the city's neighborhoods; some were published in sizes small enough to be slipped in one's pocket to take along on those walks. In 1694, an enterprising publisher began selling the first small-format map of Paris, designed specifically to help foreign tourists and businessmen navigate the city's often complicated streets.

These new guidebooks also featured a type of information that no one had given travelers before: where to shop and what to shop for during a stay in the French capital. Earlier guidebooks had never included information on shopping for the simple reason that there had not been enough information to give: Louis XIV's Paris had become the first true shopping city. More than anything else, tourist guides stressed that the sheer quantity of all there was to buy surpassed anything ever seen: the display was so dazzling that shoppers easily lost their heads in what an English visitor in 1698 termed the "whirlpool" of luxury goods, and hardly knew where to turn. "Everywhere you look, you see boutiques," one guide for German tourists remarked. A guide for Italians called Paris "the country of desire."

In addition, guidebooks noted what they saw as a new development, a phenomenon familiar to today's jaded consumers, well aware that we need almost none of the things that we continue to accumulate: French merchants were managing to convince shoppers that they absolutely had to have all sorts of completely unnecessary things. They were doing so by making those things exquisite. As a guidebook for German tourists put it, "There are shops that display essential things, but the vast majority are full of pretty baubles, things that really aren't essential in everyday life." And as a guide for English tourists warned, "When you're in Paris, you tend to buy things you had never heard of before." The seduction of the shopper with the promise of beauty and luxury that we now know so well had begun.

Parisian merchants were so successful at convincing people to buy for the sake of buying because they had made shopping glamorous, fun, and even sexy. Shopping had become the kind of experience that nations of mere shopkeepers could never understand; it had become shopping theater in which consumers were spending money because they felt that their lives were somehow being transformed by the event.

Everything that Paris still represents in terms of style is founded on a concept of value already evident in all the luxury commerce that flourished under Louis XIV's patronage. Value was not primarily about price and performance but was determined by intangible factors: it was a matter of aesthetics and elegance. Those who were successful during this emblematic age of French culture were selling much more than food and clothing: they added value by "selling" in addition the look and feel of people and places. They were making formerly everyday experiences into performance art.

Most people today would probably say that they have nothing in common with the men and women of seventeenth-century France. And yet that age's philosophy of aesthetic value has never been more alive and well. At a time when, in many sectors of the economy, increasingly brutal competition has both dramatically raised quality and driven prices down, it has become difficult for businesses to make their mark in the time-honored fashion of commerce in the United States: selling a good product for less. More and more, people have begun to chant the economic mantras of Louis XIV's France. A successful restaurant has to do more than serve good food at a good price: it has to create an environment. It's not enough to offer customers a good product: you have to make them feel special by providing a hefty dose of emotion and drama along with the merchandise.

There's no more perfect illustration of how widespread the influence of Versailles' way of doing business has become in American commerce than this recent ad campaign: "You are a work of art, so dress to be on display. . . . These aren't just shoes; they're performance art." When Payless, hardly the quintessential luxury brand, no longer markets its shoes on the grounds that they are a good value but argues that buying them will transform the quality of our lives, its media strategists are taking a page from those who wrote the book on aesthetic value. The fashionable life is clearly no longer the preserve of a moneyed elite. More of us may now be following the pied piper of Versailles than ever before.

Louis XIV gave the Western world something more durable and far more rare than the luxe goods his subjects so brilliantly crafted and marketed. He succeeded in having some of the basic activities in our daily lives redefined: rather than mundane occurrences, things we simply have to do, they have been promoted to the status of moments of sheer pleasure in which we choose to indulge ourselves. Because of the Versailles era, many of the so-called finer things in life became just that, no longer mere things but finer, aesthetically pleasurable experiences.

And every time we appreciate not only the quality of luscious chocolates but also the glorious pattern of their arrangement in the box; every time we exclaim not only over the extraordinary taste sensations particularly creative cooking gives us but also over the perfect surroundings in which it is served; every time we lust after a designer handbag when a more ordinary brand would do just as good a job of holding our possessions—well, each time we are in essence expressing desires that the Versailles era created for us. We're defining the quality of life as Louis XIV's culture taught us to do. We're hoping that a little of the sheen that those who ruled over Versailles understood so well will add a glow to the surfaces of our lives, too.

So here are the stories of the shoemaker, the hairdresser, the cosmetologist, the cookbook writers, the chef, the diamond merchant, the couturieres and the fashion queens, the inventors of the folding umbrella . . . and of champagne. Together they created a style that still shapes our ideas of elegance, sophistication, and luxury.

I

How Much Is Too Much?

The Rule of Celebrity Hairdressers

Frédéric Fekkai jets between New York and Los Angeles so that faithful clients on both coasts can have access to his hairstyling genius. On May 18, 1993, Air Force One remained parked at LAX, shutting down two of the airport's four runways and causing flights to be diverted for nearly an hour, while Cristophe of Beverly Hills clipped the locks of the president of the United States. (The *Washington Post* called the trim "the most famous haircut since Samson.") All this *Bonfire of the Vanities*–style excess was not, as we might think, unimaginable before the boom years in New York City. It has been the way of the world—or at least of a very small segment of it—ever since, in mid-seventeenth-century France, a new profession appeared on the fashion scene: ladies' hairdresser. From then on, hairdos had names, styles changed frequently, there were A-list hairdressers, and some styles were even named for those who set the tone, the celebrities of the day—the King's mistress, for example. For the first time, those who invented new styles began to make such pronouncements as *this year hair will be curlier* or *this season only long tresses are in.*

Prior to that time, the field of hairstyling was resolutely sex-specific. The first barbers were medical men, ancestors of the modern-day surgeon. Then, in 1659, a royal edict created the profession "barber–wig maker," and new-style barbers, who played no medical role and dealt exclusively with beards and men's hair, began to open shops in Paris, where they worked only on men. Women's needs were still taken care of by their ladies' maids; no one imagined that there would soon be a profession devoted to ladies' hair, much less that men would ever be allowed to engage in the intimate gesture of touching a woman's head. Women's hairdos were relatively simple affairs; there was little sense of trends; styles changed slowly and never had a broad impact. No one could have imagined a style that everyone absolutely had to have once it had been decreed to be *the* look of the season. Then, in one fell swoop, Monsieur Champagne swept away centuries of prejudice and became the original brand name in hairdressing. From that moment on, a look produced by big-ticket hairdressers earned bragging rights for the lucky few with access to the new styling magic.

The revolution in women's hairstyling that Champagne brought about was a crucial first step toward the birth of that quintessential French phenomenon, couture. Crucial to couture's stranglehold is the notion that, when a woman wears a certain style of dress, it will immediately be recognized by all those in the know as the creation of a particular designer. Haute coiffure invented this notion. For the first time ever, a stylist's name—that of Champagne—determined the value of a hairdo. As the title character in a play based on Champagne's life put it, "Other stylists may have their own ideas, / But I always know that my method / Will dictate fashion for everyone."

Before there was couture, before there were the luxe bijous of the grand joailliers, there were the new hairdos of the minute. If a woman made an appearance with her hair styled in a certain way, the ladies who lunched all identified the magic touch of le sieur Champagne, hairdresser of the rich and famous. The moment when hairstyles "signed" by their creator were first recognized clearly indicated that Frenchwomen were ready to take on what women all over the world have considered ever since to be their essential role: that of always knowing just how they have to look for every new season and also exactly which designer will guarantee that they will be instantly recognized as having that information. Couture's tyranny had begun.

A new word was created to describe Champagne's profession: *coiffeur,* the term still used in French. Coiffeur, and then its feminine form, coiffeuse, were invented to reflect the existence of a new profession: the original coiffeurs and coiffeuses worked exclusively on ladies' hairstyles and head styles. I say "head styles" because, in the seventeenth century, there was more to the coiffeur's job than just dealing with hair: the *coiffure,* which now means simply "a hairdo," referred to everything covering the head and included many things besides hair.

During the Middle Ages and the Renaissance, women all over Europe wore *coiffes*—wimples, bonnets, and other uses of fabric to cover a large part or even all of the head. (Covering the hair was considered a gesture of female modesty.) In Paris, beginning in the 1660s, the same word, coiffe, began to be used for an entirely new phenomenon, and the total production, the coiffure, began to resemble the hairdresser's masterpiece as we know it today. True, the coiffe most often still featured material. From this point on, however, the fabric—typically bits of taffeta or lace—was no longer used primarily to cover the hair but to make it look its best; it had become a fashion accessory meant to add volume to the hair or to help keep a bunch of particularly fetching curls looking as though they had just happened to fall that way naturally. The new profession caught on quickly: the term coiffeur was first used in 1663, to describe Champagne; by 1694, the French Academy's very official dictionary of the French language recognized the reign of ladies' hairdressers by speaking of "coiffeurs and coiffeuses à la mode."

The members of the new profession were the first true hair artists: it was their job not only to make their clients look as fabulous as possible but to be constantly imagining new ways of combining all kinds of hair—for coiffes could include hairpieces and what are now called extensions—and fabric. The proof of their success is the fairly dizzying progression of hair creations that followed one another on the French fashion scene at the seventeenth century's end. In each case, the minute the first woman appeared coiffed in the new way, the style received a name, and others—initially in Paris and then all over Europe—would rush to copy it. For the first time ever, there were seasons for hairstyles in the same way that we now think about fashion collections that dictate what women will wear the following year.

In the beginning, coiffeur was a profession of one. About Champagne himself, we know nothing, not even his real name. About his life as a coiffeur, however, we know a great deal. Some of the most prominent Parisiennes of the day were so outrageously enraptured with Champagne's capillary magic that his male contemporaries were driven to scathing satires of the budding relationship between hairdresser and celebrity client. The most remarkable of these is a comedy, *Champagne le coiffeur*—this seems to be the first time the word *coiffeur* was used in print—staged at the Théâtre du Marais in 1663, shortly after the real coiffeur's death.

By all accounts, Champagne could have been the model for the role of bed-hopping artist of the tresses that Warren Beatty incarnated over three centuries later in *Shampoo*. Champagne apparently bragged incessantly of having enjoyed the favors of the great ladies whose coiffes he maintained. The play turns on this image of the coiffeur as inveterate ladies' man: Champagne has convinced the only daughter of a wealthy man to elope with him. And the daughter, Elise, is surely the first hairstylist groupie; the author, Boucher, includes a list of celebrity hairstylists Elise allegedly visits on a daily basis to be certain of always being coiffed on the cutting edge. In other aspects as well, the fictional Champagne lives up to the legend of his real-life model. He boasts constantly about how desperately the rich and famous depend on him. Near the end of the play, he even launches into a detailed account of the anecdote that in his day received as much, and similarly mocking, coverage as the tale of Clinton's rendezvous with Cristophe did in our day.

When Princess Marie de Gonzague left Paris for Warsaw to marry Wladyslaw IV, king of Poland, she was considered an aging beauty—over thirty, by which time, according to seventeenth-century standards, she was disastrously near the beginning of the end. When the marriage was celebrated by proxy in Paris, Champagne helped a lady-in-waiting place the crown on the princess's head—presumably so that her coiffure wouldn't be mussed. Then, by *his* own account, the princess begged the coiffeur to accompany her to Poland in order to keep her hair, at least, perfect at all times. It was clearly the first time that anyone had considered that something as simple as a hairstyle could become an affair of state. Both contemporary newspapers and satirists of the French scene such as Gédéon Tallemant des Réaux gave Champagne considerable press, winning him the kind of status previously unimaginable for someone who worked with others' hair. In the play, for example, other characters refer to him with respect, as "Monsieur Champagne."

Celebrity status meant considerable financial rewards. The fictional Champagne says that he went along for the ride to Poland "in the hope of great gain" and adds that "he was well paid for his pains." Tallemant claimed that the real-life Champagne refused to accept money for his services—unlike other well-known coiffeurs of his day who, just as Cristophe did for the Clinton family, had service contracts with their celebrity clients. Champagne guessed—quite accurately—that his method would cause his clientele of stylish princesses to outdo one another in showering him with expensive gifts: "While he was styling a lady's hair, he would tell her about another lady's presents, and when he wasn't satisfied with them, he would add: 'She can beg me to come now; she no longer has any hold on me.'" "The foolish woman," Tallemant concludes, "terrified that he might treat her the same way, gave him twice as much as she would have done." The era of the eight-hundred-dollar haircut had dawned.

In true prima donna fashion, Champagne is said to have rewarded such slavish fidelity by humiliating his benefactors. He had all the attitude associated with today's most sought after stylists. On a whim, he would just walk out, leaving a client with her coiffe only half assembled. One day, while he was doing the hair of a woman with a particularly large nose, he suddenly turned on her: "You know, with a nose like that, you'll never look good, no matter how I style your hair." And to add insult to injury, he addressed her using the familiar *tu* form.

Champagne's high-profile styling revolutionized the way the business of doing a woman's hair took place. Until then, when a woman wanted to assemble a new coiffe, a female merchant, known as a *perruquière,* or wig maker, brought various hair ornaments to her home for her to try on. Before the end of the seventeenth century, the best-known coiffeurs and coiffeuses, while they continued to make house calls for their most famous clients, also had shops, where they could reach a far wider clientele, showing off a much expanded range of hair accessories and styling coiffes at the same time (Figure 1.1). This was the real beginning of the practice of hairdressing as we now know it: that of having one's hair done outside the home in a public place. Just that simple.

In no time at all, the situation in Paris had evolved into something very close to what we expect to find in any major capital today: there were roughly a half dozen stylists so high-profile that the addresses of their salons were listed in guides to Paris so that the well-heeled tourist would know where to turn in order to return home coiffed in the latest Parisian fashion. From Nicolas de Blégny's insider's address books of the early 1690s, we learn that the area where the luxury jewelers congregated, right around the

FIGURE 1.1. This is the earliest depiction of a hair salon. One coiffeuse is busy designing an elaborate coiffure, while on the wall behind her, on the table, and on the floor many of the accessories that enabled the first celebrity hairdressers to work their magic are displayed.

Palais Royal, close by the Louvre, was also the place to head for haute coiffure, with three of the then trendiest establishments: the shops of Mademoiselle d'Angerville, Mademoiselle Le Brun, and the trendiest of them all, Mademoiselle Canilliat, stylist to the stars for decades.

Already in January 1678, the first newspaper anywhere to provide in-depth coverage of the fashion scene, *Le Mercure galant* (Gallant Mercury), announced that Canilliat was the official coiffeuse for all the ballets held at court. (Louis XIV had a passion for ballet, so this was a high-profile assignment indeed, on the order of doing the hair of supermodels for photo shoots in *Vogue*.) Nearly twenty years later, Canilliat was still so much the celebrity coiffeuse that a character in a particularly fashion-conscious novel from 1696 was sent to her for a complete makeover. The other fashionable neighborhoods also had their boldface stylists: on the rue Saint-Honoré, a lady could entrust her tresses to Mademoiselle Poitiers, and no less a personnage than François Quentin, known professionally as La Vienne, one of the Sun King's four *premiers valets de chambre* (first personal valets), maintained a shop in Saint-Germain-des-Prés. When the reign of celebrity stylists began, women dominated the profession, but men, following Champagne's pathbreaking example, were chipping away at the old taboo.

Just as still remains true, different shops had different specialties: Versailles insiders went to Mademoiselle Cochois, whose salon was on the rue Aubry-le-Boucher near the Marais, for really big hair, elaborate mixes of fake and real, when invited to the grandest fêtes. Mademoiselle Borde and Mademoiselle Martin were all the rage in 1671, when fashionistas decided completely to abandon the traditional coiffe and to be styled *only* with their own hair, worn much curlier and a good deal shorter than ever before. This was an idea so wildly heretical that it's now hard for us to imagine its impact; the fashion for bobbing in the 1920s was nothing compared with this moment when, for the first time in modern history, aristocratic women decided that shorter hair was more attractive than longer and that they would dare appear in public with nothing covering any part of the head.

On March 18, 1671, the Marquise de Sévigné, writing to describe the new look for her daughter who lived far from the Parisian scene, at first said that the women looked "completely naked," like "little heads of cabbage," and claimed that the supreme judge, the King, "had doubled over with laughter" at the very sight of it. Sévigné detailed the suffering required to look like a head of cabbage: women were sleeping "with a hundred rollers, which make them endure mortal agony all night long." She dismissed the look's proponents with what was surely the ultimate insult for her hyperelegant, hyperfeminine age, saying they were

styled "en vrai fanfan," just like a kid—much as the original devotees of Coco Chanel's cropped hair and sporty silhouette were
labeled "garçonnes," tomboys or street urchins.

Even such extreme reactions did not stop many of the most
fashionable ladies of the day from immediately adopting the radical new style. And such was the power of la mode that, only three
days later, Sévigné was so "completely won over" that she told her
daughter that "this hairstyle is made for your face," and promised
to send her a fashion doll wearing it to make sure she got it
right. The new style—which was known as *hurlupé* or *hurluberlu*,
"tousled" or "mixed-up"—marked the first time ever that a new
look for hair became an overnight fashion event. "People around
Saint-Germain-des-Prés are talking about nothing else," Sévigné
announced. By July 1676, she penned a lengthy description of the
King's longtime mistress, the Marquise de Montespan, swanning
through a grand reception at Versailles "with no head covering
and styled with a thousand curls," and pronounced her "a tri-
umphant beauty to turn all the ambassadors' heads." The curly
look was clearly no longer just for kids. (Sévigné's personal take on
the hotly debated question: after she discussed the matter at
length with her best friend, the Comtesse de Lafayette, the century's most celebrated novelist, the two women—in 1671 they
were, respectively, forty-five and thirty-seven years old—decided
that the hairstyle was wonderful for young women but not suitable for more mature ladies like themselves.)

Once French fashionistas had pronounced all the old rules
inoperative, styling became truly the essence of hairdressing, as
fickle and as fluctuating as any domain of the then nascent fashion
industry. Styles changed so often that it's possible to date late-
seventeenth-century paintings from the way women's hair is
coiffed, just as we can date photographs on the basis of the Dior or
Saint Laurent designs that the women captured in them are wearing. Thus, we know exactly when and how the most famous of all
early hair fashions came to be.

One fine summer day in 1680, when Louis XIV returned from

his favorite pastime, hunting, he found that his mistress of the moment, the achingly beautiful seventeen-year-old Marie-Angélique de Scoraille, Duchesse de Fontanges, had tied her hair up fetchingly with a ribbon, in a way that caused her curls to spill down onto her forehead. The King asked her to wear her hair only this way; the next day, all the ladies of the court were already copying the new style, which was soon famous all over Europe and was called, naturally, the *fontange*.

The fontange remained the favorite look of the seventeenth century's final decades, and it went through endless modifications. Edme Boursault devoted entire scenes of his comedy *Les Mots à la mode* (Fashionable Words, 1694), a spoof of the new craze for high fashion, to the names of all the latest fontange-based hairdos: the list is enormous, from the *bourgogne* (Burgundy) to the *jardinière* (gardener), from the *souris* (mouse) to the *effrontée* (shameless) and the *crève-cœur* (heartbreaker). One of the most fantastic was imagined in the 1690s, as soon as the chest of drawers, or *commode*, was invented: tresses were wrapped around strips of fabric arranged one on top of another to form a series of "drawers." For the grandest evening festivities at Versailles, only "the butterfly" would do: fabulous plumelike jeweled ornaments, known as aigrettes, were sprinkled throughout ladies' hair; they were studded with rose-cut diamonds; briolette diamonds dangled fetchingly from the ends. With every turn of the head, butterfly coiffes thus sparkled in the candlelight and were reflected in the big mirrors that were becoming central to the French style of decoration. The fontange continued to spin off new variations for over thirty years: in the July 22, 1711, issue of *The Spectator*, Joseph Addison was still making fun of the increasingly exaggerated turns on the style named after Louis XIV's by then long-dead mistress.

During the decades that followed the invention of the fontange, hairstyling in France became ever more literally haute coiffure—satirists claimed that, thus coiffed, women couldn't get through many doorways. Much of the height came from a strange fabric-covered flat base made of wire netting, against which hair could be piled up or from which lace could cascade down. By the 1690s, hairstyles featuring this base were known as fontanges, even though they were clearly a far cry from the elaborately casual little do invented during the hunting party in 1680 (Figure 1.2). By the end of the long vogue of fontange-based looks, they had become so complicated that they could be over two feet high. In 1713, the Duc de Saint-Simon said that the tallest ones were veritable "edifices" and quipped that women's faces were thus "in the middle of their bodies." Much of the elevation came from wigs, hairpieces, and extensions. Wigs were just coming into fashion in the seventeenth century and remained quite controversial. (Were they suitable for priests? For servants?)

The craze for wigs began only in the 1670s; by the following decade, the demand for human hair for the ever bigger and more complicated coiffures was so great that "hair merchants" were sending out professional "cutters" all over Europe. They brought

FIGURE 1.2. Several variations on the fontange hairstyle from the 1690s. Only the lady on the right has curls spilling onto her forehead as in the original 1680 do that gave the style its name. All three coiffures use fabric to add volume. The lady on the left has chosen a somewhat lower look, featuring lace and ribbons, while the lady on the right favors the classic fabric-covered base. The style in the middle is the layered *commode* (chest of drawers) look.

pounds of hair at a time back to Paris; it had to be at least twenty-four inches long to be useful for the trendiest coiffes. The Dutch were said to produce the finest hair; within France, Norman hair won the nod. Ash blond hair—the ne plus ultra for female beauty in seventeenth-century France, undoubtedly because there were so few natural ash blonds in France—was wildly more expensive, thirty-eight times more expensive, to be exact, than ordinary brown. A pound of ash brown hair fetched up to 150 livres, roughly $7,500. (Across the channel, in England, where fair-haired women were far more common, gentlemen preferred not blonds, but raven-haired beauties. So much for wanting what we have.)

Many people liked the control offered by wigs: if you wore one at all times, you never had a bad hair day, and you never went bald, in public at least. And all over Europe, a wig began to be seen as a sign of social status and power, particularly if the wig was French made. For French wig makers, like French hairdressers, dominated the profession. M. Binet, wigmeister to the King, had a shop on the rue des Petits-Champs, where glitterati from all over Europe placed their orders. The King himself—about whom Binet once remarked, "I would strip every head in the kingdom bald in order to adorn that of His Majesty"—went in for wigs in a big way. Just off his bedroom at Versailles was the Wig Room, lined with terms, classical statues in the form of a pillar topped with a head and a torso. Each term was turned into a life-size wig stand and sported a different kind of wig—the hunting model, the stay-at-home wig, the formal one for state receptions. By the end of the century, wig making had become such big business in France that there was a true hair shortage, and some wig makers turned to horsehair to replace human hair. (Anyone who's watched Cary Grant in I Was a Male War Bride don a horsehair wig in order to pass as a woman knows how low that was sinking.)

Then, in 1713, big hair disappeared; virtually overnight, all the height and volume and high drama became radically unfashionable. Early that year, the Duke of Shrewsbury was named

English ambassador to France. His wife made fun of the by then immense fontange dos, and her mockery signaled the end of the first age of really big hair. Saint-Simon claimed that the ladies of the court abandoned the fontange "with an astounding rapidity" and jumped to the opposite end of the hairdressing spectrum, perfectly flat dos, "l'extrémité du plat." At the very end of the Sun King's reign, the beautiful people of Saint-Germain-des-Prés were under the sway of a radically new sensibility: lower, apparently more natural looks were in, and high hair was banished to a fashion hinterland from which it made a comeback only in the decades prior to the French Revolution. But the original craze for coiffure had given the fashion world a legacy still very much alive: the belief that the greatest artists of the profession will always be French. As Montesquieu phrased it in his classic 1721 novel, *The Persian Letters:* "Whenever a lady has her hair done anywhere in Europe, she slavishly respects the edicts of French coiffeuses."

Not all current visitors come to Paris hoping to have their hair styled in the latest French fashion—although, for months after the modest salon where I get my hair cut received just a small article in *Town and Country,* it was impossible for regulars to get an appointment because so many tourists were calling from abroad weeks before coming to Paris. And centuries after Champagne had princesses begging him to work his magic on their tresses, reporters covering the superstylists of the moment never fail to point out that a French accent is still a major advantage.

2

Fashion Queens

The Birth of Haute Couture

Fashion is eternal; there have always been people who dressed stylishly. The marketing of fashion, however, does have a clear beginning: in Paris in the 1670s. It was then that we can find the origins of what today is called the fashion industry, the now gigantic network of designers, manufacturers, merchants, and merchandisers who decree fashion's shifts and dictate every aspect of the official image of each new season's look. In the 1670s, a number of developments essential to the transformation of fashion into the fashion industry came together: an expanded clientele for high-fashion goods; increasingly sophisticated means of supplying the new demand; and for the first time ever, ways of disseminating news of trends in the making widely and quickly, thereby guaranteeing that the ranks of the fashion obsessed would continue to grow. And perhaps most important of all, it was then that fashionistas were introduced to what is still today the fundamental tool in the marketing of fashion: in the late 1670s, fashion seasons began.

In the 1670s, fashion first glimpsed its modern identity: it began to be transformed into couture, an industry that came into existence to supply the ever-increasing demand for high-fashion garments on the part of members of Louis XIV's court and also to market the new French fashion to an ever broader public outside the court. From the start, both the new French fashions and the new French fashion industry had an amazingly clear sense of self-definition and of mission. But perhaps what is most striking about the way couture took shape in Paris in the last three decades of the seventeenth century is how many of the concepts then invented are still key to the way we experience fashion today.

All over Europe at that moment, fashion began to be referred to by its French name, *la mode,* and to be considered something inherently and indisputably French. One of the early spoofs of fashionistas, for example, the 1690 *Fop-Dictionary,* speaks of "the Law of Mode" and presents it as part of "the Empire of the French." In addition, la mode became really à la mode, a constantly and quickly changing phenomenon whose every variation was observed and followed. All those who dreamed of becoming truly fashionable believed that to make this dream come true, they had to follow the Parisian scene, acquire French goods, and if possible, make the trip to the world's first fashion capital.

Today, we understand all too well the effects of fashion addiction: both television (*Sex and the City*) and fiction (*Bergdorf Blondes*), not to mention the fashion press, teach us more than we need to know about the lengths to which designer mania can drive its victims. We know far less about the original fashion queens and their pursuit of the trendy and the gorgeous. Enough documents have survived, however, to give us a good sense of what they wore, when they wore it, and how they came to own it. These details teach us that the Parisian fashion scene in the late seventeenth century had a great deal in common with that extraordinarily fertile period to which designers today return so often for inspiration, the moment between the two world wars when couture was completely redefined. Both periods were moments when the fashion industry was dominated by female designers. And in both cases women designers understood the needs of their female clients: the new fashion produced by women designers, in the seventeenth century as much as the twentieth, was revolutionary because it was intended to be both far more comfortable and far more body conscious than anything the women who wore it had ever known.

One anecdote from the very end of Louis XIV's reign gives us the essence of how la mode first took shape. It was July 1715, and Paris was all abuzz: fashion plates sensed that change was in the air. "Everyone was saying that there would soon be a radically new look in women's fashions," in the words of a Versailles insider, the Marquis de Dangeau. So the ladies of the court took action. The Duchesse de Berry, who had just ended her official mourning after the untimely death of her husband, the King's grandson, called a meeting, scheduled for after dinner in the privacy of her own home: she invited the reigning fashion plates, as well as "the most clever tailors and the most celebrated couturieres." Just like generals planning a military campaign, the ladies who dressed and the ladies who dressed them plotted a fashion coup: they worked together to make sure that the new fashions would be a hit with those who by then were setting the style for all the fashion-forward in the Western world, the ladies of the French court. On July 25, the meeting took place: "The princesses got together . . . and they ordered that the new designs be brought to them the instant they were ready."

Couture as we know it could only have come into being in this collaborative manner. We now think of made-to-measure as the ultimate luxury. For the first fashionistas, however, this was old hat. Before the original fashion revolution of the 1670s, made-to-measure—one-offs, as the English say—was all there was. Each lady had her frocks made by her personal tailor or seamstress; they chose the fabric and the style together. This meant that each outfit was truly unique—and that was no fun. For high fashion's thrills are all about imitation: Where to find that adorable little number you saw on a lady strolling down the Champs-Elysées? How can you know that something is the latest style if you can't see the same thing on other women? How can you establish that you got in at the beginning of a trend and were the first to have something, if others can't get the same coat or accessory that you've decided to put at the center of your winter wardrobe?

In order for these novel pleasures to exist, all the institutions now central to the fashion industry had to be created. The world acquired its first celebrity designers, brand names, fashion seasons, and above all, its first fashion queens. And the original fashion queens were willing to give up the world of one-offs for more modern pleasures such as learning which of them would set the pace for each season, or seeing an accessory they had just acquired quickly pop up all over town. And the only downside of these new satisfactions—you really couldn't go on wearing that new coat once it began to be too widely seen—was really still another upside: you went out and replaced it with another one. The age of too much muchness, the concept without which the fashion industry could never have flourished, had begun.

Once the ladies of Versailles and the first great designers began to work together in the 1670s to make fashion go public and become la mode, key ideas that we now take for granted immediately fell into place. First there was the look, the way in which everything worn from head to toe worked together, as well as those ineffable little touches of fashion magic such as the perfect way to drape the season's new scarf. Then there was the fashion season: the belief that the styles of, say, the winter of 1678 absolutely had to be different from those of the winter of 1677, or that the gray then featured couldn't possibly be the same shade that had been the hot color of the previous summer. For the first time, an ever larger population began to be collectively obsessed with questions still a staple of today's fashion press: What's in?

What's passé? What's the hottest version of the jacket of the summer, and where to find it?

By the end of Louis XIV's reign, these notions had won such widespread acceptance that those who ruled over the Parisian fashion scene had women from London to Saint Petersburg anxiously awaiting information about all the latest trends. Barely a decade later, newspapers in major U.S. cities such as Boston began to trumpet the arrival of any sign of French fashion life, so that women in the New World could demonstrate their good taste by humming the same tunes as the original fashion queens, the ladies at Versailles.

The French fashion industry reduced not only geographical distance but social distance as well, just as happens today, when couturiers adapt their ideas for moderately priced lines and market them in midlevel stores. Before the mid-seventeenth century, fashion was the exclusive preserve of a few immensely wealthy nobles: only a tiny elite had stylish garments, and even they had very few outfits, which they replaced quite rarely. Fine clothing was so prohibitively expensive that styles barely changed over long periods of time: outfits were more a display of wealth and social status than of fashion personality. (A news flash from the February 7, 1666, issue of La Gravette de Mayolas's newsletter, *La Muse historique* [The Historical Muse], proves just how valuable clothes were: a kidnapped child had just been found naked; the kidnappers had grabbed him because he was so richly dressed. Well-to-do parents were warned not to let their offspring out in public in their Sunday best.)

The vast majority of the population had only simple clothing made from coarse homespun fabrics. The rare splashes of color on their sartorial scene came from garments handed down from nobles. As soon as Paris became the world capital of style, fashion began to spread gradually through French society. The lower classes might not have been able to own much, but accessories such as ribbons and stockings—and above all, the production of less expensive fabrics with patterns and bright colors, from which they could make clothing—began to transform the appearance of the

French population. By the end of Louis XIV's reign, fashion had begun to matter to a great many of his subjects.

The French fashion industry changed everything about the experience of shopping for clothes, first of all its gendering. Until about 1650, the imbalance between men's and women's wardrobes was not terribly significant. From then on, women began to out-purchase men at an ever-growing rate. (This trend was never reversed and gradually created today's situation: women now spend three times more than men on clothes.) When the fashion press began in the 1670s, it included coverage of men's clothing, but the feature articles specifically targeted its *lectrices,* the female readers who were already known as the driving force behind the rapidly expanding market for fashion. From then on, la mode became a domain governed more and more exclusively by women's desires, and those desires never stopped growing. Within decades, the nascent fashion industry convinced its clients to give up the concept of a few outfits rarely changed in favor of multiplicity and rapid turnover. The French language quickly recognized the particularly intimate bond between women and fashion. The expression "slaves for fashion" (*esclaves de la mode*) made its inaugural appearance in 1694 (in the first edition of the venerable dictionary of the French Academy, no less), and "fashion queens" in 1719.

In 1650, style was negotiated in private; tailors came to their clients' homes to fit their clothing, a procedure that drastically discouraged innovation and change. How many samples of new cloth or new accessories could be lugged around? And how could the desire to have what someone else is buying be instilled with only one customer at a time? By century's end, shopping was becoming increasingly a public affair: aristocratic women first chose clothing outside their own homes in the chic booths merchants set up for the annual Saint-Germain Fair and, above all, in the shops dedicated to high fashion that clustered initially around the Place des Victoires and then more and more on a street whose name is still intimately linked with French haute couture, the rue Saint Honoré.

When the merchandising of fashion went public, it, too, was

gendered female. For several decades beginning in midcentury, seamstresses, who were then allowed only to do alterations, fought to obtain the right to design and make clothing. In 1675, a guild granting them official status was formed. A new word, *couturière*, celebrated the first time that women were taken seriously as creators and makers of high-fashion garments. The new term, the first word in the vocabulary of haute couture, was also used to recognize the fact that women were seen as having played the key role in turning fashion into the fashion industry. In the seventeenth century, the term *ateliers de couturières*, rather than today's *ateliers de couture*, was used to designate the workshops in which highly skilled female workers—the legendary petites mains—turned out gowns that were the stuff of dreams. Early guidebooks to Paris sang the praises of the city's "celebrated couturieres," the first celebrity designers to dictate la mode to a national and an international clientele: Madame Villeneuve, whose shop was on the Place des Victoires; Madame Rémond and Madame Prévot, both nearby on the rue des Petits-Champs; and Madame Charpentier, on the rue Montorgueil. And as soon as these women began to set the pace, fashion took on a completely new air, one that became known as quintessentially French.

The couturier, today the god of women's fashion, came into existence only in the final decades of the nineteenth century. The first couturier was an Englishman (shades of Galliano and McQueen), Charles Frederick Worth, and the first Parisian maison de couture (*that* term was initially used early in the twentieth century) was the celebrated House of Worth. It was only after Worth's phenomenal success that couturieres lost their central role and couturiers took over their place as the artists of the fashion world.

We might have trouble recognizing the manner in which la mode was initially expressed. Today it's easy to convince the fashion-obsessed of the need for new things or to signal the arrival of a new season—the skirt was big last summer, so for winter, pants will be in; if the must-have skirt for winter 2001 stops at midcalf, for winter 2002 it can end just above the knee. In the seventeenth century, all such extreme shifts were quite simply unthinkable because the parameters for possible change were tightly constrained by modesty and etiquette. Commentators on seventeenth-century fashion often remark that styles barely evolved for years at a time. There was much more variation than is usually acknowledged; it was, however, largely so subtle that, to observers accustomed to bold moves, it is often nearly imperceptible. It's possible that fashion historians of the future will say the same thing about today's more minimalist designers: think of Jil Sander and her esthetic of simplicity and her focus on fabric and detail—she is speaking the language of the first couturieres.

Today, the accessory is the backbone of the fashion industry for reasons that are easy to understand: many more women can afford a designer purse than a couture gown, and the profit margin is far higher on the bag. The accessory initially rose to prominence as the most evident way of convincing women to want superfluous things and to change simply for the sake of change. The accessory's first starring role on the couture scene was also engineered by women.

In seventeenth-century France, accessories were initially sold only by men known as *merciers*, notions sellers or haberdashers. Today, the term *mercerie* denotes a modest establishment selling small articles related to sewing. But in the seventeenth century, merceries, notions stores, were the original department stores; the best ones offered a staggering range of high-fashion accessories. The first famous accessories merchant was a haberdasher, Perdrigeon; in the mid–seventeenth century, when Molière in *Les Précieuses ridicules* (The Precious Damsels, 1659) and other authors wished to satirize women's desire for completely useless things, they always evoked his name.

Then, women decided to invade this male preserve, just as the couturieres had taken on the tailors: thanks to this second category of female entrepreneurs, the accessory became central to high fashion. Another word was invented to celebrate a new kind of expertise: *marchandes de mode*, fashion merchants. Legally, their territory was strictly limited: they could make and trim any item that women wore on their heads or on their shoulders; they could also make accessories for dresses, such as belts and ruffles. But don't cry for the marchandes de mode: they quickly made the frill the hottest thing in fashion. In addition, they learned how to sell a new type of fashion magic, one now known as accessorizing, the art of knowing how to wear each new accessory so that others can understand at a glance just how new it is. The marchandes de mode put the accessory on high fashion's map.

By century's end, the marchande de mode had taken over the role formerly played by the notions seller in satirical plays: she was portrayed as the temptress who led women into extravagance. In Florent Dancourt's 1692 comedy *Les Bourgeoises à la mode* (Middle-Class Women of Fashion), Angélique, a notary's wife, believes she's more intelligent than any aristocrat and so has decided to live as though she were to the manor born. This means most obviously that she sets out to become a fashion queen. Thus Angélique falls under the sway of Madame Amelin, marchande de mode, whom we encounter when she arrives to collect her due, coyly called a *mémoire*, a "reminder," which reminds us that it was considered indelicate to ask nobles for money, a belief that explains the situation featured in the play. For Angélique, just like the aristocrats she emulates, has run up a big tab. She owes Madame Amelin, among other things, "for having embellished Madame's left shoulder" and "for having come up with the idea for an extraordinary hairdo."

That "reminder" pinpoints the way in which the marchandes de mode had created a new profession. They sold vast quantities of accessories because they understood just where to place each of them and just how each should be arranged—the crucial importance of, say, the left shoulder in achieving a look—knowledge that, or so her contemporaries believed, only women could possess. (And so it goes still today: just recently, my favorite salesgirl at my favorite Parisian boutique convinced me to buy a new kind of belt with a phrase of which Madame Amelin would have been proud: "Accessories make the outfit.")

Edme Boursault's 1694 comedy *Les Mots à la mode* (Fashionable Words), is an extended riff on the extravagant new words with which the French language was becoming larded because of the fashion merchants' ever ingenious promotion of new accessories. A husband is baffled by the huge bills run up by the women in his family and keeps repeating lists of items recently acquired—from a *culbute* (somersault) to a *tâtez-y* (go ahead and touch it). Most of the terms were undoubtedly as incomprehensible to many in the original audience as to the husband—and to readers today. For those in the know, however—and the play is a precursor of *The Devil Wears Prada,* a spoof of the fashion industry written for an insider public—those mysterious names were really double entendres: the mots à la mode show that all the new styles were, in one way or another, all about sex.

In the case of the *gourmandine,* a slang term for a prostitute had become the name of a type of bodice that winked open to offer a glimpse of undergarments, surely the first time that high fashion had incorporated the notion of the public display of intimate apparel. Or take the *innocente,* which was in fact anything but: an ample, beltless dress closed with ribbons tied on each side and intended for indoor wear, it was the invention of Louis XIV's long-time chief mistress, the Marquise de Montespan, allegedly to hide the expanding waistline brought on by her pregnancies. Since, however, the minute she tied up those ribbons, the King's sister-in-law duly reported, everyone began to say, "Madame de Montespan has on her floppy dress, so she must be pregnant," the innocente served to advertise rather than camouflage the illicit sexual activity that had made the dress necessary. Some contended that the hardly innocent innocente would encourage out-of-wedlock pregnancies, but French fashionistas soon squashed that idea when, in the late 1680s, they made it one of the hot looks for women, pregnant or not.

Innocente, engageante (tempting), *laisse-tout-faire* (makes it possible to do anything)—the parade of accessories marketed by the ever ingenious marchandes de mode was truly over the top, and never more so than in the 1690s, one of those decades during which fashion devoted all its wiles, particularly the display of sexy looks, to escapism, as if to compensate for the horrors of the world beyond the couture microcosm. A series of brutal winters brought widespread famine to the French countryside; disastrous wars threatened to bankrupt the nation. But through it all, the Sun King kept on displaying his diamonds; writers turned to escapism and made the fairy tale the dominant literary genre—and the fashion industry found the basis for fashion statements in news from the front.

It is said that in August 1692, during the Augsburg League War against William of Orange, French generals were awakened from their sleep by the attack that began the battle of Steenkerke; they threw on their clothes and knotted their *cravates* (now a man's necktie, then a flowing neck scarf) far less tightly than usual. The following season, Parisian boutiques commemorated the battle by featuring the *stenkerke* (Figure 2.1), loosely draped neckwear for women. The stenkerke just may be the origin of the idea that Frenchwomen instinctively know how to drape scarves to create an

FIGURE 2.1. An aristocratic woman showing off the must-have accessory for 1693, the stenkerke, a long scarf loosely draped around the neck and bodice, and the hot couture detailing of that year, the falbala, or wide band of pleated fabric.

45

effect. The *falbala* illustrated in the same image refers to the wide band of pleated fabric worn around the bottom of skirts. For some reason, it was singled out as the silliest of all the countless luxury details that distinguished couture from mere clothing: in modern French, falbala designates silly, showy ornaments or trimmings in general, with a measure of the contempt also visited upon it in English in the phrase "furbelows and flounces."

The early years of the fashion industry were accessory heaven. There was so much creativity that women could legitimately have worried that they wouldn't be able to keep up. Witness an illustration from a contemporary newspaper (Figure 2.2). It uses captions indicating each of the luxe outfit's components to make sure that, point by point, fashion trendsetters would see just how to wear all the new accessories that, in the winter of 1677–1678, they were busily charging to their "mémoires." It depicts a fashionable woman modeling a look that is an essay in pure glamour. She is positively laden down with such luxury basics as diamond-studded bows for her black velvet dress, ermine trim for its black underskirt, an adorable fluff of a muff for that note of contrasting color, and hottest of all, her *palatine*—this was a trendy little fur wrap, rather like today's snugs, shown here in sable no less, named for the King's sister-in-law, the Princesse Palatine. The illustration confirms how perfectly the concept of the look was understood. Each element was essential to the overall impression produced by the outfit: the muff was as important as the black velvet dress—and the palatine was useless unless one knew just how to drape it.

Today, the fashion industry could not function without the fashion press to publicize its every move. The fashion queens and the couturieres and the marchandes de mode could never have brought couture into existence without the advocacy of the first journalist to understand the role the fashion industry could play in the modern world, Jean Donneau de Visé. In 1672, he launched a newspaper, *Le Mercure galant* (Gallant Mercury) that was, on the one hand, unlike any other early newspaper and, on the other, the first paper to have the feel of those we know now. Donneau de Visé

Habit
d'Hyuer

Grande coeffe de gaze
brodée
Palatine de Marte

Brasselets ou nœuds
de Diamans

Manchon de pluche
de couleur

Robe de velours noir
et les nœuds de diamans

Hermine sur vne
Iupe de dessous noire

FIGURE 2.2. An engraving from January 1678 showing all the hot accessories for that winter season; this was the collection that launched haute couture. The captions go through the outfit point by point to indicate the new look's essential elements, from the embroidered silk mousseline used for the coiffe to the sable snug to the diamond bracelet to the muff in a contrasting color to the black velvet dress on which diamond knot pins glittered—to the ermine trim on the black underskirt.

reported on the news of the moment; he included as well coverage of the social scene, of arts and letters, of trends in decorating and style, of all things haute. He was also the first newsman to report on the fashion scene. In so doing, Donneau de Visé helped create couture. His coverage is an essential proof that the fashion industry was coming into existence in the late 1670s: fashion could have been made newsworthy only if such key concepts as the designer and the collection had begun to become facts of life.

Donneau de Visé even used a special format to show the importance he believed that the fashion scene deserved. The first extended coverage of la mode in his newspaper was published not in the ordinary paper for January 1678 but in a new kind of supplement, which he called *extraordinaire,* or special. This was only the second time that a newspaper had turned to special issues. The newsman who invented the concept, Théophraste Renaudot, devoted special issues to hard news. Donneau de Visé focused his extraordinaires—this is the origin of the American journalistic usage of "extra"—on style coverage. Just imagine the newsboys crying, "Extra, extra, read all about" . . . not an assassination attempt, but the new look for fall.

From the start, Le Mercure galant reached out to one audience that had never previously been targeted by the press: women. A key part of that effort was news of la mode. And marketing genius that he was, Donneau de Visé aimed his coverage not at the women who could see all the new fashions for themselves, but at Emma Bovary's precursors, women stuck in the provinces and dreaming of becoming as chic as that creature who became mythic just as soon as couture came into existence, the Parisienne.

Donneau de Visé was the first to discuss in print a number of concepts now considered basic to the fashion industry's operation. Most basic of all was the notion that fashion, like the weather, had seasons. Fashion seasons officially began in January 1678 when, in his paper's first "extraordinary" supplement, Donneau de Visé announced that from then on, he would give all the information he could gather about la mode at the beginning of every season. As part of that coverage, he pronounced that to be fashionable, it was necessary to change one's garments not only and not even primarily when the weather changed, but the minute one began to notice other women dressing in a different manner. In 1678, or so Donneau de Visé reported, fashion seasons became more powerful than the four natural divisions of the year: "Spring has barely begun to be felt, and women are already dressing this way"—in other words, it wasn't yet really warm enough, but fashionistas couldn't resist parading around in the new spring styles.

His coverage sought to give the impression that the newness of each season was absolute. "Look at these sleeves," Donneau de Visé exclaimed. "I can assure you that there have never been sleeves like these before." Now it was surely not true that the look devised for spring 1678 was unlike anything ever seen. Nevertheless, the idea had been planted that such absolute newness was both possible and desirable, and that women not lucky enough to live in Paris should consult *Le Mercure galant* to see what was happening and then change their clothes to reflect what was being seen on the streets of Paris.

From this beginning, all sorts of things fell into place. There were "in" colors for each new season: fall 1678 was tinted in shades of gray—mouse gray and pearl gray, but absolutely not the linen gray featured the summer before—whereas by the following winter, the founder of the fashion press proclaimed that "everyone is wearing black." (All this change meant increased revenues for French master dye craftsmen, who dominated this profitable sector of the fashion industry until the late eighteenth century.) The wheels of color turned so quickly, in fact, that many hues didn't even last an entire season: in November 1680, fashionistas were ready to embrace color, and crimson (feu) was splashed all over the place, but by December other shades of gray were the new black. In the October 1678 issue, Donneau de Visé made room for a serious discussion of the question. "In the past two years," he wrote, "two colors have come into existence"—at which point, he observed, correctly I think, that "this is something that happens very rarely." One of the new tones, straw, seems straightforward, but the other, Prince (always written with a capital P) is more elusive: it was almost black but turned black into a color, lighting it with hints of midnight blue and crimson fire. (Prince obviously had staying power, since it was still around in the mid-eighteenth century.)

Accessories also began to be reinvented on a seasonal basis. In May 1679, *Le Mercure* warned that narrow ribbons would "reign" over summer fashions; those still wearing the wide ones that had been the thing the previous summer had better start making the switch. Even muffs changed from one winter to the next: the must-have in 1692 was the "dog muff," with a pocket to keep a lady's tiny dog warm along with her hands. Nicolas de Blégny's insider's guide to the capital informed readers that the best ones could be found in Mademoiselle Guérin's boutique on the rue du Bac.

Then, there was the craze for fancy silk stockings. At a time

when women never had the chance to show off their legs in public, this may have been the greatest proof of the nascent fashion
industry's success at convincing its addicts that something superfluous was absolutely essential. In the spring of 1673, even the
original styles reporter, Donneau de Visé, said as much: he
announced both the availability of fabulous stockings all the way
from China (then the source of the costliest imports—think fine
porcelain rather than cheap knockoffs), hand-painted with "the
most charming figures imaginable," *and* that "ladies who wear
these patterned stockings should make up their minds to show off
their legs—otherwise it would be useless to have them on."

Striped stockings soon eclipsed the Chinese models. Later, in
the winter of 1694, only solid colors were possible, and they simply had to match the outfit—green was the hottest shade of all. By
then, women had also come up with clever ways of showing off
those luxe hose. An engraving from 1694, for example, depicts the
Comtesse d'Olonne in church, taking advantage of one of the priv-
ileges of her rank. The most important ladies of the court were
known as *dames à carreau,* cushion ladies, because they were
allowed to avoid the rigor of kneeling on hard surfaces by using an
elegant velvet cushion, called a *carreau,* that one of their servants
had carried over for them. Madame d'Olonne very ingeniously
modified the carreau's function and arranged herself sidesaddle on
it, thereby providing a glimpse of those coveted green stockings
(and some killer red high-heeled mules as well).

In a move now so widespread that it is old hat, but that the
comtesse just might have invented, she may also have been taking
advantage of her role as early celebrity model to advertise herself.
In the early 1660s, the comtesse was a scarlet woman: her looser
than loose morals, as well as her "admirable breasts" and "sensa-
tional body," had been amply exposed in *The Love Lives of the
French,* a kiss-and-tell memoir so racy that Louis XIV banished its
author, the Comte de Bussy-Rabutin, from his court. But in 1694
the comtesse's raciness was surely a thing of the past: she was sixty
by then, at a time when women that age did not show themselves

off. Could the comtesse with a past have been displaying a glimpse of green stockings in the hope of a comeback?

All the luxuriously flamboyant outfits depicted in the seventeenth-century fashion press illustrate something that has served ever since to justify the expense of couture: its dependency on highly labor-intensive detailing. The first true winter collection, in 1677–1678, featured embroidery, consistently one of the glories of French haute couture, kept alive most recently by the fabled atelier run by the Lesage family. That season, skirts simply had to be literally covered with silk embroidery. For the spring-summer collection, obsessed with luxe femininity, any surface not embroidered was sheathed in lace, then the most expensive of all couture touches. The outfits of that wildly extravagant collection were so dear that, to be sure that provincial ladies would not squander their money, Donneau de Visé included an engraving with cap-

FIGURE 2.3. An engraving from April 1678 features the signature look of the new spring-summer collection. As the captions indicate, lace was everywhere—on the skirt, the gloves, the fan. The image also features the seventeenth century's most revolutionary garment, the original couturieres' most important invention, the manteau or mantua, a more loosely cut long jacket or coat worn, separates-style, over a skirt and bodice.

tions indicating exactly the right ways of wearing that wickedly costly lace (Figure 2.3). The model's fan is lace-covered, her gloves are done in lace, and her skirt—well, that is over-the-top opulence: entirely in lace and pleated, which meant that it required almost twice as much lace, it features a final dollop, a wide lace flounce. This outfit positively screams couture.

Each collection also showcased hot fabrics. For summer 1678, "almost every lady" had an outfit made from a gossamer mousseline de soie called "invisible." (This is the "gauze" pointed out in Figure 2.3.) Thus began couture's love affair with frothy, transparent fabrics that made possible a new type of layering: an underdress or skirt in a stiff fabric such as a brocade or taffeta paired with an "invisible" overdress or skirt in a diaphanously feminine mousseline, often in a contrasting color. (This may well have been the first time couture practiced the type of blending of sharply contrasting fabrics so beloved by couturiers such as Galliano today.) Sometimes the fabric season celebrated special events: in the winter of 1687, chic Parisiennes were garbed, à la Anna and the king of Siam, in a striped fabric known as Siamese cloth in honor of the first French embassy to Siam that year.

At other moments, fashionistas went wild over the equivalent of today's urban chic. For spring 1677, an inexpensive gray serge cloth known as *grisette* was the talk of the town. Grisette was normally worn only by poor shopgirls, who, because of this, were themselves referred to as grisettes. The ladies of the court were slumming it when they had elegant outfits sewn from the same fabric worn by women on the opposite end of the social spectrum. Couturieres had taken a formerly mundane fabric and surrounded it with the aura of wealth and luxury. This was the kind of blending of high and low, of class and mass, so adored by Isaac Mizrahi and other designers today—as if denim had been used to fashion a ball gown for a fête at Versailles.

Such flagrant lack of expense was, however, rare: usually, only the most deliriously dear fabrics touched the delicate skins of France's bluebloods. In April 1681, Donneau de Visé was forced to explain to provincial fashion wannabes that they would never be able to copy the luxe-on-luxe looks of the season because the hot fabrics, foreign imports all, were simply too costly for any but the noblest pocketbooks. Paris's reigning fashion queens were not, however, to be daunted by such trivial concerns: they knew that excess fabric spells status and power, particularly when the textile costs a fortune. From the beginning, *far too much makes perfect sense* was one of couture's cardinal rules, a rule that was never more ostentatiously applied than in the display of costly fabrics. And the well-trained eyes of early fashionistas didn't miss a single bit of textile overkill.

On November 10, 1679, for example, the Marquise de Sévigné described in elaborate detail the newly completed outfits for the upcoming wedding of Mademoiselle de Louvois, daughter of one of the King's longtime ministers, the Marquis de Louvois, who was about to wed the son of one of Sévigné's dearest friends, the Duc de La Rochefoucauld. "People are going to see her outfits, just as they go to the opera," she exclaimed. The seventeenth century might not have had the catwalk, but it did have its own brand of fashion tourism. And just what were they going to see? Yards and yards of "golden" fabric, textile shot through with gold thread, embroidered with more gold thread, fabrics to end all fabrics. "The least expensive of the gilded cloth," Sévigné calculated, "cost 20 louis the yard"—nearly $7,000 a yard—whereas at the time the most expensive luxe velvets and silk damasks ran to a mere $1,000 a yard.

For the bride-to-be, more was definitely more. And for the French treasury and Louis XIV's ever-vigilant minister Colbert, more was also more—as long as the deliriously expensive fabrics were made in France. On occasion, however, French designers started trends based on exotic imports, thus making money for themselves but not for their national textile industry, and that was an altogether different proposition. In 1683, for example, the head of the Parisian police informed the King that workingwomen had by then caught on to a fashion trend launched in the late 1670s and were dressing in fabrics made in China. Colbert's response? He made the sale of Oriental imports illegal. He also issued numerous decrees to French textile manufacturers, ordering them "to imitate and thereby eliminate" foreign fabrics, and thus keep all the profits from haute couture in French pockets. This was couture's financial double bind: to start trends using the most expensive materials possible, but at the same time to make sure that those wildly expensive materials had been produced by French industry.

Probably no pockets were better lined as a result of couture's excesses than those of the merchants who sold those luxe fabrics— most of all, the master of that trade, Gaultier. Every bit a worthy precursor for his namesake today, Gaultier was one of the great trendsetters for the nascent fashion industry. Donneau de Visé credits him with the invention of that mysterious color Prince (in October 1678 Gaultier was holding out on the fashion press's first star reporter: he had invented another new color but refused to reveal his secret—and now we'll never know), with having the largest stock of the most desirable fabrics, and with having launched one of the century's most memorable fads.

This was nothing less than the first time ever that Western women's high fashion had been influenced by an ethnic look. For winter 1673, *Le Mercure* reported that the chicest Parisiennes were agog over coats imported from China and covered with hand-painted exotic flowers. The new coats clearly offered the first touch of the Orient many French consumers had ever seen, and the results were predictable: Donneau de Visé soon announced that "all the streets of Paris are filled with these Chinese coats (*manteaux*)." The paper added that not all were the real thing: one had to be careful not to be fooled into buying excellent knockoffs on which the design had been printed rather than painted. To be sure, shoppers had to look to Gaultier. *Le Mercure galant* thus turned Gaultier into the original brand name. For the first time, the fashion press instructed wannabes to pay attention to the details that made a particular garment, in this case a manteau from Gaultier's boutique, superior to any other. It was also surely the first time that fashionistas had ever confronted what is now the archetypal Oscar night panic: how many ladies would show up for the party of the moment wearing the exact same coat? Off-the-peg fashion, prêt-à-porter or ready-to-wear, had arrived.

The fact that Gaultier singled out the manteau for his invention of ethnic chic was not accidental. The manteau was the most innovative garment created in seventeenth-century France, the original couture industry's most significant contribution to the history of fashion. It was also the origin of a development with an enormous future: casual dress, or dressing down. In January 1678, our man on the fashion beat calmly announced that the fashion world was about to be turned on its head: "Since everyone in France today wants to be comfortable, people hardly ever get dressed up anymore. Just about the only thing anyone wants to wear is the garment known as a manteau. Dresses are now used only for ceremonial occasions . . . and no longer when one drops in on one's friends or just to go for a walk. So when I start describing the new spring fashions for women, pay less attention to dresses than to manteaus." The manteau—which later became known as a manto, a mantoe, or a mantua in England, where its meteoric rise to prominence was charted by Addison and Steele in *The Spectator*—was far more than a mere garment: it was the beginning of a new way of life.

When the couturieres' trade guild was formed in 1675, its statutes specified that they were allowed to sew only for women and children and that they could make only certain garments. In particular, they were forbidden to design the formal dress that had been until then standard attire for aristocratic women: the dress, the most complicated and therefore the most expensive female garment, remained the exclusive property of tailors. The mantua, created shortly after the couturieres received official status, was their revenge against this division of labor—and of the pie. It became the foundation of the couturieres' fashion empire. The idea for this fashion revolution undoubtedly came both from the couturieres, who had a lot to gain from the new garment, and from the women of the court who were their active coconspirators.

Through the centuries, the word "manteau" has designated different types of clothing, among them what it still means today, outerwear or an overcoat. Donneau de Visé had in mind a newly minted use of the term. The couturieres and their clients initially turned the overcoat into indoor wear. This manteau was at first what a noblewoman wore at home in the morning, a type of dressing gown or housecoat—though French aristocratic dressing gowns were such gloriously sumptuous affairs that I hesitate to use those words to refer to them; think night at the opera rather than TV's vision of the fifties housewife. The new manteau, or housedress, continued to evolve, as fashion does: the housecoat next became the mantua, what we might call a jacket, though some of them were very long jackets indeed, the centerpiece of a new look in which the manteau was once again worn in public. This was the type of manteau that Donneau de Visé described as the "comfortable" day wear that was "the only thing anyone wants to wear."

The mantua was the most important manifestation of a truly startling new desire, surely the first time ever that noblewomen chose to be seen in public dressed not in their most formal outfits but in what they considered casual attire. In France, this was a desire with a big future: remember Marie Antoinette playing milkmaid at Versailles. The minute the fashion industry came into existence, in other words, the original female designers invented both the concept of comfortable high fashion that Coco Chanel would so brilliantly perfect in the 1920s and the two ideas that are the foundation of Chanel's long-term legacy: sportswear and separates.

Not all mantuas were created equal—some looked more like dresses tied or belted at the waist. But as Figure 2.3 on page 51 shows, the dominant mantua was something that, with only minor changes, could still be adopted today (it is in fact startlingly like a number of ensembles from Galliano's recent collections for Christian Dior): a long, supple, and loose-fitting coat worn over some sort of bodice and a long skirt. The mantua-based look lent itself to the type of small changes that may not seem earthshattering now but were highly significant to the seventeenth-century fashion industry: it was so malleable that it became an open invitation to conspicuous consumption. Ladies often pinned up their trains, creating a more rounded silhouette, a precursor of Karl Lagerfeld's hint-of-a-bustle effect. The mantua's sleeves could be tighter at the wrist and billow out around the upper arm, or the opposite could be true. Or the mantua and skirt could be made of contrasting fabrics (Figure 2.3), thereby highlighting the distinctly separate nature of the new ensemble's components. The easily modified, more relaxed style of the late 1670s thus became the springboard that launched the French fashion industry.

The mantua, basically a simple, kimonolike design, was far easier to make than the formal court dress. The dress, the tailors' preserve, was all about stitching, while the mantua was about the cut and the way it allowed glorious fabrics to fall. The couturieres who invented it were thus the true precursors of such revolutionary modern designers as Madeleine Vionnet.

The implications of this look based on flow rather than constraint went far beyond the fashion scene. The mantua was the first specifically French look, an origin of the notion still promoted by the fashion press that women should want to dress as Frenchwomen do. The mantua quickly became the prevailing style all over Europe; mantua-based looks continued to reign over European fashion for nearly forty years. This was the first time that French fashion had known such absolute, continuous domination.

In addition, the mantua was not close-fitting, so while it could be made to measure, this wasn't strictly necessary. It thus marked the first giant step toward prêt-à-porter. And since it was less expensive to produce, the mantua was the first high-fashion garment to which nonaristocratic women could aspire. They could never hope to own a mantua made from luxe fabric, but they could—and did—adopt the new style. The mantua meant that for the first time a woman's outfit did not function as an absolute class marker: from then on, it was far less easy to know at a glance who belonged where on the social spectrum.

Finally, this was the original modern fashion revolution, the first time that a garment, like all truly revolutionary styles since—think of Chanel popping women out of their corsets—gave women more freedom of movement, or at least the illusion that they enjoyed increased freedom. The dress stipulated for court wear had a completely rigid bodice with stays sewn into it, whereas the mantua was made of fabric alone. Women still wore stays, now part of a separate undergarment, a sort of camisole. The two outfits represent, however, a totally different conception of the corset: in the first, it is on the surface and gives women an untouchable look, while in the second, it becomes the hidden "secret" beneath the exterior garments. In the dress, the focus is on the outerwear. In fact, the only garment women wore under it was the all-purpose shift, intended to be neither decorative nor alluring. The overall effect of outfits based on the mantua was looser, softer, less rigid, and more curvy—in a word, sexier.

The new outfit thus began the modern conception of intimate apparel. The casual look of 1678 also launched the erotics of underwear. The loose, unboned outerwear invites the observer to imagine both that underwear—indeed, mantuas and bodices often gaped seductively to allow a glimpse of it—and the body beneath it all. *The Spectator* said of mantuas that they gave women "an air altogether galant"—meaning flirtatiously stylish—"and dégagé," meaning easy and unconstrained. Thus, the minute they got into the act, couturieres gave French fashion a new signature: adopting the latest look signaled wealth, status, and good taste—and now an air of allurement as well. In women's hands, French couture instantly became body conscious.

And the look the couturieres launched in 1678 is still playing the same subversive role. In today's Iran, proper Islamic dress code requires that whenever women leave their homes, they wear either the chador or an overcoat, called a manteau; these are meant to be shapeless. However, women are once again finding the manteau a pliant vehicle: some of the latest Iranian manteaus have ties on the legs to show off the hips, or an elastic under the bust to show off a breast's curve. It's the Marquise de Montespan's innocente all over again.

The hot new silhouette of 1678 marked the first giant step toward brand recognition, a phenomenon upon which the fashion industry has always been dependent. It's no accident that Donneau de Visé concluded his initial feature story on the mantua by instructing his readers that if they wanted to be certain that their new outfit looked just like those being worn by the ladies of the court, they absolutely had to have it made by Madame du Creux, in her boutique on the rue Traversine. He was warning his readers that true fashion slaves had to learn to recognize all the little touches that meant that a mantua was a du Creux. The mantua thus launched fashion on its modern path. It would no longer be primarily about the one-off but about styles that could be copied and marketed to an increasingly wide audience.

When *Le Mercure galant* began its coverage of the fashion scene, it promoted two messages. First, styles are changing faster than ever before, and you absolutely have to keep informed or risk appearing completely out of it. Second, there is "a certain air" about garments made and worn in France that cannot be found elsewhere: only in Paris do they get it right. By the end of Louis XIV's reign, all over the West people were saying the same things. One guidebook advised German tourists to come to the source to experience firsthand "the particularly subtle taste" with which the French dress and informed them that the first thing to do upon arriving was to "buy new clothes in the style of the current season." In London, *The Spectator* told its readers that they simply had to experience for themselves "that goût that they do in France." You can just imagine the Cole Porter lyrics—sort of a cross between "Anything Goes" and "You're the Top."

3

Fashion Slaves

Marketing la Mode

Today, we see high fashion everywhere we turn. Fashion ads preside over the pages of even the most venerable newspapers. A new fashion magazine seems to hit the newsstands every month. And giant billboards—advertising current styles as well as the models wearing them—figure prominently in our cityscapes. It may be hard for us to imagine, therefore, a time when visual reminders of what the celebrity designers of the moment have in mind for us this season were not omnipresent. And yet in 1675 the original couturieres were operating in a city in which the only visual publicity for the latest looks was on the backs of the trend-setters who appeared at chic soirées dressed to the nines.

When the fashion industry was coming into existence, in Paris in the last three decades of the seventeenth century, its creators were quick to learn a number of lessons that those who market styles today probably think were invented only in the twentieth century. First, high fashion must advertise. Without advertising, la mode simply cannot exist. Without advertising, who would think to buy a Rolex rather than an ordinary watch? If there are no brand names, no must-have accessories of the season, no in colors, and if all these things are not instantly recognizable by those who aspire to being à la mode, then the fashion game and the fashion industry have no meaning. Only advertising can guarantee brand recognition on a scale large enough to support an industry. Second, in the case of high fashion, the familiar adage that an image is worth a thousand words is certainly true; no journalist has the ability to convey the details of an outfit the way even the crudest image can. And finally, nothing sells fashion more effectively than that heady mixture: sex and celebrity.

Had la mode's original creators not learned these lessons quickly and well, Paris would not have become the birthplace of the fashion industry. Other cities—for example, sixteenth-century Venice—had played the role of style center for the Western world before Paris; none, however, had tried to market high fashion, and their reigns had thus been short-lived. No one before the late-seventeenth-century Parisian fashion merchants had been able to conceive of fashion as a medium for the desires and the imaginings of strangers.

"Stranger" is the operative word here. For it is only by constantly striving to broaden the clientele for its goods that the fashion industry can ever hope to be able to produce those goods on a scale that allows it to survive. The initial public for the new French fashion was limited to the chic Parisiennes able to shop in the first trendy boutiques, a clientele probably comparable to the roughly two hundred women who actually buy couture ensembles today. But as is still the case, the romance of high fashion quickly proved to be a powerful stimulus for the production of luxury goods of all kinds, goods that were marketed far beyond couture's core clientele.

Couture could in fact exist only once it was able to reach an audience outside Paris. That audience initially turned to the coverage of the French scene provided by Jean Donneau de Visé, the first journalist to understand the new phenomenon taking shape in Paris. Beginning in the early 1670s, the newspaper he founded, *Le Mercure galant,* reported on all the latest looks. Yet Donneau de Visé saw that print coverage had its limits as far as fashion was concerned: in the late 1670s, he included in every issue in which a new season was previewed an engraving illustrating its outstanding innovations. Since at the time it was prohibitively expensive to mix engravings and print, this visionary approach was soon abandoned. But couture's visual culture had been launched. Before the century's end, two major new ways had been developed to market style to the ever-expanding ranks of foreign fashionistas: fashion dolls and fashion plates.

The fashion doll was the first marketing device that specifically targeted an international clientele. The earliest dolls to be decked out in the latest French fashions had been destined only for private use. In 1600, Henri IV had figurines dressed so that his fiancée, Marie de Medici, would be up on the latest French fashion trends when she arrived at court. In the early 1670s, when the Marquise de Sévigné was concerned that her description of the latest look would not be clear enough and that her daughter, stuck because of her marriage in the far reaches of Provence, would end up looking ridiculous rather than a perfect copy of Parisian chic, she would mail her dolls. In the late 1670s, when Donneau de Visé was preparing his coverage of a new fashion season, designers sent him small mannequins decked out in the latest styles; he had Louis XIV's favorite designer, Jean Bérain, sketch the dolls as a basis for the engravings used to illustrate his articles.

Then, in the final decades of the seventeenth century, early fashion moguls realized that these tiny models could be sent to shops around the world to show off the look of a new season to foreign ladies—a sort of miniature trunk show. Their arrival was always anxiously awaited, an event covered in contemporary newspapers as though a real-life supermodel had come to town.

The earliest fashion dolls, made entirely of wood, are now exceedingly rare. Some scholars believe that once their advertising mission had been accomplished, they were handed on to children as toys and thereby condemned to a short, hard life. One early French fashion doll (Figure 3.1) is two feet high and made of wood, has human hair—which was sometimes added so that the mannequin could do double duty and advertise the latest hairdos fashionable in Paris as well—and glass eyes. She wears a style from the early 1760s known simply as à la française, and her outfit—

FIGURE 3.1. This French fashion doll from the mid-eighteenth century is decked out in a casual take on a formal court style, in a cotton dress and mittens. Her outfit is a kind of aristocratic sportswear.

which is accurate down to the last furbelow and the smallest detail—is a perfect example of the aristocratic dressing down that, from the first, was promoted by French couture. Her dress's style is a model of the fashionable set's formal day wear, but it is made in cotton, a fabric normally used only for informal garments. This cotton, however, is so luxe that it is printed with exactly the kind of pattern then found on the finest silks. Everything about the figurine's ensemble—even her trendy cotton mittens—shows that she was created to make a highly individual fashion statement, to give a formal style a modern, sporty feel.

Many early fashion dolls were articulated and thus were called "jointed babies" in English. (They were also referred to as "mannequins"; the word "doll" appeared only around 1750.) An even older French fashion doll, from the turn of the eighteenth century (Figure 3.2), fourteen inches tall and entirely in wood, corresponds perfectly to the description given in *The Spectator* on January 17, 1712, of a doll that was her exact contemporary, the "jointed Baby" that had then just reached London.

That figurine, decked out in a fully accessorized cherry red ensemble "à la mode de Paris," was newly arrived at the shop of a milliner, Betty Cross-stitch (a.k.a. Charlotte Wood), near Covent Garden, a well-known purveyor of fine laces and fabrics. Ladies of fashion were flocking there to study every detail of her outfit, especially the exceptionally "dégagé" cut of her mantua. Both dolls were articulated, with metal rings serving as joints. (Articulation was a feature apparently introduced to make it easier to dress the original mannequins.) Both had anatomically correct bodies. (The male reporter in *The Spectator* admits to having been embarrassed by the body under the elaborate garments.) And both had garters painted on their wooden legs and tied in a "very curious manner." Like "the French baby" le tout Londres rushed to see in 1712, the surviving doll was undoubtedly dressed by "the most celebrated mantua-makers in Paris." Her original outfit has not survived, and today she is garbed in finery from later in the eighteenth century (Figure 3.3).

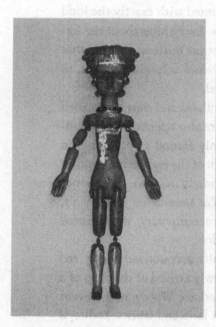

FIGURE 3.2. Perhaps the oldest surviving fashion doll, from the turn of the eighteenth century. The doll is articulated and is anatomically correct. Her intricately patterned garters are painted on, as was her makeup, traces of which are still visible.

FIGURE 3.3. The articulated fashion doll is shown dressed in her only surviving ensemble; the dress is more recent and was made perhaps a half century after the doll's initial voyage in the service of the French fashion industry.

Contemporary newspapers tell us that by the early eighteenth century, the traffic in fashion dolls was brisk; they reached London every month. The arrival of a mannequin in 1712 was particularly noteworthy because the established pattern had been interrupted for some time before that. During the War of the Spanish Succession (Queen Anne's War, 1702–1713), England and France led opposing coalitions. The military conflict spilled over into trade wars: the English, for example, imposed far lower taxes on the wines of Portugal (a member of its coalition) than on those of France, and port became the less expensive—and the patriotic—drink. The London Custom-House clamped down on the circulation of French fashion, and fashion dolls were suddenly no longer able to reach English shores, causing, as *The Spectator* put it, London's fashion slaves to become hopelessly out of it, "ridiculously tressed up." *The Spectator*'s coverage claims that ladies of fashion had protested this war effort and had even offered money (bribes?) so that "the wooden Mademoiselle" would be allowed to return.

According to Addison and Steele's French confrere Abbé Antoine-François Prévost, reporting in *Le Pour et Contre*, their efforts were successful. Despite the fact that "all English writers were openly attacking everything that could be seen as French," the English ambassador granted the ladies of London a special favor: the doll was awarded an "inviolable passport" and became, during the conflict's final months, the only commodity whose safe passage was respected by both camps. The jointed baby's return to the London scene the year before the war's end was seen by the French journalist as a diplomatic triumph for French style. And fashion dolls were soon making much longer journeys—going along on the return voyage to Salem with sea captains; arriving in shops in Boston and New York, where fashion wannabes had to pay a fixed sum just to see the doll, and three times more to take her home for closer inspection.

Those viewing charges highlight the figurines' limitations as a marketing tool: they could never be seen by a broad international clientele. For that, Parisian merchants relied on another medium: *gravures de mode,* fashion engravings, or fashion plates. These images could be quickly and frequently changed; they could be reproduced in as many copies as necessary. They played for the original high fashion the role photography plays today: they taught a broad audience about the latest fashion trends. As has been true in the world of fashion photography, each of the best-known engravers approached the marketing of la mode in a highly personal manner. During the final decades of the seventeenth century, the world of Parisian engraving evolved just as high-fashion photography has over the past half century. In the 1670s, the first great fashion engravers highlighted the clothes alone. The dresses, however, were soon no longer the real stars of fashion plates: by the 1690s, it was not always clear if the engravings were attempting to advertise a product or to promote a vision of the way in which the glitterati who could afford to own high-fashion garments lived their lives.

Fashion plates put all of advertising's potential at the fashion industry's feet: because of them, it became possible to stage what we would recognize as advertising campaigns, in particular the type of promotion used so brilliantly by designers such as Ralph Lauren to promote a total concept, a way of life, rather than a single outfit. In the pages of *Le Mercure galant* in the 1670s, Donneau de Visé suggested to his readers that they might get an authentic court look if they chose their clothes in a particular boutique. By the end of the seventeenth century, fashion plates went one step further and intimated that if consumers acquired the new outfit being depicted, they might at the same time acquire a share in the lifestyle of the person shown wearing it. Fashion plates began selling the French aristocratic way of life. They were also simultaneously confirming and marketing the notion that France and the French had a monopoly on style, sophistication, and luxury. In the terms of couture's original visual culture, to look like a fashion plate was to look perfectly French.

The golden age of fashion plates began in Paris in the 1670s when the engravings were first used to guide sartorial taste and change the way people dressed. By the 1680s, the equivalent of *Vogue* or *Elle* was in place—or rather in two places. A woman could turn to *Le Mercure galant* for print coverage, to the plates for the visual—and voilà: she had a fashion magazine. Each medium even actively publicized the other's efforts. Donneau de Visé would run a piece that began, "Such and such an engraver has just published six new plates," and then go on to describe each outfit depicted in detail. And a well-known engraver (Figure 3.4) portrayed an aristocratic lady relaxing on a sofa (then a hot new piece of furniture; like the mantua, it was less rigid than the highly formal official seat, the armchair, and therefore had sexy overtones), dressed to kill and reading the April 1688 issue of *Le Mercure galant*. When images of current fashions were for the first time ever made widely available, every player in the new enterprise hoped to benefit from the exposure.

Dame de Qualité sur vn Cannapé lisant le Mercure galand En Auril 1688.

FIGURE 3.4. This engraving, dating from barely a decade after the fashion press began, is the first depiction of a woman reading a fashion publication. She is dressed in the height of current fashion—note her "chest of drawers" hairstyle and the trendy little apron look—and is curled up on a then innovative piece of furniture, a sofa, with one leg propped up under her (the better to show off her high-fashion shoe), engrossed in the accounts of the new styles for the summer of 1688.

We know very little about the economics of fashion engravings. In the case of the early images that are straightforward depictions of a new look, fabric merchants or the merchants who fashioned and sold the scarf or stole or skirt of the moment were obviously behind their diffusion. But in the case of the many engravings from the 1690s that are far more interested in conveying information about a lifestyle or a mood than about a particular garment, it's not easy to guess why the image was marketed. Imagine many of the photos that appear in any fashion magazine today allegedly to advertise the latest look from Calvin Klein, or Prada, or Dior but that depict much more obviously an elaborately staged scene of nightlife or high life—if you saw the image without the caption, would you always know right away what it was intended to sell?

Just as fashion shots are now propelling photographers to superstardom, engravers could make names for themselves by helping to market the original high fashion. Like classic fashion photographers such as Edward Steichen or Cecil Beaton, the first star of fashion illustration, Jean Dieu de Saint-Jean, was a purist who produced images of controlled elegance. Saint-Jean made fashion engraving into an art form. Like Steichen and Beaton, Saint-Jean focused the viewer's attention on the clothes, on all those little touches that draw fashionistas to couture. (See Figure 2.1 on page 45.) *Le Mercure galant* claimed that his were also the most accurate renderings of la mode as it then functioned. Saint-Jean kept the setting, almost always indoors, simple: he generally used only a plain background with at most a floor sketched in to hint at perspective and suggest the play of light and shadow.

The other stars of the original world of fashion illustration had a style as unlike that of Saint-Jean as Helmut Newton or Guy Bourdin are different from their precursors of the 1930s and 1940s. Their name has become synonymous with French fashion plates, so much so that such engravings are sometimes referred to generically as "Bonnarts." There were in fact four Bonnart brothers, engravers all, and two of them, Henri and Nicolas, reproduced more fashion than anyone else. They began production—which they sold in their shop on the rue Saint-Jacques, the nerve center of Parisian engraving—just as the fashion industry was taking shape; in the 1690s, they redefined the genre. Unlike Saint-Jean, who almost always preferred the mystery of anonymity and displayed high fashion on unidentified aristocrats, the Bonnarts were selling celebrity at least as much as the clothes on the models' backs. And like their twentieth-century heirs, they used their illustrations to tell a story.

Before then, there had been only individual prints—a lady with the latest muff, for instance. The Bonnarts began issuing their prints in series—the princes of the French court, the great ladies of the court—in which each item would have a caption on the order of "You can buy additional portraits of members of the court at . . ." They thereby sold more engravings—it was a bit like playing cards; you wanted to have the entire deck. And so they moved the genre away from the individual print and in the direction of the portfolio or the book. Indeed, some merchants gathered together the work of different engravers into books—one ad from the end of the century promoted a nine-hundred-page volume; this gives some idea of both the total production and of the genre's sales potential. Above all, these series identified fashion with specific individuals—and with their lifestyles, or at least the viewer's fantasy of their lifestyles. Each outfit was shown off on the shoulders of one of the most important ladies at Versailles. It was as if Saint Laurent had managed to get Lady Di to be photographed in one of his famous smokings.

Or at least so the Bonnarts wanted fashion slaves to believe. In fact, it's highly unlikely that the engravers ever met any of their illustrious models; at best, they copied their faces from portraits; at worst, they simply made them up. But those who purchased these series would never have suspected the hoax. For them, the prints were the closest they would ever get to a glimpse of the lifestyles of the rich and famous. And this is where the Bonnarts' next innovation came into play. Whereas Saint-Jean had displayed

his anonymous models against a plain white backdrop, the Bonnarts and the engravers who rushed in to follow in their footsteps
showed off their aristocratic stars standing in front of their magnificent châteaus or in their fabulous gardens—or better yet, in the
privacy of their bedrooms.

Imagine the thrill of seeing just how to wear a relentlessly
trendy outfit and, at the same time, seeing Madame la Comtesse
de Mailly (Figure 3.5), a real-life countess and, better yet, as the
caption tells us, "lady-in-waiting to the Princesse de Savoie," as
she's sitting in front of a brand-new piece of furniture, her dressing table, engaged in the intimate activity of arranging her
makeup and her jewelry. The advertising agency that in the mid-
1960s launched Estée Lauder's first higher-priced fragrances with
a campaign featuring Lauder herself in her own home surrounded
by her personal artwork and rugs was practicing the Bonnarts'
brand of marketing. The countess is portrayed in a pose so casual
that it proves to viewers both that they are seeing her as only her
closest friends are able to and that, if you're someone really important, you don't have to be seen only in your most perfect state;
you'll look great even in your at-home attire. This view of the
Comtesse de Mailly's boudoir glows with the sheen of effective
promotion; it could have been the model for a Ralph Lauren ad.
We see her surrounded by lots of those lovely mirrors and little
bottles and pots that, as we all know, cover every available surface
in any great family's château, exactly the fancy doodads that the
earliest French antique dealers were just then beginning to sell.

These engravings used the implicit patronage of the French
aristocracy to market fashion: after all, whatever the Comtesse de
Mailly wore simply *had* to be elegant. Thus, hot accessories were
often named for court figures or for the most famous actresses of
the day or even for the roles that had made those actresses
famous—something that was happening in cuisine as well, when
for the first time new preparations were christened with the name
of important contemporary personages (Béchamel and Colbert, for
instance). Fashion plates also, by the way, had something to offer

Se vend à Paris chez BERET Graveur rüe S.t Jacques à vis la vüe de la Parchemiñerie a la Princesse de Savoye Avec Privilege

Madame la Comtesse de Mailly

Dame d'attour de Madame la Princesse de Savoye

FIGURE 3.5. A fashion plate depicts the Comtesse de Mailly in the privacy of her bedroom putting the finishing touches to her makeup and jewelry. The ad shows off a high-fashion look and at the same time tantalizes viewers with what it suggests is an insider's view of life at Versailles.

their subjects, who were undoubtedly VIPs within, let's face it, the very tiny world of Versailles, but hardly household names to the wide world outside, to which they became far more familiar thanks to these engravings. And some of them had a lot to gain from the exposure.

Take the case of the Comtesse de Mailly. When the engraving was published, she was the wife of a wealthy and famously elegant aristocrat (a contemporary painting, *The Family of Louis, Comte de Mailly,* shows off his progeny surrounded by all the trappings of his rank). She was also a true Versailles insider: Louis XIV often found room for her in his carriage, a rare honor. But it had not always been thus. She had arrived at Versailles as Mademoiselle de Saint-Hermine, a penniless provincial girl; she owed all her status to the influence of her cousin Madame de Maintenon, who, as Louis's not-so-secret secret wife, was the most powerful woman in the kingdom—she had forced the Comte de Mailly to marry her young cousin, of whom one contemporary wag remarked: "She had brought to Versailles all her country manners." To those in the know, making Madame de Mailly into a model of elegance would have seemed a joke, and black humor at that in the 1690s, when she was spending a fortune—every last penny of it the King's money—to have her apartment at Versailles, including that elegant boudoir, redecorated *every year.* Because of her excesses, in 1700 the King announced that he would no longer pay for such expenses. The countess, however, could have seen the image as public proof that you could take the country out of the girl.

Fashion plates thus invented the notion, ever more familiar to us today, of conjured celebrity. The original fashion industry may not have had the runway at its disposal, but it did have the first supermodels, women such as Madame de Mailly who, once couture had reinvented her, was transported from barefoot contessa to someone so famous for being famous that her image was passed around and put on display in countless households, where it fed the inhabitants' fantasies of luxe living. Fashion plates also played a crucial role in initiating a phenomenon that is now omnipresent, the fixation on celebrities: these images are one origin of celebrity journalism. It's hardly surprising, therefore, that the mediatization of war heroes is first visible in fashion engravings.

In 1696, France was nearing the end of almost a decade of the conflict that had set new standards for bloodshed, the War of the Great Alliance, and the man of the hour was Jean Bart, the naval hero who had defended Dunkirk against repeated English attacks the previous year. The year before that, when France was threatened by famine, he took on a Dutch squadron, overpowered the enemy flagship, and brought home to his starving countrymen a convoy of 130 ships stuffed to the gills with Polish wheat; his exploit had saved tens of thousands of lives.

In 1696, the fashion industry decided—just as their twentieth-century heirs imagined the transformation of World War II hero Audie Murphy into a movie star—that Jean Bart could model the latest menswear. A number of rival engravers, practitioners all of the dramatic school of fashion illustration, made the naval hero the focus of a veritable media blitz. Nicolas Bonnart's print shows him luxuriating on board ship, every inch the grand seigneur (Louis XIV had ennobled him, as the caption reminds us, after the grain escapade), with a manservant to pour his ale, a gentleman's plumed hat, a sensuously draped cravate, and a pocket watch (an expensive new luxury toy). The pipes master and servant are smoking provide both an exotic touch to hint at the seafaring life and just the right note of casual chic. All this, *and* he's decked out in the kind of French fashion that the gentlemen of the countries France had just defeated would have killed to own.

A rival engraver, Jean Mariette, offered an action-packed vision of the man still another engraver called "the terror of our seafaring enemies" (Figure 3.6). (France had a huge complex, richly deserved, about the naval superiority of the English and the Dutch.) His Jean Bart is a dashing swashbuckler—sword in hand, he's clearly just finished doing in an entire enemy fleet, shown sinking in the background, and he's done it all in the latest sleeves, with his buttons placed just so, putting a nicely rakish

FIGURE 3.6. France's greatest naval hero of all time, Jean Bart, is portrayed winning his most celebrated victory, over a squadron of Dutch ships. The image proves that war heroes, French ones at least, could also be fashion plates: Bart is ready to take on the enemy in man-to-man combat attired in full court regalia—he wears a formal wig and even the same shoes the King wore at Versailles. Only his drawn sword and clenched fists betray any hint of battle readiness.

Monfieur le Chevalier Jean Bart

spin on full court regalia. The fashion engravings of the 1690s promoted the message that if you were a French celebrity, you were fashionable and perfectly turned out at all times, in the privacy of your own home and even in the heat of battle.

Those crafty admen also capitalized on the fame of those who were the rock stars of the day: the singers and dancers of the Paris Opera. It was then considered risqué for a woman to appear on the stage; to make matters worse, in the 1690s, the first professional ballerinas in France, the original stars of the Paris Opera Ballet, became the first women to show off their ankles (and when their skirts twirled, most of their calves as well) in public. Opera stars such as the Loison sisters and ballerinas such as Mademoiselle de Subligny thus lent an illicit thrill to the outfits they modeled— such as the "in" sleeve for 1684, named the Amadis sleeve after Jean-Baptiste Lully's opera *Amadis des Gaules,* first staged on

January 18 of that year. (The sleeves were tight and buttoned up very high on the arm.) And nothing provided more illicit thrills than the concept of what became known as a *déshabillé*.

It comes from the verb *se déshabiller*, to undress. A déshabillé (then a recently created word) initially meant the elegant little nothings that the fashionista slipped into in her boudoir, what is now called a negligee. The aristocratic fashion queens began to use the word in another way, as part of their campaign for casual Fridays. In their usage, when a woman was dressed *en déshabillé*, she was less dressed up, wearing an outfit more casual than formal court dress.

There was nothing undressed or boudoirlike about the first publicly worn déshabillés, but the use of the same word for boudoir fashion and outdoor fashion reminds us that at the time, there was something more than slightly illicit about seeing aristocratic women strolling around in public in dress that wasn't tightly constrained. The déshabillé was another indoor look transformed into an outdoor one. All these trends were a flagrant transgression of the boundary between private and public. As the King's sister-in-law, the Princesse Palatine, remarked in April 1712 of a subsequent boudoir look that had become street fashion: "The ladies look as if they are about to go to bed." The fashion engravers went wild over the déshabillé and took full advantage of its illicit thrills because they grasped that advertising rule so overused today: sex sells.

Even the illustrations of the most apparently innocent déshabillés follow this rule. The lady reading *Le Mercure galant* (Figure 3.4) is depicted indoors and fully clothed. And yet, in an age in which portraits of noblewomen always show them in totally correct posture—backs straight, knees together—this one is relaxed, nonchalant: her body is the opposite of rigidly closed; it is open, available, particularly because her legs are separated and one is jauntily propped up on the sofa.

And when the déshabillé became the déshabillé *négligé*, or simply the *négligé*, the new "carelessly undressed" look inspired the most overtly erotic engravings anyone dared publish at a time when the censorship of visual imagery was outrageously severe in France: these fashion plates neatly prefigure fashion photography's recent glissade into pornography.

In the September 1693 issue of *Le Mercure galant,* Donneau de Visé devoted a long article to a newly published series of fashion plates by his favorite illustrator, Saint-Jean. He led off with "Noblewoman wearing a déshabillé négligé," and it's easy to see why: in the 1690s, this was as erotic as imagery could be (Figure 3.7). In fact, the woman here is so extraordinarily undone that the reporter feels obliged to justify his public display of private life and intimate apparel. Before the justification, however, he takes full advantage of the possibility for titillation by describing her outfit in detail. He lingers in particular over the new type of corset she is wearing, known as *respirant,* breathing, because it is *entr'ouvert,* gap-

Femme de qualité en deshabillé negligé

FIGURE 3.7. A noblewoman showing off the height of boudoir fashion. In seventeenth-century terms, the image was as shocking as any recent fashion photos: the décolletage of her bustier is impressive; her crossed-leg pose manages both to outline her trim leg and to display her sexy mules, which feature the original spike heels.

ing. (The lace-up look, so like today's bustiers, was quickly adopted for many seventeenth-century négligés.) Only then does he get to the justification: it's all right to be seen in a state of semiundress if you've just had bad news. "In order to show off this new type of outfit," Donneau de Visé explains, the artist "imagined that the lady had just read a distressing letter; this is evident from the expression on her face and from the rest of her pose."

The newsman was calling attention to the fact that for this image Saint-Jean, who normally avoided props and extraneous drama, did indeed invent a story: he clearly sensed that the déshabillé négligé was taking high fashion and its illustration onto dangerous new ground. But neither the fiction of bad news nor the new style the lady is wearing can explain the engraver's most transgressive move: in a period when Emily Post's precursors decreed in no uncertain terms that no woman in high society was ever allowed to cross her legs, this noblewoman is seen crossing hers, not at the ankle, which would have been a bit daring but still on the better side of propriety, but at the thigh—furthermore, since her gesture traps the material of her dress between her legs, she reveals exactly what all the luxe fabric was supposed to hide, the very shapely contour of her leg.

In a related image, Saint-Jean took the implications of the new craze for negligent high fashion to the limit. To do so, he was forced to break completely with his preference for studio scenes without props. He portrayed an aristocratic fashionista not only outdoors but in Paris's Tuileries gardens. And this makes her outfit's carelessness—the fact that it was artfully arranged to slip down and reveal more than was necessary or fitting of her left breast—all the more transgressive. A lady of the court showing off a bit of boudoir undress in a completely public setting—she's even taken off the mask with which French noblewomen usually covered their faces when they appeared in public—signified to a contemporary audience far more than the scenes of tasteful scandal now being staged by photographers such as Giles Dufour. This was a gesture without precedent.

In the final years of his career, Saint-Jean was clearly selling much more than luxe ensembles: he was marketing an idea that has continued to be promoted ever since: chic Parisiennes were both sexier and more sexually knowing than women anywhere else. On this, one final note. Whereas seventeenth-century paintings portray most of the age's beauties as pleasingly plump, as round or rounder than those across the channel, fashion plates all show off the ancestors of today's fashionable Parisiennes: there is not a trace of dimpled flesh on their trim figures. It seems that as soon as there was a fashion industry and a fashion press to publicize it, they began to lay down what remains the basic law of high fashion: to wear the most sophisticated ensembles one simply had to be slim. Is it possible that the body type exemplified by today's Parisiennes somehow developed to conform to this image promoted by fashion plates? If so, hats off to the admen.

It's been said that the moment in the 1980s and 1990s when Italy became the first country ever to challenge the French domination over the fashion industry was brought about by marketing: Italian designers, or so it is said, sensed that couture would henceforth be defined by the image it projects and no longer by the service it provides, as if marketing and style had until then made strange bedfellows. Anyone who says this doesn't know how the French created the fashion industry in the first place.

Those who planned the first couture ad campaigns had thought of everything marketing could do for fashion. They instantly saw that the connection between aristocratic chic and stealth populism was essential to fashion's survival—after all, who would want to own dozens of images depicting court figures? Not the people at court, that's for sure. From the start, proclamations of the season's must-haves were directed at those lower down on the social scale. Fashion engravers instinctively knew something that Madison Avenue claims to be discovering only now: ads must create a lifestyle; consumers are looking for a brand that suggests the universe to which they aspire. Nor would those who first marketed high fashion have batted an eye at the most sexually suggestive of today's ads: that aristocratic breast slipping oh so seductively out in a public garden may well have been more daring in its day than total nudity is in ours. They would not have been surprised to learn that some of their successors today think that the stars of pornographic films could well become the next supermodels.

They saw that high fashion properly marketed could play a significant role in carving a new economic niche for France—and even this message inspired a fashion plate. This image was originally part of what was then a stock subject for engravers, the continents, a series of plates portraying stereotypical views (exotically garbed Africans cavorting with lions, and so forth) of the peoples of the world. This particular series proposed a decidedly new stereotype, Europe in thrall to French fashion. It depicted a scene straight out of a fashion plate: a slave to French fashion, decked to the gills with furbelows and flounces, shows off her outfit and her château. A caption tells a less typical tale: "Each new style keeps money flowing out of pocketbooks and into craftsmen's pockets." Fashion ads portrayed all the figures of the French court as though each person's role was defined solely by trendy clothes, and the court allowed itself to be marketed in this way, the plate implies, because everyone understood that the fashion game could prove essential to the economic well-being of the French nation.

There is no greater proof of the success of the marketing strategies devised by those who could be seen as Madison Avenue's founding fathers than the records that have come down to us documenting the massive consumption of French fashion all over Europe as soon as fashion had begun to advertise. From the 1670s on, for example, England imported more than twenty times more luxury goods than it exported to France, leading to a colossal trade imbalance between the two countries. In the final three months of 1682 alone, a London fashion queen extraordinaire, the Countess of Pembroke (she was the sister of Charles II's French mistress,

Louise de Kéroualle), bought from just one Parisian accessories boutique—that of Lesgu and his wife, Jaquillon Laurent—ninety-nine pairs of gloves (one pair, covered with silver and gold, cost almost $1,500), twenty sashes "in various embroideries and brocades," fans, fontanges, silk stockings, a dainty rose-colored apron "covered with silver clouds," etc., etc., etc. When, after King Charles's death, the countess left England to return to France, she had to charter several ships to bring all the goods back home.

Fashion slaves indeed.

4

Cinderella's Slipper and the King's Boots

Shoes, Boots—and Mules

Diamonds may no longer be the proverbial girl's best friend: her Jimmy Choos and her Christian Louboutins just may have become dearer to her heart. Remember the episode of *Sex and the City* in which Carrie Bradshaw agreed to hand over to a mugger her jewelry and her money—"but not my Manolos"?

This is the story of how today's obsession with shoes began. Without the shoemakers of Louis XIV's reign—and without the Sun King's personal passion for haute pumps—Carrie Bradshaw would have held back something else, and Imelda Marcos would have filled her closets with Dior gowns. The transformation of the shoe industry that made possible the current craze for luxe footwear began, not only during Louis XIV's reign, but because the Sun King was himself a shoe addict of the first order.

Louis XIV had great legs. His contemporaries often said so, and he himself must have believed this was the case because he seems never to have missed an occasion to show them off. He was also fortunate enough to have lived in an age when men's fashions focused attention on their legs (and naturally, he encouraged the spread of this new fashion): the fabulously embroidered and decorated doublets and waistcoats stopped, most conveniently for a king who considered his gams his best feature, high enough to expose a nice expanse of leg. In his father's day, men, nobles and bourgeois alike, covered up their legs with boots, usually dramatically tall models that rode up well over the knee, which they wore for all but the grandest occasions. Louis XIV relegated boots to the limited place they still occupy today, reserving them for riding and hunting. This allowed him to show off, instead, all manner of elaborate pumps. Until February 13, 1669, when he danced in public for the last time, the King often displayed his legs, his fancy footwork, and his fancy footwear by taking the lead role in numerous court ballets. And in what is undoubtedly the most famous portrait of the Sun King in all his glory (Figure 4.1), exe-

FIGURE 4.1. An official portrait of Louis XIV displaying all the trappings of the monarchy. His boot shoes are a featured attraction: they are adorned with diamond buckles and the oversized bows known as windmill ties, here in bright scarlet to match his crimson high heels.

:uted by Hyacinthe Rigaud in 1701, Louis still pulled off a perfect dancer's turnout, despite the fact that by his period's standards, at age sixty-three he was already an old man.

It seems only natural that such a monarch presided over one of
the best-heeled ages of all time. Until the seventeenth century,
footwear was virtually identical for both sexes: indeed, since
women's shoes were hidden by their long skirts, they were often
less decorated than men's. As the seventeenth century unfolded,
the variety of styles available to women became ever greater. The
last decades of the seventeenth century and the early decades of the
eighteenth mark what is widely considered the most glorious era
in the history of footwear.

During the first half of the seventeenth century, footwear
became an essential component of the new French look, as well as
still another domain in which French craftsmen excelled. During
Louis XIV's reign, almost all the types of shoes and boots worn ever
since were invented. From what became known as the "Louis" or the
"Louis French" heel—a gracefully curving heel in which the sole
continues up and under the arch and down the front of the heel,
which gave women's shoes a lighter, more slender look (the fashionista engrossed in the fashion press [Figure 3.4, page 69] is showing
off the trendy curvy heel that was taking Europe by storm)—to the
age's emblematic shoe, the mule, all the era's best-loved styles were
imagined by French cobblers (Figure 4.2).

FIGURE 4.2. One of the earliest
surviving French luxe mules, just
the kind of slipper Cinderella
wore to the ball, is a study in
green and white. Made of white
leather with a green leather welt
and green embroidery, it features
the curvy Louis heel.

Article 35 of the statutes that governed the guild of *cordonniers* (shoemakers) specified that every shoe produced by guild members had to be stamped with "a special mark that made it possible to determine the shop where it had been made." This mark can be seen as the origin of modern brand-name footwear. The seventeenth century was nonetheless not yet fully an age of haute cobblers, shoemakers so celebrated that their names have entered the language. There was, however, one striking exception to this rule, a shoemaker who rose to such heights of glory that he can be said to have out-Manoloed Blahnik: Nicolas Lestage, the official bootmeister to the King. For his royal patron, Lestage invented what is surely the most legendary pair of boots of all time.

Lestage's story reads like a real-life version of "Puss in Boots," the classic fairy tale of a penniless miller's son who ends his life as a marquis, all because of a cat who knew how to make the most of a pair of boots. And Lestage found the way to use boots to win a monarch's heart all on his own, without the help of a wily cat. When we first pick up Lestage's trail, he was a big fish in a small fashion pond, the city of Bordeaux. His shop on the rue du Parlement—even his shop sign reeks of the fairy tale: "Loup Botté" (Wolf in Boots)—was so successful that Lestage had twenty workers in his employ. He was described by his contemporaries as being "pour la régale né" (a born host, the ultimate party boy and party planner). Lestage's involvement with the King who, during the long years of his reign, was destined to prove that he, too, was "pour la régale né," began right at the start, even before the King's marriage and his independent reign.

In 1659, Louis XIV was in Bordeaux. Officially, his visit was related to the negotiations for his upcoming marriage to the infanta of Spain. Very, very unofficially, it seems that he was saying his (as far as we know) last good-byes to the great love of his youth, Marie Mancini. She had been banished from Paris by her uncle, France's prime minister, Cardinal Mazarin, to eliminate the main obstacle to a great political match. Lestage, as quick as the fairy tale's crafty puss, saw his chance. He confected ("without even having measured the royal foot") a pair of men's pumps described as truly breathtaking: "Pumps upon which lilies [literally *lys*, as in the fleur-de-lys, the stylized three-petaled iris flower that was the heraldic emblem of the kings of France] were heaped upon lilies, / [Pumps] burnished by solid gold (there *might* have been a bit of exaggeration there), / [Pumps] made of honey-colored Oriental silk / Lined with taffeta in the monarch's color" (royal blue?). Eat your heart out, Carrie Bradshaw.

Despite the lack of measurements, the shoes were a perfect fit. (I did say this was a fairy tale.) The young King was so enamored of the glorious pumps that they may even have helped him put the girl of his dreams solidly into his past. He wore them, not to impress the dazzling young-Elizabeth Taylor-style beauty, Marie Mancini, but for his marriage to the rather homely Spanish infanta (who, by the way, all her life apparently adored her husband despite his legendary philandering). On his wedding day, some said that Louis thought about his new shoes as much as his bride: "In the midst of the solemnity / Of the great day of his marriage, / He was enraptured with Lestage's work."

Naturally, this was the beginning of a beautiful relationship. Nearly four years after the encounter in Bordeaux, on June 26, 1663, Lestage showed up in Paris with still another princely gift, the boots upon which his reputation is based. Jean Loret closed the August 5 issue of his gazette, *La Muse historique* (The Historical Muse), with a news flash: "All the court is abuzz with talk about an astonishing masterpiece, an invention so novel that nothing like it has ever been seen." What was the "marvel" turning all heads? "Was it a giant diamond? Was it some exotic beast? Was it a new rose from America? It was none of the above."

"But what was it, for pity's sake?"

"It was, I swear to you"—the newsman about town finally tipped his hand—"seamless boots for His Majesty's pleasure."

"Des bottes sans couture," seamless boots. What quickly became known as "Lestage's masterpiece" "so thoroughly won the prince's heart, / That Lestage had the honor of being chosen / As the only one able to make footwear for the greatest of kings." So complete was his elevation that on April 8, 1665, Lestage assembled the highest legal authorities of his native province in order to make a formal announcement of his new status, both professional and social: Louis had bestowed on him the title "master shoemaker" and had raised him to noble rank. (Jimmy Choo, by contrast, has thus far only been made an officer of the Order of the British Empire.) As a permanent reminder of his new rank, the King ordered a coat of arms established for the royal cobbler—a boot topped with a crown against a background, once again in royal blue, adorned with fleurs-de-lys—and sent Lestage a carpet "strewn with fleurs-de-lys," which Lestage proudly featured on the wall of his now hot boutique, with a portrait of his monarch hanging over it. Louis returned the favor by displaying a portrait of Lestage in a picture gallery: it was labeled "Maître Nicolas Lestage, il est miracle de son âge" (Master Nicolas Lestage, he is a miracle of his age).

We know so much about the fairy-tale existence of the first celebrity shoemaker because of still another proof of Lestage's impact on his era. Sure, Manolo Blahnik has had a retrospective of his work at London's Design Museum, and yes, a selection of his shoe designs is now in print. But can any of today's shoemakers to the stars boast of having a hundred-page volume of poetry published in their honor, to which dozens of poets contributed verse celebrating their craftsmanship? Oh, the poetry is often dreadful—those less than sparkly lines quoted in the past few pages, full of information about Lestage's biography, are all from this volume, which appeared in 1666—but the fact remains that that one pair of boots had clearly tickled the fancy of a very fancy age.

No artist could ask for a more complete tribute to the status won by virtue of his creations. The volume's frontispiece is a rendition, albeit crude, of the royal shoemaker's coat of arms. And then there is Lestage's portrait, in which, proudly assuming the grandeur of his new station—"Sir Lestage, the King's Shoemaker, 1665"—he looks us in the eye with all the dignity befitting the first cobbler ever to have his likeness passed down to posterity.

The poems that follow are truly shameless in their acclaim. Their authors present the seamless boots as a wonder of the modern world: "Antiquity had nothing to equal them; posterity cannot hope to do better." "Invincible Romans, celebrate your monuments, / It is nonetheless time to yield your place: your glory is now tarnished. / This boot that today is displayed before our eyes / Exhausts reason and all of nature." Puffery aside, the fact remains that no one was able to figure out just how Lestage had managed to make a boot completely free of stitching. One poem reports some of the theories devised to explain what all agreed was a "miracle of the cobbler's art." Someone said that he had used a section of an elephant's trunk; another poet suggested that he had taken the skin of a doe or a fawn's neck. One wit wondered if Lestage hadn't copied the technique of glassblowers and somehow "created his work of art with one breath." Someone even proposed the idea that Lestage had used skin from the feet of one of the hangman's victims—although, since Louis's boots were never described as having separate compartments to accommodate each toe, it's hard to imagine just how this would have worked. The most generally accepted view held that each boot had been shaped from a skinned calf's foot.

One of Lestage's Parisian rivals challenged him to a sort of shoe fight: he promised to duplicate Lestage's feat and produce a pair of bottes sans couture—size 10. Lestage's anonymous rival was so sure of himself that he had a formal contract drawn up: he promised to deliver his product in six months (by March 1666); at that time, Lestage would owe him the princely sum of 300 livres, roughly $15,000. If he failed, he would pay Lestage a tenth of that amount "for damages." The little duel in the sun came to a bizarre end. The Parisian was only a windbag: he started playing fast and loose, asked to be paid in advance, and never delivered the goods.

To this day, the mystery of Lestage's achievement remains unsolved. In 1804, it was announced with great fanfare that a cobbler named Colman, whose shop was in the Palais Royal, was selling seamless boots for 600 francs—and that "he was displaying a pair under glass." (From this, we infer that the modern practice of displaying luxe shoes in glass display cases began in the early nineteenth century.) Colman's boots, however, were apparently merely crude approximations, truly made from calf's trotters. In the 1860s, it was once again announced that a shoemaker had duplicated Lestage's feat, but these seamless boots were never documented. Indeed, it was only in 1930 that one of the luxe cobblers of the day, Luigi Di Mauro, at last became Lestage's equal: he created, not a boot, but a woman's shoe, glorious in its seamless simplicity and rising high on the instep.

As for Lestage, it's not clear what the wages of such overnight celebrity might have been. After taking Paris by storm, he hastily returned to Bordeaux, driven from the capital, it was rumored, by the jealous hatred of Parisian shoemakers. One poem in the volume published in his honor reads like a rather primitive ad for Lestage's shop in his native city: "If you're looking for stylish shoes, / Entrust your feet to this rare artisan. / His work is guaranteed to please." Lestage was reportedly offered vast sums for a second pair of "the miracle of our age." The King, however, expressly forbade him to make them for anyone else. And there is no record of a second royal purchase. For boots, no matter how miraculous, did cover up those handsome royal legs.

In addition, boots, like any footwear made from leather, could neither be decorated as extravagantly as fabric shoes nor as exactly matched to an individual outfit. And it was considered essential that shoes be seen as an integral part of each new look: the Versailles era created the concept of matching shoes. Thus, in an age when fragility was not a factor, since aristocrats could avoid walking outside their homes and be transported whenever they chose, most men's shoes and nearly all women's were fashioned from brocades and silks and satin.

And the emphasis was truly on the detail. At Louis XIV's court, for example, a craze for fancy buckles began: diamonds were, of course, de rigueur. Late in the seventeenth century, a kind of wildly oversized bow, known as a windmill tie, became fashionable for men's shoes—the King sports them in his portrait by Rigaud (Figure 4.1). The Rigaud portrait is designed to display Louis in all his princely glory: he is draped in ermine, the fur of kings, and his person and the entire staging area alike are "strewn," as the saying went, with fleurs-de-lys. His windmill ties are a bright blood red, the better to call attention to that one scarlet heel, strategically positioned dead center in the portrait's footwear zone.

From the beginning, the King had favored heels. Jean Bérain, Louis's favorite designer for court masques and later the chief designer for the original Paris Opera, always included high heels in the outfits he created for the King's dance performances. For his appearance in the Ballet of the Night in 1653, for example, the young King was costumed as the Sun (this was an early use of Louis's emblem); his shoes featured high heels and huge, gilded sun buckles, right down to the rays. Some historians claim that Louis XIV always wore heels because he was so short, about five feet five and a half inches, even though this would have been an average height for a man in his day. Others contend that the King was much taller, closer to five feet eleven, in fact, which would mean that his stature was very imposing indeed, particularly with the added advantage of heels.

Early in his reign, Louis decided that the heels of men's shoes simply had to be the scarlet we see in Rigaud's portrait. He was not, as is often reported, the first to wear red heels. Some say those originally appeared in Venice in the sixteenth century; others say it was in England in the early seventeenth century; still others say that the new fashion was introduced in Sweden. Louis XIV's name is so widely associated with those flaming red heels because he gave them a clear, unequivocal meaning, one that they kept until Louis XVI's day. In France they were literally status heels, a sign of nobility, a flamboyantly visible indicator of social status. A man of low birth could be called a *pied plat,* a flatfoot; he wore shoes without high heels. (In England, by contrast, red heels became the mark of the dandy, the kind of man who was a slave to French fashion.)

FIGURE 4.3. Rider's shoes or boot shoes were the height of men's fashion in the late seventeenth century.

As if to direct attention even more pointedly to those status heels, men's shoes began to sport additional scarlet touches: one style rode up very high on the ankle in a tab that was called in English a "tongue" and in French *oreilles* (ears); this tab was often folded forward, in order to display a lining that was just as red as the heels. Such shoes could be thought of as boots for the man who wanted to show off his legs. Known as "rider's shoes" or *souliers de bottes* (boot shoes), they immediately became trendy all over Europe (Figure 4.3). Louis's cousin Charles II brought the new fashion back to England; in a 1661 coronation portrait by J. M. Wright that is as over the top as any concocted for the Sun King, he sports the shoes of the moment; the high tongue is not folded over, so attention is focused solely on the fancy buckles set with red and blue stones. (Charles II did not have the diamond reserves that his French cousin was beginning to acquire.) In that portrait Charles's heels are a good deal higher than those favored by the Sun King.

In the last years of his reign, Louis did invent a new fashion for heels: he had his adorned with elaborate miniature paintings. Since, as ever, only the best would do, the finest artists of the age were put to work decorating the royal footwear. Adam Frans van der Meulen, celebrated for the canvases of Louis's greatest battles that he executed for Versailles, reproduced the same scenes on the Sun King's heels. It is even reported—though the evidence for this seems shakier—that the greatest European artist of the early eighteenth century, Antoine Watteau, covered other royal heels with tiny renditions of his signature visions of bucolic love among shepherds.

With its monarch so passionately devoted to footwear, it's no wonder that Paris became what it remains today, a city that gives visitors the impression that chic footwear is all around them. On April 9, 1671, the Marquise de Sévigné wrote her daughter with good news: a friend was about to make the long journey to Provence. The century's most doting mother gives a half dozen reasons why she's sure that her daughter will be delighted to see him, but she saves the best for last: he's agreed to slip into his luggage "two pairs of shoes made by Georget"—the haut monde's designer of that decade.

In the 1691 edition of Nicolas de Blégny's insider address book for Paris, he is categoric: the finest men's shoes were crafted by Le Poitevin on the rue Mazarine. The most glorious women's shoes came from the shop of Des Noyers on the rue Sainte-Anne and cost exactly twice as much as men's—close to $650. The following year, numerous cordonniers appeared on Blégny's cult list: in 1692, the two top places for men were near each other but quite a distance from what was clearly emerging as the nerve center for high-fashion footwear, the neighborhood around Saint-Germain-des-Prés. The shops of Sir Lucas (apparently another gentleman cobbler) on the rue Vieille du Temple and Perrot on the rue de la Verrerie were his top picks. Also highly recommended: Loziers on the rue de Seine and a slew of boutiques on the rue de Buci—Malbeau, Le Breton, Poirée, Soyer, Parent, and Le Basque. (The rue de Buci, today home to an about-to-become-no-longer-famous market, is a very short street; at the turn of the eighteenth century, it must have been wall-to-wall fancy men's footwear.) A number of new contenders for women had likewise popped up on Blégny's screen—Raveneau on the rue des Cordeliers, Bisbot on the rue Dauphine, and several shops on what was clearly the equivalent of the rue de Buci for women, the rue des Fossés Saint-Germain: Vernon, Gaborry, and Couteaux. This time, Blégny's picks were clearly right on the money: when Louis Liger published his guide to Paris for foreign tourists in 1715, he stood by Blégny's rankings.

Both Blégny and Liger also devoted space to recent innovations in the shoe trade. Liger informed his readers that waterproof footwear was now available on the rue Mazarine: this may have been the first time that waterproof shoes, which became common only in the nineteenth century, had been marketed. The new rainwear may well have been a sign that well-heeled tourists were beginning to do what visitors to Paris still do today—tour its sights, no matter what the weather; if so, another invention first marketed during Louis XIV's reign, the folding umbrella, would have made their rainy-day walking possible. And the two guides include a brand-new category, what Blégny terms "ready-made shoes." (This was then clearly quite a novel concept, as both guides go to a lot of trouble explaining, for example, that such shoes "really feel comfortable when you wear them.") The lower-end trade in footwear clustered near the city's legendary market, Les Halles. Liger makes it clear that less expensive need not necessarily mean mere plain, serviceable footwear: he directs women in search of embroidered shoes and fancy mules "in all sizes" to a shop near the Montagne Sainte-Geneviève. Might this have been the first chic resale boutique, the place where tourists with flair could unearth bargains and bring home trendy pumps unloaded by the Versailles glitterati after only "gentle" use?

Even today, when the arrival of the long-awaited latest model can work the shoe-obsessed into a white-hot frenzy, it would be hard to argue that footwear collections change as dramatically from year to year as dress styles. This was far more visibly true in the seventeenth century, when the case for radical change was just beginning to be made. Take the example of the heel. Whereas men's footwear, particularly boots, had featured heels since the Middle Ages—one theory, hotly debated, has it that the heel was a Persian invention, probably in the tenth century, designed to help riders keep their feet firmly in the stirrup—the first heels for women's shoes appeared only in the early seventeenth century. Even then, they were not yet true heels, but wedges slipped in between the heel of the foot and the sole of the shoe to make women appear taller. Exterior heels were originally used on women's shoes soon after: in Louis XIV's Paris, they became the springboard that made possible the first golden age of women's footwear.

On the there's-always-bad-news-as-well-as-good front: the arrival of the heel spelled the end of the distinction between left and right shoes, which had been widely practiced at many different periods. Shoemakers seem to have decided that it would be too costly to make all the lasts or forms required both for shoes with heels and shoes shaped for each foot; they chose the heel over the left-right distinction and began to manufacture only what were known as straight lasts. Shoes were once again shaped for each foot only in the early nineteenth century: the first set of left-right lasts in over two centuries was produced in 1822 by William Young of Philadelphia. Young's reinvention of the wheel spread quickly back to Europe, but it was only in the second half of the nineteenth century that it once again became standard practice to distinguish left shoe from right.

When Jean Donneau de Visé began the fashion press in the early 1670s, he always included information on the shoe styles of the season. Thus we learn that in 1673, women favored square-toed shoes and models inspired by such shoe fashions for men as boot shoes. His newspaper proclaimed 1677 "the year of the shoe": "Elegance is in the shoe, in the beauty of its fabric." The must-have model for that summer was a cunning little number that laced up on the side and had a tiny heel. And yes, its elegance was in the beauty of its fabric: "The most magnificent ones are made from toile de Marseilles; the cloth's pattern is overstitched or quilted; they are trimmed with an old-fashioned rose crafted from French lace."

The following summer, all that hyperfemininity had been replaced by relative sobriety: "Women are wearing shoes in white or cream-colored leather trimmed with a knot of ribbons on the side." The summer of 1678 did feature one fancier model, presumably to go with the fabulously expensive lace-covered ensemble that was every fashion queen's dream of that moment. Like the outfit itself, they must have pushed the concept of tasteful opulence to the limit: in front, they were completely "bedecked" with two different kinds of lace; behind, they featured "gold or silver buttons all up and down the heel." A tad vulgar perhaps? Or couldn't we say, as John Galliano recently did in describing his summer 2004 collection in an interview with French national television: "Who can say what's good taste and what's bad? Sometimes, in order to shake things up, you have to toss a bit of bad taste into the mix." So much wild extravagance immediately won the hearts of women all over Europe. Donneau de Visé reported that "German ladies are so enamored with French shoes that I have just seen two *tonneaux* [a shipping container that held twenty-eight cubic feet or two thousand pounds] filled with them for shipment to Germany."

Of all the styles that tickled the fancy of the age, none proved more enduring—and none came to be considered more quintessentially French—than what may well be quite simply the sexiest footwear of all time: the mule. Now the mule was not a seventeenth-century French invention. Mules existed in antiquity: the Egyptians, the Greeks, and the Romans in particular all favored flat, backless sandals. Mules also have a rich ecclesiastical history, above all as the footwear traditionally worn by popes. "Mule" comes from the Latin *mulleus calceus,* the name for the red slippers worn by Roman patricians. There was also a second type of mule popular in Rome; called *soccus* or *socculus,* it was made of either very soft leather or fabric, sometimes richly embroidered: the *soccus* was worn exclusively by women and exclusively in their own homes—only courtesans dared to wear them in public.

Perhaps because of this association, already in Rome near the beginning of its long history, the mule was the foot fetishist's dream. Witness the example of Lucius Vitellius, three-time consul, governor of Syria, and head of the government during the emperor Claudius's long absence while he was off on the expedition to Britannia. In his *Lives of the Twelve Caesars,* Suetonius lets readers in on the not-so-secret secret life of Lucius Vitellius. He carried with him at all times, tucked between his toga and his tunic, the *socculus dexter*—the mule made for the right foot (for the Romans, unlike the seventeenth-century French, maintained the left-right distinction in shoes)—of the emperor's third wife, Valeria Messalina. (She was subsequently executed after having been convicted of plotting to kill her husband.) Vitellius was often seen in public taking out that little mule "and covering it with kisses."

The term "mule" began to be used only in the mid–sixteenth century. Until well into the seventeenth century, mules were more often referred to in English as pantobles, or pantofles, or pantoufles, all of which, like the French *pantoufle,* a bedroom slipper, point to the fact that mules, like the Roman *soccus,* were considered strictly indoor wear, footwear reserved for lounging around the house. Shoe historians maintain that it was only in the nineteenth century that mules were first worn in public. They obviously have never looked closely at the French fashion engravings of the 1690s.

Fashion plates make it clear that the mule was the footwear of choice to accompany that revolutionary new way of dressing, the déshabillé, the casual look whose arrival was announced with great fanfare in the January 1678 issue of *Le Mercure galant.* Mules, often with devilishly high heels, were de rigueur with the déshabillé, and in particular with the sexiest of all the new styles, the déshabillé négligé, and they were also paired up with outfits based on the mantua. And just as the déshabillé, originally reserved for the boudoir, soon began to be seen in public, so did the mule. Fashion plates depict aristocratic women giving the mule a very public airing indeed: one hand-tinted engraving features the Comtesse d'Olonne proudly displaying, in church no less, her red highheeled mules. She was literally making a display of herself, ostentatiously showing off in public footwear made flagrantly sexy by its links to the intimacy of the boudoir.

In late-seventeenth-century France, the mule at long last came definitively out of the bedroom and triumphantly into its own—having lost none of the powerful erotic charge bestowed on it in ancient Rome. Once the most daring, the loosest, ladies of the court, such as the Comtesse d'Olonne, had paved the way, fashionistas soon made the mule—decked out as never before in fabulous fabrics, gem encrusted, and covered with lace and embroidery—*the* status footwear for balls and glam soirées. Leaving the foot half undressed, half exposed; easily kicked off; ideal for dangling provocatively from the toes—in seventeenth-century Paris the mule quickly left behind its past as a humble bedroom slipper and became the déshabillé négligé of footwear, the sexiest shoe in town.

Mules also became a quintessentially French style. Genre painting—those elegantly sparkly canvases that, from the mid-seventeenth century to the Revolution of 1789, lusciously flaunted the high jinks and the high life of the French aristocracy and promoted thereby what is still considered the most typical French look of all time—well, the masters of genre painting found the mule irresistible. And no painting makes this more evident than one of genre painting's last great masterpieces, Jean-Honoré Fragonard's *The Swing* (Figure 4.4). The woman, a frilly pink bonbon of mid-eighteenth-century furbelows and frills, is swinging with abandon high in the air, while her lover—no fashion slouch himself, in a sleek ensemble of pearly gray silk with a pink rosette in his lapel—lounges on the ground below. The woman's left leg is extended, sending her adorably frothy pink mule flying into the air; her right leg is bent at the knee, leaving the companion mule dangling—precariously and seductively. Her lover is looking up rapturously. I had always assumed that he was taking advantage of his position to get a glimpse of those intimate parts of the woman's body exposed by the swinging movement. However, no less an authority on the eroticism of feet, and of footwear, than Manolo Blahnik is convinced that Fragonard portrayed not so much a rapturous gallant as a foot fetishist in the throes of his passion: "The man is looking at the foot and the little pump."

FIGURE 4.4. Fragonard's *The Swing* (late 1760s) is French painting's most eloquent tribute to the golden age of the world's sexiest shoe, the mule. The canvas portrays the lady's dainty little pink mule as a tool of seduction; it flies through the air and attracts her lover's rapturous gaze.

Fragonard's saucy canvas hints at the end of the golden age of the mule, the century inaugurated by the Comtesse d'Olonne's killer red model and brought to an abrupt end by the French Revolution. During the century prior to the French Revolution, everyone wore mules, even the Sun King himself: according to the *Etat de la France*—literally, the "State of France," a blend of *Burke's Peerage* with an account of the state of the nation and especially of its monarch's activities and projects—the first thing the King did when he got out of bed was "to slip on his mules." And in one of the greatest portraits of the age, Nicolas de Largillierre's luxurious depiction of Louis XIV's favorite painter, Charles Le Brun, the artist is shown surrounded by his canvases and his props, but the viewer's gaze is focused on the painter's outfit. The opulent folds of his red velvet overgarment are draped in such a way as to draw particular attention to his footwear: one of the principal creators of the Versailles style is wearing boots that, even though they clearly have seams, are to die for: of glowing two-toned (brown and crimson) leather, and with elaborate stenciling in the manner of today's cowboy boots, they are not shoe boots, but boot mules—boots designed to pass for those scarlet mules in which scarlet ladies were just beginning to take on the town.

As Cole Porter said: "The world has gone mad today"—shoe crazy, that is. Even without Carrie Bradshaw and her friends, we'd still be inundated with tales of the ultimate stiletto or the killer vamp. Today's tales are told, however, with decidedly less imagination than those of that earlier shoe-obsessed age, the Versailles era. All our fictions of shoe mania are told from the point of view of the Imelda Marcos figure, as though women alone understand the obsession to fill closets with more pairs of irresistibly gorgeous and impossibly expensive shoes than they could ever hope to wear, much less wear out. We even choose to remember that classic fairy tale, "Cinderella," as a decidedly staid and cautionary vision of the power of shoes.

Cinderella was still another creation of Louis XIV's reign. This now legendary story is famous to readers today as it was told by Charles Perrault. Perrault was a major propagandist for Louis XIV's reign: he celebrated the accomplishments of his monarch, as well as those of the French fashion industry. In 1697, Perrault published "Cendrillon ou la petite pantoufle de verre" (Cinderella, or, The Little Glass Slipper), giving a version of the folktales about Cinderella that had previously circulated orally a new life in print.

In Perrault's version, an exquisitely beautiful young woman, condemned to a life of poverty and drudgery by her wicked stepsisters, with the help of her fairy godmother is able to attend a ball decked out in finery finer than that worn by any of the hautmonde notables in attendance. That night, Cinderella meets the handsome prince who is also heir to the kingdom. When she is obliged to rush off before the magic hour at which her glamorous attire will cease to exist, Cinderella "lets drop," on purpose, one of "a pair of the most beautiful glass *pantoufles* in the world." In the vision represented by Perrault's "Cinderella," only women have a relation to shoes, and that relation is resolutely bleak. Women will go to any ends—even, most recently, a controversial new type of foot surgery designed to remove bunions—in order to stuff their feet into their beloved Roger Viviers, when all that agony may well be pointless: they'll only find that fabled prince charming if they are to the slipper born.

Perrault's "Cinderella" was intially one of two often contradictory versions of this archetypal fairy tale. At the time of its initial publication, "Cendrillon" had competition from an alternate account of the Cinderella legend, this one by a woman, Marie-Catherine de Barneville, Comtesse d'Aulnoy. (Perrault's and d'Aulnoy's versions were published within months of each other, so it's impossible to say which was the original version of the tale.) D'Aulnoy's "Finette Cendron" (the title means something like "Wily Cinderella") puts the shoe at the center of the Cinderella story. To begin with, D'Aulnoy presents a very different vision of the story's famous ball: the Cinderella figure and the prince don't even meet, much less dance. The scene functions solely to advertise the Parisian fashion industry; Cinderella twirls in order to show off an extraordinary outfit confected by the most talented petites mains of all, fairy hands, right down to her "red velvet mules completely encrusted with pearls." She loses her slipper, not intentionally—*that* would be like imagining Carrie Bradshaw handing over her luxe pumps to the mugger—but by accident, in her haste to get home before her evil sisters.

The next day, the king's eldest son, Prince Chéri (his name is probably the origin of our modern cliché "Prince Charming," but it actually means "cherished" or "beloved" and is closer to momma's boy than to glamour boy and the man of a woman's dreams), finds "the tiny, lovely" mule. Whereas, in Perrault's version, the prince shows no interest in the shoe and thinks only of the woman who left it behind, d'Aulnoy gives us a prince for whom the mule is the ultimate object of desire. A worthy successor to the Roman instep man, Lucius Vitellius, Beloved Prince "held the mule up, turned it this way and that, kissed it, caressed it, and took it home with him"— all the while without giving a thought to the woman who had worn it. From then on, he is in the throes of his obsession with the most beautiful *shoe* in the world: he becomes "a completely different person"; he stops eating and refuses to go out, living for the shoe alone. Finally the king and queen, in a panic over how all this will end, call in the best doctors from Paris (for this fairy tale is proudly set in the land of designer shoes) to check out their country's heir apparent.

The specialists keep him under observation for three days and three nights before they put a positive spin on his advanced case of foot fetishism and declare that Prince Beloved is in love. When his mother begs her boy for the girl's name, he pulls out from under his pillow "his little baby, this darling, tiny mule," and announces: "Madame, this is the cause of my sickness." Still without ever having seen or given the shoe's owner a thought, he declares that he will marry only the woman who can wear the beloved shoe (thereby guaranteeing, of course, that he can have closetfuls of "baby" mules, all in the same tiny size). It is the terrified parents who send out their troops in search of the girl with the pearl mule. When she is brought to the palace, their subjects are screaming with joy; the queen "takes her in her arms and calls her her daughter; . . . the king outdoes her efforts." And Prince Chéri? He does manage to drag himself out of bed and to give his bride-to-be a kiss—but only on the hand. "She finds him handsome"; he gives her "mille amitiés," his compliments, and that's the last we hear of him.

Today, the word Perrault used for Cinderella's footwear, *pantoufle*, is translated as "slipper," whereas in 1697 a pantoufle worn to a ball was clearly a high-heeled mule (much easier to slip out of, by the way, in seemingly accidental fashion than a conventional ball slipper). When the ladies of Louis XIV's court, Cinderella-like, wore their pearl-covered mules to some of the greatest balls of all time, they were advertising in still another way the sexy new image of the chic Parisienne. They were making themselves into an open invitation to men whose heads could be turned by a well-turned ankle. The shoe-obsessed who were unable to get their hands on the real thing, Cinderella's velvet mule, soon were able to begin their collections of those tiny china and porcelain shoes that are a staple of the collectibles industry today: by the early eighteenth century, workshops in Delft began to export itty-bitty mules that faithfully reproduced the latest models from Paris. The mule has a long history, as I've said. But at no other moment was the sexy shoe so brazenly flaunted: as the Delft porcelain industry understood, the mule had become the symbol of the new dominance of French haute cobblers and of the magic they could work for their clients male and female.

D'Aulnoy's alternate version of the Cinderella story is the perfect icon for what can be seen as the first shoe-obsessed age. In a country ruled by a monarch who never tired of displaying his footwear, shoes became central to every outfit and to many psyches. The fashion-forward at the court of Versailles were the first generation able to understand the sentiment widely expressed by devotees interviewed at a recent fashion-insider shoe event, who said of their favorite models: "I don't wear them, but they are objects of desire. Look at the shape of the heels."

The Sun King became a model for fashionistas and fetishists alike. On the one hand, he was and still is seen as the best-heeled of monarchs. The darling of the French shoe scene today, Christian Louboutin, whose original boutique was located just off Paris's Place des Victoires, identifies as "one of my favorite shoes" the sandals worn by Louis XIV in the giant equestrian statue that dominates that elegant circular Place. And on the other: when near the end of his reign, in 1713, Louis XIV founded the Ecole de Danse, the origin of today's Paris Opera Ballet School, he provided instep men of his day and for centuries to come with a glorious new focus for their obsession.

5

From the French Cook to Crème Brûlée

How Cooking Became Haute Cuisine

Photo courtesy of The Ram's Head Inn, Shelter Island, NY

Bernard Loiseau is shooting for the stars." In January 1991, the *Economist* used this caption to identify the celebrity chef of the restaurant La Côte d'Or in the Burgundian village of Saulieu; Loiseau ("bird" in French) was photographed brandishing a hunting rifle. The phrase referred to the rumor, which became a reality two months later, that Loiseau was about to receive his third star, the highest rating possible, from the most powerful restaurant guide in the world, the red Michelin Guide, sometimes called the bible of gastronomes (high French for food-obsessed). No one could have foreseen how ironic the formula would appear a dozen years later.

On February 24, 2002, in his home near his by then world-famous restaurant, Loiseau used that hunting rifle to shoot himself. The event dominated the French media for days. Commentators kept repeating that no one could be sure why he had committed suicide, but Loiseau's fellow chefs had no doubt—it was because of the stars. "Il avait des soucis"—he was worried, as his close friend and the most famous French chef of all, Paul Bocuse, put it in an interview immediately after the suicide. Bocuse had in mind what many in France termed Loiseau's recent "disgrace": in the 2003 edition of France's second-most-powerful guide, the GaultMillau, his rating had dropped from 19 (out of a possible 20) to 17, with the comment that his cuisine was "agreeable but nothing more." In addition, as France 2, the state-sponsored TV channel, said in the news break announcing his suicide, Loiseau was afraid that he was about to be "dégradé," a term used when an officer has his rank stripped from him. The phrase referred, of course, to the widespread rumor that Loiseau was on the verge of a far worse disgrace than the GaultMillau drop, losing that third star he had been shooting for in 1991. This time, the rumor turned out to be false. When, four days after Loiseau's suicide, the 2003 edition of the Michelin Guide was published, La Côte d'Or had retained all its stars.

In France, no one had any problem understanding how ratings could drive someone to suicide. Marc Veyrat, who runs two three-star establishments, admitted that "for the two months before the guide comes out, I can't sleep." Another three-star chef, Pierre Gagnaire, described theirs as a "profession in which there is suffering, fatigue behind the façade," brought on by "the combination of commerce and art that keeps you always on the razor's edge," and added that "I understand his despair so well; when you've given everything to a profession, . . . and all of a sudden, people love you less, criticize you. . . ." Even the French ministers of agriculture and culture went on record to say that Loiseau's name alone evoked culinary perfection and to laud "this extremely difficult profession that has done so much for France."

Across the channel, however, commentators were having none of it—and this, despite the fact that English chefs also have to deal with the particular brand of tyranny that the Michelin Guide exercises. There, reporters and chefs alike agreed that if the pressure to maintain the ratings became too great, one should simply turn in one's stars. Marco Pierre White, formerly a three-star chef with a trendy establishment in Knightsbridge, reported that he had done just that because he was tired of "being judged by people with less knowledge than myself of how to cook." *The Independent* summed it up this way: "The Michelin-GaultMillau standard was born in France, has existed for centuries and will always belong in that place where gastronomy is a matter of life and death."

In the United States, no one even tried to understand what could cause a celebrated chef with a fabulous restaurant and hotel (newly modernized to the tune of $3 million) and at the top of his powers to kill himself rather than face criticism. Indeed, the angle taken by those covering Loiseau's suicide for the U.S. press was often radically different from the perspective adopted in France: in this country, commentators played down the role of the ratings and stressed that Loiseau had a history of depression.

The process by which France became a culinary world apart, ruled by "the Michelin-GaultMillau standard," a place where food preparation can be literally a matter of life and death, all began in 1651 with the publication of a cookbook. This was in fact the first great cookbook, the first modern cookbook, and the harbinger of a culinary revolution as a result of which food became cuisine and cuisine became French. From this moment on, the recipes that are still the foundation of traditional French cuisine began to exist as part of a permanent record. In 1651, François Pierre was a professional chef (in the seventeenth century this meant someone who ran the kitchen of a noble household) who borrowed the name of an illustrious precursor, that of Henri IV's cuisinier, La Varenne, and used it to sign a work with a title that is a marketing dream, pure Julia Child well avant la lettre: *Le Cuisinier français,* The French Chef.

During the second half of the seventeenth century, a new science began to be explored, one that much later was named gastronomy. La Varenne's cookbook initiated the culinary revolution that culminated in the creation of gastronomy. As a result of the process that began in 1651, cooking and eating began more and more to be thought of no longer as a simple necessity but as a domain in which sophistication was possible and desirable. From then on, the domain of cuisine was ruled by values such as refinement and elegance. During the second half of the seventeenth century, French cuisine began to be described with terms never before part of the food writer's vocabulary: "dainty," "delicate," "refined," "courteous," "civilized." The movement that started with La Varenne made food share in the values promoted by all the standard-bearers of the new French style, from couture to cafés; it made food essential to the new civilization of good (French) taste. Also during the second half of the seventeenth century and as an integral part of the same process, Paris became enshrined as gastronomy's international capital: the age of celebrity chefs, of the restaurant, and of must-have dishes had begun.

Because of the movement that began with La Varenne, an absolute distinction was put into place between food and fine food, what we refer to, appropriately, with a French word, "cuisine." From the beginning, the only true cuisine, the only haute cuisine, was French: La Varenne's first words are "our France," a prelude to an extended eulogy of the superiority of the French "way of life." As a result, all other cooking began to be considered inferior, as Italian cookbooks—formerly the greatest cookbook tradition in Europe—soon began to say, to food prepared "alla francese" or "perfezionato a Parigi," in the French or Parisian manner. The French way of preparing food, which by 1750 was known as *la cuisine française,* quickly became dominant all over Western Europe. That doctrine was accepted virtually without question for three and a half centuries, the longest reign of any national tradition over the culinary world.

Hand in hand with this doctrine went a second: the French are the only true masters of haute cuisine—hence La Varenne's title. (Note that the book refers to a *cuisinier* and never admits the possibility of a *cuisinière:* from that point on, the best houses and the finest families had men running their kitchens; women return, and timidly at that, to the scene of haute cuisine only in the twentieth century.) This idea was originally proclaimed in England in 1653, when La Varenne was published there—this was the first time ever that a French cookbook had been translated—under the title *The French Cook:* "Of all cooks in the world, the French are esteemed the best." (Think of it: London in 1653 under Puritan rule and just four years after the beheading of its king. Many say that Izaak Walton's *The Compleat Angler* is the most important book published that year; the translation of La Varenne is surely a contender for that title.) Fifty years later, French chefs already had the possibility of the type of career three-star cuisiniers enjoy today: the best known were international celebrities, and European aristocrats, particularly the English, fought to have them rule over their tables and paid a fortune to enjoy haute cuisine's tyranny.

The most evident characteristic of the new French cuisine was newness itself. During the second half of the seventeenth century, either the kinds of foods the French liked suddenly changed in radical fashion or the numerous books on cookery and food in general published after the success of La Varenne's cookbook quickly gave the French more sophisticated tastes. Whether the impetus came from diners or from chefs, the fact remains that in France during that half century almost everything about the way food was prepared and consumed was radically remodeled.

When *Le Cuisinier français* appeared, no new cookbook had been published in France for more than a hundred years. By the century's end, books on food preparation had become an important sector of the French publishing industry. La Varenne's book was reprinted twelve times in the first five years alone, forty-six times before 1700. It was quickly translated into every major European language; never before had a cookbook gained an international following. For the next fifteen years, books about food poured off the presses in France. It is estimated that over ninety thousand copies of these new titles circulated there during the second half of the seventeenth century, an enormous figure at a time when a thousand copies constituted an excellent print run. We don't know who was reading these books, but the subject obviously interested many outside the limited circle of professional chefs. The new cookbooks had tapped the earliest mass market for publications on food; for the first time, nonprofessional cooks were collecting and consulting cookbooks, as we still do.

The French Cook announced to the world the arrival of a new culinary experience, a single style of fine food and fine dining available to and accepted by a wide international public. Before the mid–seventeenth century, very few people anywhere had ever had access to exquisite meals beautifully prepared and served. In 1650, the portals of culinary perfection were suddenly opened to an ever broader clientele. The new cookbooks had created a particular geographical definition for fine food that was unlike anything that had existed before but that has remained in place ever since: first, if diners saw that the menu being served was French, they knew that the meal would be elegant; second, from the start, this sophisticated French food was produced not only in France, but wherever there were French chefs and faithful followers of *The French Cook.* When one style of fine dining finally became universally accepted, it was always defined as French, but its practice was never confined within French borders.

It's easy to see why *The French Cook* became such a sensation: it was quite simply the most revolutionary cookbook of all time. Previous cookbooks were mere compilations, collections of randomly selected recipes, loosely organized. Earlier French cookbooks give no sense of participation in a culinary tradition: their authors do not expect their readers to share common values or to know basic techniques. In fact, before 1650, there had been fewer signs of the emergence of a national culinary tradition in France than in other European countries. La Varenne proved in one fell swoop that France was becoming the first country to develop a true culinary art.

For the first time, La Varenne codified techniques and recipes, a process that had to begin before concepts such as haute cuisine and French cuisine could make any sense. La Varenne first made public the techniques that have served ever since as the building blocks on which professional culinary practice is founded: he opened his book, for example, with an explanation of the preparation and the use of stocks. He was then able to codify recipes that required the knowledge of these standard techniques, of basic mixtures such as the herb blend now called a bouquet garni, and of classic raw materials. Haute cuisine was initially more open to variation than was subsequently the case: bouquets garnis, for example, were not yet all identical—the now classic bay leaf, for instance, was first mentioned only in Menon's 1746 cookbook; some called them *bouquets*, others *paquets*; some even said *nouets*, or "knotted." But from then on, the author of a cookbook could be sure that his readers knew certain universally accepted rules.

La Varenne included numerous cross-references; for the first time, its author conceived of a cookbook as a unified whole, rather than a simple accumulation of recipes. This is also the original user-friendly cookbook: recipes are clear and easy to follow; they are grouped in sections and numbered; for the second edition, La Varenne added something we take for granted but that no one had thought to include before: an alphabetical list of recipes. Whereas all previous cookbooks were produced by mere compilers, La Varenne presented himself as an author: he spoke in the first person and provided a personal vision of how classic cuisine should be prepared. And last but certainly not least, the outlines of modern French cuisine are already evident in this 1651 volume. Anyone who has frequented Julia Child's books will recognize many recipes that by now are old favorites; most of them were originally codified by La Varenne, and others seem to have been his creations—*boeuf à la mode, poissons au bleu, œufs à la neige.*

Le Cuisinier français was followed two years later by an almost equally revolutionary volume, *Le Pâtissier français* (The French Pastry Chef), the earliest book to be devoted entirely to pastry, then defined as the art of making everything with a crust (meat pies were a big item). There are almost no recipes for pastry in medieval collections; scattered recipes appear in the sixteenth century; La Varenne included some baked goods but few desserts. Pastry was then so little known that the publisher of the first Dutch edition of *The French Pastry Chef* (1655) claimed that there were "many major European cities where there is no one who can practice this art." Like La Varenne, the anonymous author of *The French Pastry Chef* knew that he was trailblazing; like La Varenne, he identified himself as French and his art as quintessentially French. (At the period, anonymous publication was extremely common and not at all surprising for a new genre such as the cookbook.) Like La Varenne's, the volume is user-friendly: recipes are numbered and named; the book is divided into chapters, each of which begins by codifying the basic preparations necessary for that category—*crème de pâtissier* (today's *crème pâtissière*), *glace de sucre* (our *glaçage*).

Before this, we have no way of knowing how any of the standard types of dough were made. *The French Pastry Chef* gives the original explanation of all the basic tricks of the pastry chef's trade. The modern way of making *pâte feuilletée* (exclusively with butter and with the precise way of interweaving to obtain the same number of layers of butter and dough) was initially codified here, as were many classics of the pastry chef's repertoire: *beignets, chaussons aux pommes, choux, gaufres.* Never before had there been recipes for *gâteaux* that we would still recognize as cakes. There are fruit pies, in particular an apple pie that anyone would love. The author is far more precise than La Varenne: for the first time ever, a cookbook indicates exact cooking times, heat levels, and the precise quantity of each ingredient used. Some say that all the precision means that the book was intended for amateur as well as professional chefs; others say that any true pastry chef knows that this is one domain in which improvisation is not possible.

By the end of Louis XIV's reign, the French style of food preparation had become an essential part of Paris's image as the capital of elegance and luxury. For the first time ever, food became a tourist attraction. Guidebooks told tourists they simply had to visit Paris to taste the new dishes prepared à la mode de France. In 1670, two decades after La Varenne had announced the French assault on the world's taste buds, Savinien d'Alquié reported in the first gastronomic guide to France that foreigners visiting Paris said that "the thing they want most in the world is to have a hundred stomachs so that they could eat everything that is put in front of them, since they've never before had anything so good." By then, readers all over Europe would have believed him when he bragged that "the best food in the world is found in France." In two short decades, as a result of the revolution started by La Varenne, the basic rules that had governed the world of food for centuries had been rewritten.

French chefs were the first to reduce radically and often to eliminate the spices from the Orient—nutmeg, cinnamon, ginger, and so forth—that were the dominant flavor in medieval cooking all over Europe. In a Eurocentric gesture that parallels Louis XIV's decision to begin manufacturing in France exotic luxury goods such as porcelain, they replaced foreign spices with indigenous herbs, in particular parsley—called by one author "our French spice"—thyme, chives, and scallions. Among Oriental spices, pepper alone remained in favor: it moved up from a rarely used seasoning to the position it still occupies today, salt's coequal.

For the first time in Western cooking, a radical separation between sugar and salt went into effect. Before the birth of haute cuisine, sweet dishes were part of every course. The new French chefs allowed salt and pepper to dominate until the end of the meal and gradually moved sweet dishes to the last course, which began to be called *le dessert*. They also redefined sweetness: sugar, readily available in France for the first time because of its New World colonies, replaced honey in recipes. (Sugar was never overused in classic French cuisine because it was so dear: at its high point, in 1711, it rose to over $600 a pound.) Prior to the French culinary revolution, sweet-and-sour mixtures—often based on vinegar and honey—were a staple of food preparation. These blends were generally replaced by one ingredient alone, the ingredient that today most often stands for classic French cuisine: butter. In the Middle Ages, poor people cooked with butter, while the rich preferred oil or lard. Butter was occasionally used in sixteenth-century recipes. *The French Cook* shows that butter had come into its own: nearly half of La Varenne's recipes call for it.

Partly under butter's influence, sauces began to play the central role they still occupy in haute cuisine. Until midcentury, they were served on the side as completely separate relishes meant to enhance flavor. During Louis XIV's reign, the sauce increasingly became an integral part of the dish. New ways of thickening sauces helped make this possible. La Varenne's is the first cookbook to describe a roux. Pierre de Lune in 1656 and François Massialot in 1691 popularized the use of meat and fish reductions and of *coulis,* rich stocks they thickened with flour or powdered nuts. The sauce began to be taken seriously as a mark of fine cuisine: in 1670 one food writer said that in Paris you ate sauces so exquisite that they "could bring those on death's doorstep back to life."

The types of food eaten changed radically, too. The big birds such as peacocks that were traditional banquet fare in the Middle Ages disappeared from aristocratic tables. The new French cookbooks featured mainly veal, lamb, fowl, and game birds. For the first time, the upper classes began to eat pork. Beef, which now seems the quintessential French meat—after all, what is more basic bistro fare than *steak-frites?*—was used mainly for making stock. In the new cookbooks, some of the now classic beef preparations were first codified—*bœuf à la mode* (La Varenne), *bœuf bourguignon* (in 1656, Pierre de Lune specified that Charolais beef and marc de Bourgogne should be used)—but the French passion for *la vache* really began only in the eighteenth century, and under the influence of the national cuisine the French most love to denigrate, the English. In 1735, the *Cuisinier moderne* of Vincent La Chapelle, who had worked in London, introduced the French to *bifteck*. The medieval taste for seal, porpoise, and whale also vanished; seventeenth-century aristocrats preferred the fish that fine restaurants still serve: sole, turbot, trout.

In the Middle Ages, vegetables were thought to be indigestible, coarse fare fit for peasants. As for fruit—well, it was only in 1683 that Dr. Nicolas Venette became the first medical authority to say that it was good for you. He thereby made official the message that food writers had begun to preach in midcentury. In companion volumes, the 1651 *Le Jardinier français* (The French Gardener) and the 1654 *Les Délices de la campagne* (The Delights of the Countryside), Nicolas de Bonnefons became the spokesperson for a vision of food and its preparation at the same time completely unlike anything previously imagined and uncannily familiar to us today because of food gurus such as Alice Waters: the finest, freshest ingredients prepared in the simplest possible way. Bonnefons was the first to encourage aristocrats to cultivate their gardens. During the second half of the century, kitchen gardens and fruit orchards sprang up on great estates all over France (the most famous of which, *le potager du roi,* the King's vegetable garden, has recently been re-created at Versailles). He also encouraged his readers to savor the full flavor of the glorious primary ingredients that they could produce in this manner. All his recipes concentrated on bringing out "the authentic taste that must be given to each ingredient" and on rejecting the use of extraneous flavorings that "disguise the central taste." He complained that other cooks give all their soups the same flavor, whereas "a cabbage soup must be completely infused with the essence of cabbage, a turnip soup with turnip."

The second half of the seventeenth century was a golden age for fruits and vegetables. Many more varieties than ever before began to be cultivated: sixty kinds of pears were available in France at the beginning of the seventeenth century, but nearly four hundred in Bonnefons's day. Asparagus, artichokes, and spinach originally became important in French cuisine; the strawberry was mentioned for the first time in a cookbook in *The French Cook*. Young, tender vegetables were the rage, which explains how the green pea became the superstar of them all. A crate of baby peas was formally presented to Louis XIV at Versailles in 1660; he adored them, and the royal craving set off a mania that lasted for half a century. Comedies lampooned the "madmen" willing to pay any price to get their hands on the first of the season; in May 1696, the King's morganatic wife, the Marquise de Maintenon, portrayed the court as in a "frenzy": no one could talk about anything but the peas "already eaten, being eaten, and about to be eaten." Better fruits and readily available sugar spelled jams and jellies. Today, French confitures are considered among the finest anywhere; their reputation began along with the craze for fine fruit, with the appearance of a number of books called *confituriers* that described ways of drying and preserving—"en leur naturel," in Bonnefons's expression—all the newly abundant fruit.

By the end of the Sun King's reign, his countrymen were eating many of the dishes that are still featured on the menus of restaurants today. In this respect, no cookbook was more of a trendsetter than François Massialot's 1691 volume, *Le Cuisinier royal et bourgeois* (Cooking for Royalty and for the Bourgeoisie). This was the next culinary bestseller after *The French Cook;* it was constantly reedited until the mid-eighteenth century. Massialot's immensely readable book breaks new ground in many ways. It marks the consecration of a preparation that has played ever since a starring role in French cuisine: the stew. A few stewlike recipes—called *hachis* or *haricots*—had appeared in the sixteenth century. In the seventeenth century's final decades, the modern word *ragoût* began to be used, no longer as La Varenne still did, to mean a sauce or a seasoning added to a preparation to give it what his English translator called a "haut goût," a taste that whet the appetite, but in its modern meaning, "a stew."

The new approach to cooking meat might well have been helped along by what is surely the seventeenth century's most original culinary invention: the pressure cooker. Still today, no cooks make even remotely as great a use of this device as French cooks; they turn to it in particular when they want to serve a stew and can't be in the kitchen all day long. The new invention made it possible, in the words of its creator, Denis Papin, to cook "all types of meat in very little time." (Papin also came up with a system of evaporative cooling that is still considered the earliest precursor of air-conditioning.) In 1682, Papin published a book explaining his invention, truly a dead ringer for the modern pressure cooker (Figure 5.1); he informed readers that they could have one made by Mr. Houdry, a master welder, on the rue de la Ferronerie. (Pressure cookers, by the way, are still known in German and other languages as "Papin's pots.")

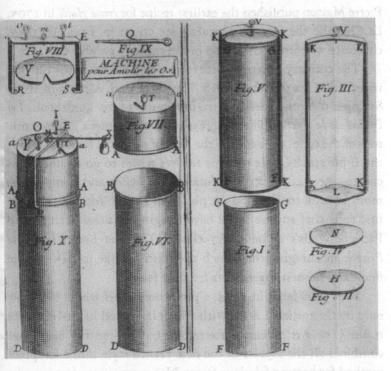

FIGURE 5.1. The diagram for the original pressure cooker, described in 1682 by its inventor, Denis Papin, as a "machine for softening bones and for cooking all types of meat in very little time."

Massialot was also one of the major innovators of all time in the dessert realm. He introduced meringues and what is apparently the most frequently ordered dessert in fine restaurants in the United States today, crème brûlée (including some nice variations such as à l'orange, with bits of orange peel). And it is in his cookbook that the ingredient now considered essential to any elegant sweet course made its inaugural appearance: Massialot's recipe for a *crème de chocolat* could still be used today. (Massialot also added a bit of chocolate to one of his many stews, just as French cooks often still do when making a *bœuf bourguignon*.) During the second half of the seventeenth century, ice became for the first time commonly available in France. At the end of the century, it began to be used to make frozen desserts—first sorbets and then ice creams. Pierre Masson published the earliest recipe for *crème glacée* in 1705, La Chapelle the first for chocolate ice cream in 1735. By then, chocolate was firmly enshrined in the culinary pantheon.

The culinary doctrines first formulated in the 1650s quickly transformed the way the French thought of food. Already in 1670, Savinien d'Alquié turned a sizable chunk of his guidebook, *Les Délices de la France* (The Delights of France), into a gastronomic tour of the country he called "the land of milk and honey of which the Bible speaks." He told his readers where to go for the finest cheese—he was particularly fond of Roquefort and Cantal—the most flavorful truffles, and the plumpest game birds. This was the first time that anyone could have imagined a mission similar to Patricia Wells's in her 1987 classic, *The Food Lover's Guide to France:* encouraging the French and tourists alike to seek out the finest and freshest ingredients for their feasts.

Four years later, in 1674, a professional chef whom we know only by the initials L.S.R., with which he signed his *L'Art de bien traiter* (The Art of Fine Entertaining), delivered the book that combines all the aspects of the new French style into a foolproof method for hosting fabulous feasts. Not exactly a modest man, he calls his method a "science"; this is the first indisputable indication that gastronomy would be an inevitable consequence of the new cuisine. L.S.R. sounds for all the world like the twentieth-century proponents of nouvelle cuisine railing against what they saw as the excess of traditional cuisine: he advocated elegant simplicity.

To make your guests feel like kings, it's not necessary to crowd the table with an overabundance of dishes and to cram into every dish as many expensive ingredients as one can think of. No: an "exquisite choice" of the freshest seasonal foods cooked "without destroying their true taste" will do it every time. The best way to eat meat? Rare and right off the grill in its own *jus*. Asparagus should be *croquantes* and served at room temperature with just oil and vinegar or hot with a sauce that is a proto-hollandaise. (L.S.R. won my Southern heart by including a recipe for a mean fried chicken—surely the first time *that* dish had appeared in print and something that proves that initially the culture of culinary refinement was considerably broader-minded than subsequent tyrants of haute cuisine would have admitted. He served it with a dipping sauce or just plain with lemon and a bit of fried parsley.) It's hard to imagine a vision of a great meal more radically different from all prior definitions of a banquet.

L.S.R. extended the doctrine of elegant simplicity to every aspect of throwing a good party—from how to choose a melon to how to seat guests around an oval or a square table to how to adopt a menu devised for eight guests if two others have to be included at the last minute. More than any other writer of the age, he is attentive to the presentation of food, to how it is arranged on the plate and on the table, and to how it is served. L.S.R. laid out a streamlined version of the highly elaborate way of serving a fancy meal, known as *service à la française*, that was practiced all over Europe until the nineteenth century, when it was replaced by what was called Russian service. In French service, one served oneself from platters in the middle of the table, while in Russian service, a servant held the platter for each guest. In the soup course in French service, for example, a variety of soups was laid out: guests then selected the soup or soups that appealed to them and that were within their reach. In today's terms, a classical French banquet was closer to eating in a restaurant than in a private home: you were often not eating the same things as the other guests at your table. You were also able to try a bit of several dishes proposed for each course: this was an age that understood, every bit as much as ours, the attraction of grazing.

Initially, French service was an orchestrated ritual that dictated with absolute precision both the order in which courses were served and the symmetrical arrangement on the table of the dishes that composed each course. The diners' plates lined the edges of the table and serving dishes occupied its center in a precise pattern. Each course was composed of the exact same number of big, middle, and small dishes, each of which occupied the same place on the table for each course. (Even the size of serving dishes was codified: big ones measured sixteen and a half inches in diameter, medium fifteen, and small twelve.)

The banquet's quality was judged both by the way in which all the different dishes in each course, as well as those in all the different courses, worked together, and by the geometrical pattern formed by the arrangement of dishes on the table (Figure 5.2). To us, this last part doesn't sound particularly complicated; it's hard to imagine that the way serving dishes were laid out could be among the principal measures of a fine feast and of a chef's worth. Seventeenth-century works such as *The Art of Fine Entertaining* stress, however, that the most important guests will never be satisfied with a less than spectacular table composition—a dress rehearsal is even advised to make sure that the design mapped out will live up to expectations. The diagram in Figure 5.2 displays the military precision with which every aspect of a table's arrangement, from the precise number of each kind of dish to the table's exact dimensions, was calculated.

Because *The Art of Fine Entertaining* contains tips on entertaining as well as recipes, it is often considered part of still another category of food publications prominent in the seventeenth century, books that give advice to the maître d'hôtel, the individual

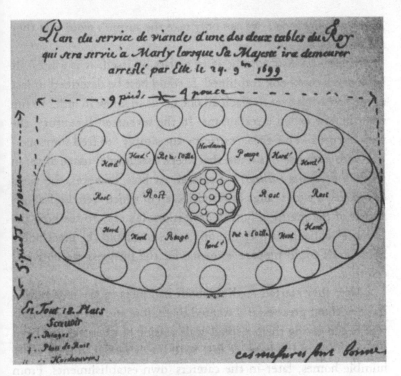

FIGURE 5.2. The design for a meat course planned for one of Louis XIV's banquets, on September 24, 1699. Note the precise measurements and, in the bottom right corner, the phrase "These arrangements are perfect" in the King's handwriting, which shows that the Sun King had personally checked over the table plan.

who oversaw every aspect of dining and entertaining in a great household. (He bought the food, planned the menus, supervised the personnel, planned the table designs, and so forth.) The best guides for aspiring maîtres d'hôtel—by Pierre de Lune in 1662 and Audiger in 1692—gave tips on everything from what they should budget for the staff's weekly consumption of red wine to the fine art of folding napkins. (Some of the patterns described in the 1659 volume Le Maître d'hôtel—the rooster, the hen with her little chicks, the suckling pig—seem incredible; since no diagrams were included, we can only take the author's word that they are possible.)

In fact, L.S.R.'s volume is in a class by itself: it is a lifestyle book and a cookbook combined. It could best be described in fact as the first book ever to teach all one needs to know in order to run what is now called a restaurant. In the seventeenth century, the verb featured in his title, *traiter*, meant simply "to feed someone." The verb gave rise to a noun that keeps that former usage alive: in modern French a *traiteur* is a caterer. At first, however, the word designated a wider range of activities, all of which were logical off-shoots of the maître d'hôtel's profession. It's easy to see how the "science" of banquet preparation for the court and the great noble households could prepare someone for the business we now call catering.

After they started reading about banquets in the new books, those without great estates wanted them, too, and one type of trai-teur began giving them a small-scale version of what was practiced for the lords of the land, at first with meals served in their more humble homes, later in the caterers' own establishments. From that point on, traiteurs became the precursors of those we call chefs; they opened the first establishments of the sort now known as restaurants. Individuals began to frequent them not only to cel-ebrate a wedding or some other special event, but simply when they wanted a fine meal served outside their home. There's no evi-dence that most traiteurs did much of what they mainly do in France today: prepare dishes that one purchased at their shops and then ate in the privacy of one's home. The luxury provided by the first caterers was not only that of preparing food, as it is for us today; it was that of serving food with elegance—à la française.

In seventeenth-century Paris, food was served in public in a variety of places—inns, cafés, cabarets (the precursors of our bars). Nobles, however, ate out only "chez le traiteur." This was the first time ever that aristocrats had dined in a public place; it marked the beginning of something we take for granted today, eating out as a form of entertainment. This was a practice so revolutionary that one of the food-obsessed noblemen who are the characters in the anonymous 1665 comedy *Les Côteaux* has to explain it to his fellow foodies: "Do you know, Marquis, what we should do? / Let's go to a traiteur and we'll dine there. / We can eat whenever we like." The new activity took off because traiteurs had to know how to do far more than merely put food on the table. As continues to be the case in all French restaurants that aspire to the standards of haute cuisine, they were also dealing in atmosphere. Their conviction that the way in which the plate and the food were displayed was as important as what was on the plate paid off handsomely, and traiteurs were soon doing a brisk business all over the city.

By the early 1690s, Nicolas de Blégny's guide to the French capital's best addresses listed thirty-four traiteurs whom he recommended when people wanted "to treat themselves to a fine meal": the niche that the Michelin Guide was created to fill in 1900 had been invented. Those Blégny singled out were located all over town: Aux Bons Enfants near the Palais Royal, A la Galerie on the rue de Seine, Aux Bâtons Royaux on the rue Saint-Honoré. Also among the trendiest, and the most expensive, eateries were Gerbois on the rue Saint-Honoré and Meunier on the rue du Temple. The chicest of them all soon clustered in the newly fashionable Saint-Germain neighborhood. One person could dine handsomely for about $100, modestly for half that price—and the least expensive meal possible in a respectable establishment cost $25. By the end of Louis XIV's reign, the first restaurant scene had developed in Paris. It was soon duly chronicled by Abbé Antoine-François Prévost, who set an episode of his most famous novel, *Mémoires et aventures d'un homme de qualité* (Memoirs and Adventures of a Man of Quality), in the 1680s and in the establishment of one of the best-known traiteurs of that day, Fracin.

The rise of the restaurant meant that the pleasures of the table were no longer reserved exclusively for the happy few invited to attend the great banquets at Versailles and other châteaus. As a result, virtually everything about what the French ate and how and where they ate it would never again be the same. Before the advent of haute cuisine, homes did not contain a dining room. The earliest architectural treatise that included a dining room as part of a floor plan appeared at the same moment as *The French Cook*. In 1661, when Louis XIV's then superintendent of finance, Nicolas Fouquet, made Vaux-le-Vicomte the first château with a dining room, he was far ahead of his time. Louis XIV's Versailles still had no room reserved for dining: any public feasting took place in part of a vast reception space; the King took most of his meals alone in his bedroom. It was only during the early eighteenth century that dining rooms began to be common, only in 1735 that Louis XV made room in Versailles's vastness for a space reserved exclusively for culinary pleasures.

Prior to the age of haute cuisine, even the grandest banquets were served on simple tabletops set up on trestles. Since these table-tops were always covered with long cloths, no one cared what they were made of or how they looked. The earliest tables made especially for dining were for one person: Louis XIV got his first one in 1673. Full-sized dining tables appeared only in the 1770s. Even then, their owners wanted them to take as little space as possible: their sides collapsed, so they could be pushed against the wall when not in use. It was only after the French Revolution that stationary tables became the center of attention in French dining rooms.

The center of the table was the focal point of seventeenth-century tables rather than individual place settings (Figure 5.3). Glasses were left on a sideboard; when guests wanted something to drink, they called for a servant to bring one over. Until the 1690s, when porcelain began to be produced in France, only metal plates existed—gold for the king, silver for the very wealthy, pewter for the less rich. Soup bowls were introduced during the second half of the century; until then soup was served in rimless bowls from which one drank.

Soup bowls led to an increased use of individual spoons, thereby creating a distinction between them and serving spoons. Emily Post's seventeenth-century precursors worked hard to convince their readers that it was horribly rude to take a spoon out of

FIGURE 5.3. Louis XIV and members of his court à table in 1687, at a banquet given in his honor at Paris's Hôtel de Ville. Note the elaborate arrangement of dishes on the table and the fact that glasses are arriving from behind. Curiously, the engraving depicts a fork beside each plate, whereas diners are clearly using their fingers to pick up food. One lady is serving herself from the dish in front of her and is using her own fork rather than one of the new serving spoons.

their mouths and use it to serve someone else a bit of the sauce they found so delicious. Antoine Courtin's 1671 *Nouveau traité de la civilité qui se pratique en France* (A New Treatise on the Rules of Politeness in France) was adamant that diners must stop using their fingers to get food from the serving dish to their plates and must use serving spoons instead. He didn't even bother trying to fight the practice of using one's fingers to get food from the individual plate to the mouth.

The fork was introduced in the seventeenth century (initially with three tines), but it was not widely adopted until the eighteenth. Standard place settings included only knives and spoons—already positioned as the French still do today, with the bowl down. It is said that Louis XIV never touched a fork in his life. As late as 1713, his sister-in-law remarked that most of those who dined at the King's table used only their knives and their fingers.

French cuisine created a new type of diner, no longer someone who merely ate, but someone who ate with refinement and discernment, an individual for whom only the French have a name: "gourmet." Gourmets have nothing in common with either those who eat only because they have to or those who stuff in everything in sight (a category for which we do have a word in English: gluttons). Gourmets were the citizens of the new world capital of gastronomy that Paris had become. The word was created in the late seventeenth century: the first gourmets were those who were so knowledgeable about wine that they could tell immediately if a wine had been adulterated or if it would age well. Those able to discern the finest foods were called at first *côteaux* (in reference to the "hills" or "sloping vineyards" on which the grapes are grown to produce many of France's finest wines). Soon the two words were used interchangeably. (Gourmets were also known as *friands*, those who really like food a lot, or the food obsessed.)

These particularly obsessed foodies immediately began to do what gourments still do today: police the world of fine food in order to dictate in all categories—from restaurants to wines—what's in and what's out. *Les Côteaux* was the earliest send-up of the French obsession with cuisine. It may well be the first play entirely devoted to food and those who live to eat. Its characters act as people often do around French dinner tables today: they pay lip service to other interests (there's a truly minimal love plot) but really only want to talk food—other meals they've eaten, where to get the most delectable duck, the latest way to prepare chicken, the perfect wine to drink with a particular dish. The gourmets were more than mere foodies: they claimed to have palates that were both preternaturally sensitive and highly trained. They believed, as did the author of *The Art of Fine Entertaining*, in a "science" of food.

The French culinary revolution naturally created the first celebrity chef.

When historians today speak of François Vatel, they often stress that he was a maître d'hôtel and so really not a chef. This is true, if by chef one means someone who stays in the kitchen. Yet modern three-star chefs do much more than that. Accounts of Loiseau's suicide stressed that famous chefs actually run a small business: typically, they have a staff of fifty to eighty working for them; they supervise all aspects of the dining experience, from the creation of menus to the floral arrangements in the dining room. The Michelin Guide's darlings are very much Vatel's heirs.

When haute cuisine was young, from the late 1650s to the early 1670s, Vatel orchestrated some of the grandest fêtes of an age that set new standards for entertaining on a grand scale. He was in charge of food preparation for two of the most prestigious domains in France: Vaux-le-Vicomte, the estate built by Nicolas Fouquet, and Chantilly, the ancestral home of the prince de Condé, head of a family many considered nobler than the ruling Bourbons. Vatel's genius was legendary: the century's equivalent of GaultMillau, contemporary journalists such as Jean Loret gave their highest rating to the pleasures both gustatory and visual that awaited guests at his performances.

Vatel twice was put to the ultimate test for any maître d'hôtel when Louis XIV and all the major figures of his court visited first Vaux and then Chantilly. Such a royal visit meant organizing several elaborate meals a day (even a *collation,* or snack, served after a stroll through the estate's gardens involved a complicated table arrangement and dozens of dishes). The court's stay at Vaux in 1661 was a fabled success: according to Loret, the main banquet's perfection was simply "inconceivable." The visit has become the stuff of legend: it is said that Louis XIV found everything so much to his taste that it was in a fit of jealous rage that he had Fouquet imprisoned the following month on charges of embezzlement. He then proceeded to move right over to Versailles everything from Vaux that he could get his hands on—Fouquet's architects, his statues, even his orange trees.

Vatel, however, got away: he is believed to have slipped out of the country; he resurfaced only in 1669, in the employ of the Condé family. Thus it was that he found himself, a decade after the Vaux extravaganza, running an even more intricate state visit for the monarch, who by this time had far higher standards for grandeur. Louis XIV and his court arrived on Thursday, April 23. That evening's festivities unfolded like a charm: a hunting party was lit by the moon and by lanterns carried by an army of servants; fireworks exploded over Chantilly's extensive gardens, freshly carpeted with jonquils for the occasion. The weather was a dream, certainly not a given in France in April. Vatel was thus able to serve a collation outdoors: the King and his entourage, out for a stroll, "happened" upon a grove as ornately decorated as a stage set with orange trees, lemon trees, thirty chandeliers, thirty candelabra, sixty huge porcelain vases (ruinously expensive Chinese porcelain, since no one in Europe had yet discovered how to manufacture it) filled with spring flowers—and in the middle, a fountain of marble and gold that let water cascade down onto a series of marble seashells. Music by the greatest composer of the age, Jean-Baptiste Lully, played in the background as guests snacked on a variety of newly invented sweetmeats.

Everyone agreed that the banquet that evening was pure magic, "enchanted," a fairy tale come true, culinary excess refined beyond any food guru's dreams—and this despite the fact that Vatel had faced the maître d'hôtel's worst nightmare: so many unexpected guests arrived with the royal party that sixty tables were required to seat them all, whereas Vatel had been told to plan for only twenty-five. As a result, two of the tables didn't get any of the most elaborate meat dishes. Even though the prince assured him that the King's supper had been flawless, Vatel kept repeating that he "had lost his honor" and could not survive such a "humiliation."

Things went from bad to worse. The next day was a Friday and therefore a meatless day in officially Roman Catholic France. This meant that all meals had to be built around seafood. Vatel, just like today's three-star chefs, had a vast network of suppliers all over the country and had sent out runners to numerous French seaports. At four in the morning, the first runner arrived at Chantilly with only a small amount of seafood. Vatel asked how much more was on its way; thinking he was asking only about the port from which this batch had come, the young man replied that there would be no more. Several hours later, when seafood started arriving from all over France, his staff went to Vatel's room to look for him: they found him swimming in his own blood. He had propped his sword against the door and driven it through his heart.

Newspapers today delight in catastrophe's ability to sell papers; Vatel's suicide would be front-page news, just as Bernard Loiseau's was. In seventeenth-century France, when actors left the stage to kill themselves in the wings so that the audience would not be confronted with even the illusion of bloodshed, official coverage of the King's visit naturally did not mention Vatel's violent end. We know the story only because of two magnificent letters in which the Marquise de Sévigné reported on the events at Chantilly. Her account helps us see why suicide would have seemed the logical response for a maître d'hôtel who had failed to give the prince and his royal guests the meal that had been planned for them.

In a country in which Catholicism was the official religion, we might think that suicide would have been considered at least as great a sin as eating meat on Friday. Upon hearing of Vatel's death, however, no one evoked Christian blame. Most worried about whether, without him, the show would go on. The Condé family indulged in a collective cry of anguish, frantic about all the parties in the pipeline. Then there was the more immediate concern of the royal visit—reported to have cost well over a million dollars. But Vatel had trained his staff with care, and—just as in the case of Loiseau's restaurant, where it was business as usual the night of his suicide—it all came off without a hitch: the King "ate very well; the perfume of jonquils filled the air; it was enchanting." In the aftermath of Vatel's suicide, some tried to shift the blame by saying that he had of late been depressed. (These accounts sound remarkably like U.S. reports of Loiseau's death.) Louis XIV, however, would have none of it. The period's greatest expert on points of honor, the King understood Vatel's agony just as Vatel had, "praised him highly," and said: "He had his own kind of honor."

And the issue of how culinary honor could justify suicide may well be the main thing to take away from the first years of haute cuisine. From the start, the new food, which was promoted as quintessentially French, was bound up with the very honor of the French nation. As a character in Montesquieu's 1721 novel, *The Persian Letters,* phrases it: "Nothing makes the French prouder than to see the taste of their chefs rule the world from North to South." And the maître d'hôtel's status was the perfect reflection of this (for Anglo-Saxons at least) strange situation of the status accorded culinary genius. Although a maître d'hôtel was in service to an aristocratic family, he had his own valet. As a badge of his culinary affiliation, he wore a white towel folded lengthwise on one shoulder, while over the other he draped the kind of flowing cape nobles wore. He wore the kind of hat nobles did, and even had the right, normally reserved strictly for aristocrats, to wear a sword. It was truly as if the status suddenly given to food had conferred on the new artists of its preparation such as Vatel their "own kind of nobility."

Vatel's decision to use the sword to which he had a right as a member of the culinary rather than the landed gentry to preserve that honor was thus completely appropriate. The "burden" of his task had simply been "too great," as the King also pointed out. (He might have been Bocuse speaking of Loiseau.) Vatel, as he himself said, simply could not "live with" the idea that he would be publicly humiliated, lose both his honor and his ranking.

Ever since, the foremost French chefs have understood his decision. Each time I walk into one of the great French palaces of gastronomy, I think of Vatel—"a man of such genius that he was capable of running a small country," as Sévigné said—and of the cost in human terms that his heirs have always paid to maintain the highly codified and refined culinary elegance now inherent to civilization à la française.

For the first three centuries of its existence, French cuisine touched few North American lives. That situation began to change rapidly with the arrival of mass air travel in the 1960s: just like their English and German precursors in the late seventeenth century, American tourists came back from trips to Paris with a new conviction, that "the best food in the world is found in France." Soon, French chefs and French restaurants became part of the culinary landscape in the United States. Soon, eating out became dining out, the evening's main event and one of life's special pleasures. Soon, French cuisine found its place on the tables and in the vocabulary of a nation where culinary sophistication had never before been widely desired.

The process by which haute cuisine first took on an American accent began with the publication of Simone Beck, Louisette Bertholle, and Julia Child's *Mastering the Art of French Cooking*, volume 1, in 1961, almost exactly three centuries after La Varenne's *The French Cook*. *Mastering the Art of French Cooking* was the culmination of the French culinary revolution launched by *The French Cook*: it made the mysteries of haute cuisine accessible to a mass audience La Varenne could never have dreamed of—to servantless cooks, to cooks who shopped in supermarkets rather than outdoor markets. It succeeded in doing so because its authors carried on La Varenne's mission: as they announced in their volume's foreword, "Anyone can cook in the French manner anywhere, with the right instruction." Beck, Bertholle, and Child presented haute cuisine as above all an affair of techniques and rules, for the most part the very techniques and rules originally codified by La Varenne in 1651. And from the moment just over forty years ago when Julia Child began her appearances on public television in *The French Chef,* the message initially formulated in Louis XIV's France became part of our culinary heritage. By now, the fine food we serve is often French food with only a hint of an accent. But from the moment *The French Chef* first aired, no one on this side of the Atlantic forgot that all fine chefs are French cooks at heart.

6

The World's First
High-Priced Lattes

Chic Cafés

Ours has always been a nation of coffee lovers. In 1670, barely six years after the British takeover of Dutch New Amsterdam, coffee controlled the niche formerly occupied by beer as the New Yorker's breakfast drink of choice. The first coffeehouse in North America was founded in Boston in 1689. Coffee was thus drunk in public in the New World not long after the coffeehouse reached the two cities today considered the pillars of café society, Paris (1675) and Vienna (1683), and long before it had begun its life in such European cities as Berlin (1721). New York got its first coffeehouse in 1696, Philadelphia in 1700. Well before there was much in the way of culture on these shores, America's coffee culture had begun.

After this promising start, our love affair with coffee then kept a very low profile indeed for some three hundred years. No one—certainly not the European visitors who shuddered at the thought of American coffee—would ever have dreamed that on January 16, 2004, a Starbucks would open on Paris's Avenue de l'Opéra. By introducing Paris, the original home of high-priced coffee, to a typically American way of marketing the brew, Starbucks was showing the world that the formerly lowly American coffee had come a long way indeed.

Sometimes we call them coffee shops; at others, coffeehouses or even coffee bars. Most often we use their French name, cafés. All these names point to one of the most significant recent changes in our cityscapes, the highly visible way in which the consumption of coffee now marks our cities great and small. Currently there seems no end to the proliferation of spots where one can linger over an espresso, and perhaps a light snack or a delicious dessert, in a setting heavy on ambiance, be it elegant or edgy—in other words, the New World's answer to the legendary cafés of Paris and Vienna. When high-end coffee to go was first marketed in the early 1970s in Seattle and the Starbucks phenomenon was launched, could any of those who were bringing European-style coffee to the United States have imagined that only a few decades later, this country would have a real café scene?

All over the country today, people are ready to pay prices that would have seemed inconceivable a decade ago in order to drink excellent coffee and to drink it in sophisticated surroundings. Thus, in Boston the niche once occupied by the country's first coffeehouse has been taken over by the far trendier Café Vanille. The nation's other first cities of coffee also favor coffeeing holes with an Old World feel. New York City has Cafe Lalo and Café Gitane, while in Philadelphia coffee lovers linger at La Colombe and Café Lutécia. The coffee capitals of today tell a similar tale: in San Francisco the Zuni Café is in, and in Seattle patrons turn to Café Campagne. In New Orleans, the courtyard of the Croissant d'Or is the place to go for French coffee and French pastry, while in Washington, D.C., Café Bonaparte fills this role. And in Jacksonville, one goes to Fuel Coffeehouse to ease into a velvet chair and nibble on a torte while sipping a glass of sherry. In all these places and countless others, the phenomenon is the same: we want coffee at all hours, but we want only the right kind of coffee served with the right kind of nibbles and in the right kind of place.

Our desire was invented, and style and coffee were originally marketed together, in Louis XIV's Paris.

Coffee was first served in France in private homes in the 1640s, when French voyagers to the Orient brought beans back as souvenirs and prepared the exotic new beverage for their friends: Pierre de La Roque began this practice, in 1644 in Marseilles, the port that remained the center of the French coffee trade. By the 1660s, coffee was being prepared in two kinds of Parisian homes, those of merchants who traded with the Orient and those of a few great lords who imported Italian coffee chefs to oversee the trendy operation. Coffee was then as wildly expensive as the rarest caviar today: a pound of beans fetched the truly princely sum of eighty livres—nearly $4,000—ten times the price of the most expensive bottle of champagne when the bubbly was brand-new. And then, in 1669, the Orient came to Paris, and the city's endless love affair with coffee began.

At that point, Franco-Turkish relations were so severely strained that Sultan Mohammed IV sent an ambassador, Suleiman Aga Mustapha Raca, to meet with Louis XIV. His diplomatic mission over, the fifty-year-old ambassador settled in Paris for a year; he immediately became high society's darling of the moment. His receptions were apparently particularly popular with aristocratic women: coffee was prepared with great flourish and then served by young and handsome slaves, dressed in flowing Turkish robes, who passed around gold-fringed damask napkins and poured the exotic new beverage into delicate cups. After the dashing ambassador's departure in late 1670, society ladies began to entertain their guests with coffee ceremonies (minus, presumably, the handsome slaves).

In the early years, the new "in" drink was marketed to potential customers in wildly different ways. In the December 2, 1666, issue of his gazette, *La Muse de la cour* (The Muse of the Court), newsman Adrien Perdou de Subligny billed the hot new "Turkish liqueur" as the seventeenth century's Viagra: "For a woman it works miracles / When her husband drinks it." In his 1671 treatise, Jacob Du Four provided an extensive discussion of coffee's many medicinal properties: it could cure migraines and stop constipation, regulate menstruation and put an end to monthly cramps, stimulate one's appetite—in 1671, coffee's promoters were selling it as an almost universal panacea.

They also realized that consumers had to be trained to deal with the new drink. Du Four thus explained that it should be drunk as hot as possible—though he warned his readers that they might burn their tongue if they used it to take a little taste of the strange-looking brew—and served in a porcelain cup, "the rim of which should be positioned between the tongue and the upper and lower lips." Coffee, he also cautioned, will have a bitter taste: "If it weren't bitter it wouldn't be good," he pronounced with somewhat circular reasoning. Those who really couldn't take it were advised to add a bit of sugar. The practice of adding sugar, then still another expensive, exotic commodity, which began in the 1670s, was said to have been much favored by women. The first lattes appeared only about 1685; in a letter from January 29, 1690, the Marquise de Sévigné referred to the resulting mixture as "coffeed milk" or "milked coffee."

Think of it: all this hype, and almost no one in Paris had as yet been able to taste the new drink. Then, in the spring of 1671, at the Saint-Germain Fair—an annual event held near Saint-Germain-des-Prés Abbey at which all ranks of society gathered to stroll by booths displaying everything from wild animals to old master paintings—an Armenian whose real name was Harouthioun but who called himself Pascal opened a new kind of booth, which he called a *maison du café*. (See Figure 12.2

on page 240.) Thus, coffee was first consumed in public in Paris only steps away from the most legendary cafés of modern Paris, Les Deux Magots and Café Flore, the cafés that were a mecca for the "lost generation" in the 1920s, the cafés that, after World War II, were the gathering spot of the great French writers and artists of that generation—from Sartre to Picasso—the cafés that, ever since, have been an obligatory stop on every first trip to Paris. Nearly three and a half centuries after the opening of the first maison du café, in our image of Paris, the bond between coffee and Paris's Left Bank remains intact.

During the second half of the seventeenth century, coffeehouses were springing up all over Europe. Those created in Paris were a world apart, however, from their counterparts in other major cities. Indeed the concept of gathering in a public place to drink coffee took hold in Paris only after the previously humble coffeehouse, a setting in which coffee became popular as an inexpensive alternative to beer, was elevated to previously unimagined heights of style and luxury.

The first known coffeehouse was founded in 1650 or 1652 in Oxford, by someone identified as "Jacob, one Jew," in a rented room in the Angel Inn on High Street. In 1652, Bowman's coffeehouse opened in Saint Michael's Alley in London. From there, the institution spread through England, the Low Countries, and Germany. The French, however, took no interest in the coffeehouse as it functioned elsewhere in Europe: it was twenty years before coffee was drunk in public in Paris.

In the early to mid-1670s, Pascal and several fellow Armenians opened coffeehouses near Saint-Germain-des-Prés, but none of them could make a go of it. Jean de La Roque, son of the man who introduced coffee to France and its first European historian, attributed their failure to the fact that they were too like English coffeehouses—they served beer; they were too smoke-filled, too dirty, and altogether not "exquisite" enough. The secret recipe that made the coffeehouse into a chic café, the formula that is being rediscovered all over the United States today, was found by

Francesco Procopio dei Coltelli, a Sicilian who began his career working for Pascal at the Saint-Germain Fair and then used his savings to open, in 1675 or 1676, his own establishment, once again near Saint-Germain-des-Prés, on the rue de Tournon.

From the start, Parisian cafés had a style all their own. The founder of the first café in the city had a vision for it identical to that of the Costes brothers, today's trendsetters on the Parisian café scene, creators of such "in" spots as the Café Beaubourg and the Café Marly: the Parisian café was to be glamorous and elegant, a place where patrons would linger in order to see and be seen. Cafés thus participated fully in the creation of the new French style: they were a showcase for the luxury goods for which Paris was becoming famous. Because of this, the new cafés attracted a new clientele, elegant women in particular, people who would never have dreamed of setting foot in a coffeehouse.

Procopio—who soon Gallicized his name as Procope—set out to make his establishment different from those that were flourishing elsewhere in Europe: smoking was not allowed (one thing at least has changed since that time!); beer was not served. Above all, Procope realized, just as his heirs do today, that people would pay for a setting glamorous enough that they would want to linger in it. Coffee was served from silver pots; tables were made of marble; chandeliers hung from the ceiling. And on the walls he displayed the latest status symbol: mirrors, mirrors made in France and not in his native Italy. The French royal company, established in 1665, had been able to produce glass of the quality and quantity needed to satisfy French demand only since 1672, so Procope's café was surely among the first commercial establishments to feature the latest French-made luxury commodity. Those mirrors on the wall would have served as a highly visible sign of his support for Louis XIV and Colbert's determination to control high-end trade.

Procope's waiters were dressed in a version of the exotic garb in which garçons had served coffee at the Saint-Germain Fair. Coiffed in fur-trimmed hats and wearing flowing caftans, presumably in homage to the Armenians who had been the first Parisian coffee purveyors, they obviously fulfilled a common fantasy of Armenian dress, because the strange outfit was used in all the original luxe cafés. Soon, when a playwright wanted to show that a character was a garçon de café, as in Florent Dancourt's 1696 comedy, *La Foire Saint-Germain* (The Saint-Germain Fair), he was costumed "en Arménien" so as to be immediately identifiable by the audience. In popular slang of the day, "going to the Armenians" meant going to a café.

In the mid-1670s, coffee was made publicly available in a second way. Itinerant coffee sellers hawked their service from the street. They carried a tray with a small brazier and all the necessary apparatus, which they would carry up to private apartments in order to brew a cup on the spot. They wore black and had a very large, very clean white napkin tied around their waist; this is still the traditional outfit for waiters in today's high-end establishments. In seventeenth-century Paris, everything related to coffee just had to be elegant: even street vendors felt obliged to live up to the new drink's standards. And soon those really on the go could buy the "portable coffeemaker, small enough to fit into a pocket," and yet containing everything right down to the coffee, the spoon, and the original to-go cup, advertised in Nicolas de Blégny's 1692 Paris guidebook. This may well have been the first coffeemaker invented in the West, the prototype for all the fancy espresso machines on the market today. It proves that, from the start, there were those who absolutely had to have fine coffee wherever they went.

The Café Procope remained on the rue de Tournon until 1686, when it moved a few minutes away to the rue des Fossés Saint-Germain (today's rue de l'Ancienne Comédie, where the establishment, by now the oldest continually functioning café in the world, can still be found at number 13). In 1689, the city's most famous theater, the Comédie Française, took up new quarters right across the street. From then on, the café became *the* place for actors and the before- and after-theater crowd. On April 18, when the new theater opened with a gala performance of Racine's *Phèdre*, featuring his muse, Champmeslé—then forty-five and near the end of her glorious reign over the Parisian stage—in the title role, Procope was there, front and center. Ever inventive, he set up a small stand where he served (garbed en Arménien?) light refreshments. Thus began a continuing tradition of providing Parisian audiences with a snack when they attend a performance.

Other cafés quickly followed in Procope's footsteps. In 1690, François Laurent opened the Café Laurent at the corner of the rue Christine and the rue Dauphine; it quickly became known as a spot where writers gathered. When Joachim Christoph Nemeitz published his 1718 guidebook, *A Paris Sojourn,* he informed foreign visitors that because "almost everyone" went out for coffee after lunch, one found "an endless number of cafés in Paris." Nemeitz's claim, that there were "ten, twelve, or even more in a single street," was surely a bit of an exaggeration. But according to official estimates, in 1715, only forty years after Procope had opened his doors, there were already between 300 and 350 cafés in Paris. In seventeenth-century terms, this was a triumph as resounding as Starbucks. From the start, everyone agreed that luxury was the secret to success in Paris. In 1759, the *Dictionnaire universel du commerce* (Universal Dictionary of Commerce) declared that "almost all Parisian cafés are magnificently decorated."

The earliest depiction of a Parisian café, the frontispiece to Louis de Mailly's 1702 *Entretiens sur les cafés* (Conversations About Cafés), proves just how completely Procope's model had carried the day (Figure 6.1). The scene is set in the evening in a typical Parisian café, where the décor is elegant indeed. The walls are hung with tapestries, elaborately framed paintings, and on the back wall, mirrors. There are comfortable armchairs, flowering plants; the room is softly lit by a posh chandelier as well as candles. The exotically dressed garçon, carrying a silver coffeepot, completes the picture.

The engraving also highlights the singularity of Parisian café society. In other European countries, women appeared in coffeehouses only very rarely, if at all. In contrast, all early accounts of

FIGURE 6.1. The earliest image of a Parisian café focuses on the stylishness of both the clientele and the décor. It portrays going out in the evening for a coffee and an elegant snack as a favorite pastime of Paris's fashionable set.

the cafés of Paris describe them as, to cite an anonymous pamphlet from 1700, *Le Portefeuille galant* (The Portfolio of Style), "places frequented by well-born people of both sexes." Indeed, the women featured in the engraving are not mere generic women, but noblewomen: their clothes and jewels, and in particular their elaborate hairstyles, known as fontanges after the mistress of Louis XIV who had invented the look, are all signs of social status. (Jean-Baptiste Rousseau's 1694 comedy, *Le Café,* suggests that there were fixed times of day, "women's hours," when women were particularly likely to frequent cafés.) The presence of a young cleric adds additional respectability to their outing.

In the background, men play sedately at cards and a board game, pastimes altogether different from those enjoyed in contemporary English or German coffeehouses, where men smoked pipes or gambled actively. In seventeenth-century Paris, the role of the coffeehouse was performed by cabarets, where an all-male clientele went to share a drink and perhaps a bit of hearty fare, mainly sausages, to go with their liquid consumption. The cabaret, like the coffeehouse, was a rather rough-and-tumble milieu, one in which style had no place; the café was the essence of style. A wide range of the luxury goods for which Paris was becoming famous were on display there, either as part of the décor or on the patrons' backs.

By including small plates and cutlery on the table in the foreground, the engraving features one final particularity of Parisian cafés, the fact that from the beginning they were, albeit in a modest way, restaurants, that is, places where you could have a snack at any hour. (This is undoubtedly why, in the United States today, the word "café" is often used to refer to an informal restaurant.) And the food one ate in a café was as unusual as the setting itself. Parisian cafés were the first public establishments ever to specialize in nibbles, fare both light and elegant.

As is still true all over the world today, from the start pastries were a specialty of chic cafés. The pairing of coffee and pastry, which seems so logical to us now, was invented in the original high-end cafés about two decades after the publication of the first cookbook devoted entirely to pastry. Thus, in Paris in the seventeenth century's final decades, coffee and pastry went public together. Initially, all baked goods were prepared on the premises, but by 1691, Nicolas de Blégny—author of a treatise on coffee as well as an insider's guide to Paris—lists several shops that made all manner of pastry in bulk for resale in cafés. In addition, cafés offered an impressive selection of ice creams and sherbets, with offerings such as amber or musk sherbet and carnation ice cream.

Even more impressive was the range of beverages that could be ordered at the Café Procope and other early cafés. There were, of course, the staples: coffee, tea, and chocolate. As of 1676, the crown awarded the right to "make and sell coffee as well as coffee beans" to the newly established guild of *distillateurs-limonadiers* (distillers and soft drink sellers). This explains why Procope and other café owners were referred to for nearly a century as *limonadiers,* or soft drink merchants. (The modern term *cafetier* came into general use only around 1750.) Limonadier can, however, be misleading. Cafés did sell various soft drinks, but even many of their lemonades contained alcohol. And the vast majority of the truly astonishing number of beverages they proposed were what we would call cocktails, and very exotic ones at that.

Take the example of the concoction known as a *rossoly (rosée du soleil,* or "dew of the sun"), personal favorite of the Sun King himself, who is reported to have indulged his taste for it as prodigiously as he did all his appetites. For a rossoly, fennel, anise, coriander, dill, and caraway seeds were crushed together, then mascerated in the sun—with a healthy dose of brandy added. Then there was the *populo,* a combination of musk, amber, pepper, sugar, anise, coriander, lemon oil, and wine spirits. When lemon oil was colored red with a dye made from dried cochineals, the populo became "the elixir of perfect love." In this same vein, there was also "Venus's oil," a mixture of cinnamon water, carnation water, vanilla, and sugar said to have been particularly popular with women. Since the "waters" used had been distilled with either brandy or wine spirits and aged for up to ten years, the ladies' choice was perhaps the most potent of all these early cocktails. This explains its name suggesting that it possessed aphrodisiac properties. The same thing was said of champagne, which was invented just in time to be served in the first cafés.

Still another element that now seems to us part and parcel of the chic café experience was also there from the start. Late-seventeenth-century engravings show that the fashionable set quickly saw that an alfresco setting was particularly appropriate for all those exotic new beverages (Figure 6.2). They began to have tables, chairs, and all the café accouterments set up under trees or on outdoor colonnades, creating in effect the original sidewalk cafés.

FIGURE 6.2. Late-seventeenth-century fashion prints advertised the trendiness of exotic new beverages such as coffee by showing how the best-dressed members of Louis XIV's court took theirs: alfresco and dressed to the nines.

As for coffee as it was then prepared, it's not clear that it would stand up to today's best-rated espresso. It was brewed Turkish-style: an ounce of ground coffee was added to a pint of water, and the mixture was brought to a full boil—ten times. It was then strained and served. The resulting brew is said to have been light and weak by modern standards, but also less bitter. It was only around 1760 that the infusion method was first used to prepare coffee. During Louis XIV's reign, all the coffee in France was Arabian. With the Regency, Indian coffee came on the scene, a newly exotic complement to the wild years of the Mississippi Bubble. Later in the eighteenth century, just as slavery first became a public issue in France, coffee from its colonies in the Caribbean became the rage.

It was surely no accident that the launching of cafés also coincided with that of daily newspapers. The Procope had hardly opened its doors when the first Parisian daily, François Colletet's *Le Journal* (The Daily)—so named because each issue was to contain "l'histoire de chaque jour" (the story of each day)—appeared on June 27, 1676. (This particular paper was around for only a week: its issues were mainly devoted to the heat wave that scorched Paris that summer and to the hundreds of deaths caused when people who didn't know how to swim tried to cool off in the Seine.) By 1686, the Café Procope had begun to post the news of the day printed on a single sheet and pasted up on the pipes of the stove used to heat water to make coffee. Paperboys stopped by the cafés with newspapers, in particular the first ancestor of *Women's Wear Daily*—*Le Mercure galant*, which featured all the latest French fashions and luxury goods. As a result, the style setters who frequented cafés in order to show off their attire didn't waste time while they sipped "Venus's oil."

Coffee made its first appearance on Louis XIV's breakfast menu in 1696. A decade later, as the Duc de Saint-Simon reports in his memoirs, every day after lunch with the King small tables were set up around the room with a complete coffee service: "You just went and served yourself." As usual, his subjects followed their monarch's example. Over the next century, coffee and chocolate became the nation's breakfast drinks, gradually replacing bread dunked in wine, the traditional morning fare known as a soup.

All the while, cafés continued to invade Paris: in 1728, there were 380 of them; 1,800 in 1788—and 4,000 in 1807. (For comparison's sake, it was estimated that there were 7,000 restaurants in the infinitely more populous New York City of 1997.) And that was only the beginning. Their heyday came in 1915 when, according to figures published in the Parisian daily *Le Monde,* there were 350,000 places where one could buy coffee in Paris. (Not all modern establishments, needless to say, are as luxurious as their seventeenth-century precursors.) According to a 1995 study, 25 percent of French adults go to a café every day.

Today, spending time in a café is part of every tourist's visit to Paris. Modern tourists are doing what tourists have done since the café's invention: for over three centuries, visitors to the capital have clearly felt that if they frequented its cafés, they could soak up some of that elusive French style. Already in 1685 and again in 1701, the chief of the Paris police received memos warning that it might be dangerous to have "so many foreigners" gathering together, and suggesting that all cafés be closed. We don't know why the authorities made no effort to stop the irresistible rise of the Parisian café. However, Louis XIV and Colbert, the two individuals who did more than anyone else to reinvent Paris as world capital of luxury, surely understood that Procope and his followers had succeeded in creating, perhaps for the first time ever, what would now be called a scene—places where the people others wanted to see (those the French today refer to as *pipole,* the rich, the beautiful, and the famous) wanted to spend time, to eat and drink, and to be seen. They would have understood the vital role that these establishments could play creating the legend that nothing could be as elegant as things French and in spreading all over Europe the word of the new kind of capital Paris had become.

The original stylish cafés prefigured the trendy establishments popping up in this country today in still another way: their espresso and their lattes were high-priced indeed. The first cups of coffee sold in Parisian cafés cost two and a half sous—a bit over $6—at a time when a pound of meat from one of the city's top butchers could be had for just twice that sum. Coffee thus began its public life in France as one of the most expensive luxury drinks of all time. Of course, the first customers were paying for a taste sensation unlike anything previously known in the West, as well as for a type of entertainment similarly unlike anything previously known in the West.

At present, an espresso served at Paris's Café Les Deux Magots, around the corner from the spot where Procope hung out his sign, goes for 4 euros, more than $5 in the spring of 2005. Patrons are served by garçons wearing white floor-length aprons and black vests that continue the tradition of the itinerant coffee sellers of the 1670s. For the price, they can dream of Hemingway, who was a regular in the post–World War I years and went there to read aloud from his writing. And while those who sip their high-priced lattes in the stylish spots now run all over the States by Procope's successors aren't free to picture themselves in the exact spot where Hemingway sat, they can remember that they're doing what trendy city dwellers have done ever since 1675. Now if someone would only bring back those Armenian outfits for waiters. . . .

7

The Night They
Invented Champagne

*When the Bubbly Became an
Overnight Sensation*

It didn't happen *quite* the way it's been described: champagne
was not invented in a single night. The secret of sparkling wine
was, however, discovered quickly, over a period of experimenta-
tion that lasted only some three to four years, which is virtually
overnight if we keep in mind that this was one of the most revolutionary ideas in the entire history of wine making. In 1669,
champagne did not yet exist. By 1674, it not only existed but was
being celebrated in the original guide to trendy food and wine as

149

the "in" wine of the moment and one of the finest wines of France. From then on, champagne's rise to prominence was unstoppable.

Few things evoke a sense of luxury the way that champagne does. What is perhaps most amazing about its well over three-hundred-year-long history is that there hasn't been a moment when this was not the case. By the turn of the eighteenth century, the bubbly was enshrined in a special niche, one it still occupies today: it had become the wine that was served at all the grandest and the most memorable occasions of public and private life. From the late seventeenth century on, no ceremony or celebration was considered perfect if champagne was not poured. In addition, the bubbly new wine had become an integral part of the dazzling new image of France and the French that Louis XIV had set out to create. As Voltaire put it in his poem "Le Mondain" (The Man of the World): "The sparkling foam of this frosty wine / Is the brilliant image of our Frenchmen." A frothy, sophisticated wine for a brightly stylish nation. It was a pairing almost too good to be true.

The new French national wine was the creation of one man, still another of those visionary innovators who helped Louis XIV's reign sparkle. The man who invented champagne was a most unlikely candidate for the job, a far cry from the marketing geniuses who introduced the world to everything from folding umbrellas to stylish cafés. He was a Benedictine monk, content to work magic with grapes and with no desire for personal fame. Had his fellow monks not recorded his exploits for posterity, we would not know that what we think of as one of the most prominent brand names in the champagne industry, Dom Pérignon, is also the name of the individual who gave the world the secret of sparkling wine.

In the late 1660s, Dom (Father) Pierre Pérignon became cellar master at the Abbey of Hautvillers, near Rheims. He remained there until his death, in 1715; his reign and that of Louis XIV were conterminous. Champagne was thus invented at the precise moment when the conditions that made its phenomenal success story possible were being created, just in time to become the shimmering wine for a glittering age, the wine that could, and did, scintillate by candlelight and mirror light.

Before the late 1660s, when people spoke of *vin de Champagne*, they were referring to wine from the Champagne region in general, most of which was either light red or pink still wine made from pinot noir grapes. During Dom Pérignon's tenure at Hautvillers, the region was moving massively to white wine. Champagne's wine makers were turning in particular to a rather unusual white wine, known as *vin gris* (gray wine). Since this white wine was made almost exclusively from red grapes, its color was a different shade from that expected of white wine—hence the label "gray wine."

The winds of change do not blow often through the most venerable wine-producing regions in France. Dom Pérignon arrived at just the right time to take advantage of one of those rare moments during which centuries-old techniques and habits were being transformed: he also did a great deal to hurry the sea change along and to guarantee its success. By the time that revolution was complete, it had become customary to speak, as we do today, simply of "champagne" (lowercase) when one wanted to refer to a special category of the new gray wine, the small part of the production that had been made effervescent. It was this particular product that put the Champagne region on the international trade map and that quickly became responsible for a wildly disproportionate share of its revenues.

It is clear that Dom Pérignon developed techniques that no one could duplicate for some time, so much so that his name was at first a brand name, synonymous with sparkling wine, which in the Champagne region initially was often called simply "Pérignon's wine." It was only early in the eighteenth century that Dom Thierry Ruinart, another Benedictine, who had frequented Hautvillers, shared the abbey's secrets with his family of wine makers, who in 1729 founded the first firm, known as a *maison*, devoted exclusively to the production of champagne. (The Maison Ruinart still produces champagne today.)

A good deal of information has come down to us about the innovations in wine making for which Dom Pérignon was responsible. We know that he was a proponent of a then revolutionary practice: he blended grapes from different vineyards, grapes of different quality and of different degrees of ripeness. (He realized that, if grapes were picked when not quite ripe, the wine made from them was more likely to sparkle.) He was also perhaps the first wine maker in France to believe that wine should be stored in bottles rather than in casks. It was only logical that a champagne producer first understood this concept. In other regions, bottling is important because wine ages more successfully in a bottle than in a cask. When making champagne, however, it is essential that the still wine be enclosed in a bottle in order to contain the bubbles. He also promoted the aging of bottled wine in good cellars: in 1673, he had new ones dug in order to store champagne's original vintages. Most significantly, Dom Pérignon was the first to realize that a double fermentation process is essential to turn still wine into bubbly.

The Champagne region is among the coldest wine-producing areas anywhere. By late fall, when the harvest and wine making are completed, the low temperatures in the region halt the wine's natural fermentation before all the grape sugar has been processed. With warmer weather, generally shortly after Easter, a second fermentation begins, a process that does not occur in wines from other regions in France. Wine makers had to learn to control this phenomenon before still wine could be made frothy. Those who produce champagne today, following in Dom Pérignon's footsteps, make their wine in the fall but hold off the bottling until early spring, when warmer weather induces fermentation. Dom Pérignon waited longer, even until late summer, to allow the second fermentation to advance naturally as far as it could. In addition, he realized that to guarantee effervescence, it was necessary to help nature along. Dom Pérignon invented in fact what is now the patented method for making champagne: he added a mixture of alcohol and sugar that assured the success of the second fermentation. This was the most significant of all the wine-making techniques he developed, the single invention without which champagne could not have been produced.

As early as 1718, in the book that may well mark the beginning of wine literature in print, *La Manière de cultiver la vigne et de faire le vin en Champagne* (How to Manage a Vineyard and Make Wine in the Champagne Region), Dom Pérignon was identified as the originator of the technique that put the frothiness in champagne. The book's author, another cleric from the Rheims region, Canon Jean Godinot, divulged "the secret of the famous Dom Pérignon." He claimed that on his deathbed, the cellar master of Hautvillers had asked one of his fellow Benedictines to write it down:

> *To a bottle of wine, add a pound of sugar, 5–6 pitted peaches, powdered nutmeg and cinnamon. Once the ingredients are well mixed, add a half bottle of good brandy and bring the mixture to a boil. Strain the mixture through a fine cloth and bring it to a boil again.*

Dom Pérignon was thus the first to understand that what champagne producers now refer to as a *liqueur de tirage* had to be added to the still wine to be certain that the essential second fermentation process would take place.

In the Champagne region today, just before bottling, wine makers still follow Dom Pérignon's example: they add to the vatted wine a liqueur de tirage, now a mixture of yeast and a blend of wine and sugar. They understand what Dom Pérignon intuited: the liqueur helps the residual yeasts in the still wine produce the second fermentation. As a result, the added sugar in the liqueur de tirage is converted into alcohol and natural carbon dioxide gas. When these are trapped inside a bottle, effervescent wine results. Today, the process by which a second fermentation is induced has been patented as *la méthode champenoise* and is officially recognized as the only means of making true champagne—all of which, of course, is French.

The speed with which "Pérignon's wine" created a new market

was impressive even by today's standards. Indeed, virtually the minute that the frothy beverage began to be drunk, it began to acquire an almost legendary status, as though it were not just a wine but the key to a new way of life. Already in 1674, *The Art of Fine Entertaining,* among the first books to announce the arrival of the new French cuisine, pronounced champagne "the hottest thing," saying that "its taste is so charming and its aroma so sweet that it can revive a dead man," and adding that it was "the noblest and most delicious of drinks, next to which all others taste like plonk."

Meanwhile, across the channel, English Restoration comedy was spreading the word that sophisticated partygoers could count on the scintillating new wine to renew their vitality, even after a long evening of excess. In *The Man of Mode,* his 1676 satire of those who live in relentless pursuit of the latest fashion, Sir George Etheredge enshrined "sparkling champagne" as the drink of choice when fashionable gentlemen meet for nightcaps: "It quickly recovers / Poor languishing lovers / Makes us frolick and gay and drowns all our sorrows." Just as was true for coffee, another new drink coming onto the scene at the same moment, the public was willing to believe that champagne's bubbliness could act as an aphrodisiac. (Etheredge's world-weary men of the world could have been speaking for Brigitte Bardot, who, just before turning fifty, said of champagne that it was "the one thing that gives me zest when I feel tired.")

In the late 1690s and early 1700s, a slew of French comedies were performed that lampooned the lengths to which the fashionable set was prepared to go in order to satisfy its desire for all the newly invented upmarket goods. Jean-François Regnard put champagne center stage in one after another of the turn-of-the-century comedies in which he portrayed the dissipated jeunesse dorée of Paris ostentatiously spending money like it was going out of style. In his plays, those who insist on only the best and most expensive in all categories always drink what they refer to with a then newly minted phrase, *vin mousseux,* "the wine that foams."

By the first decade of the eighteenth century, champagne was making regular appearances in a new kind of *chanson à boire*, the frothily sophisticated drinking songs then wildly popular in French high society. Time after time, these airs repeat the message of Etheredge's *The Man of Mode*—champagne is the ideal pick-me-up after a long night of partying: "It's time for the champagne to wake up our meal" (Jean-Baptiste Drouart de Bousset, 1711). "Drinkers, wake up! They're bringing out the champagne!" (Louis Lemaire, 1715).

In short order, the original cookbooks then preaching the gospel that there was no cuisine but French cuisine began to invent ways of bringing the new luxury wine into the kitchen. For the 1712 edition of his *Cooking for Royalty and for the Bourgeoisie*, for example, François Massialot added a series of recipes that, we are told, *can*, of course, be made with white wine if one should need to scrimp, but are naturally infinitely better when prepared with champagne. Thus, a simple but elegant preparation for sole filets (which is also adapted for trout, salmon filets, and oysters) instructs the would-be cook to brown them in butter with mushrooms, then to poach them in a half bottle of champagne, and finally to thicken the sauce with a crayfish coulis.

Champagne's reputation as the ultimate status drink was bolstered by the fact that, for a long while, demand continually wildly outstripped supply. During the decades when the bubbly was acquiring its image as the most sophisticated of drinks, production was severely limited because of the many problems in bottling and storing posed by the new type of wine. Today, the immense pressure that builds up in a bottle of champagne—ninety pounds per square inch during the second fermentation—can be rigorously controlled. But this exactitude, founded on a scientific understanding of the fermentation process made possible by Pasteur's discoveries, dates only from the turn of the twentieth century. At first, it was truly hit or miss, and so many bottles exploded in the abbey's cellars that Dom Pérignon tried seemingly everything to stem the loss from breakage.

It was quickly evident that sparkling wine called for far more resistant glass than was otherwise used for early wine bottles. At the time when champagne was being created, the French government was doing everything it could to encourage the development of the country's glassmaking industry; a number of new factories were founded in the Hautvillers region. By 1711, Dom Pérignon's congregation had at last convinced nearby glassblowers to produce bottles that were both strong enough to withstand the pressure and completely opaque, to limit deterioration. Until then, they had regularly lost 30 percent, and some years up to 90 percent, of their production when bottles exploded in their cellars. The monks also learned that frothy wine required a bottle of different design. The very first champagne came in what were known as apple-shaped bottles; they were ten inches high and had a long (four to five inches) neck. The shape apparently didn't allow the bubbles to circulate freely, so that it was difficult to uncork these bottles. Thus, the pear-shaped bottle still in use today was gradually adopted in the course of the eighteenth century. The first bottles were yellow or blue, but dark green quickly won out as the color of choice.

Until the late seventeenth century, wine bottles were usually plugged either with bits of hemp soaked in oil or with a *broquelet,* a wooden stopper coated with tallow and driven into the neck. Without a hermetic seal, however, the bubbles produced by the second fermentation would have been lost. The Spanish cork industry has long venerated Dom Pérignon as the individual who put it on the map when he realized that corks were necessary to keep in champagne's fizz. The sound of corks popping was, therefore, immediately an inherent part of the champagne experience.

Because the much-touted wine was in such short supply, it instantly fetched truly exorbitant prices. In 1694, for example, champagne was selling for nine times the price of the best wine for which the Champagne region had previously been known—and this was when one bought directly from the cellars near Rheims; Parisian merchants regularly doubled, and even quadrupled, those prices. In the early eighteenth century, at the height of the craze, a bottle of champagne sold for up to 8 livres—nearly $400—in Paris. And this at a time when it was estimated that all the wine drunk in a day by the thirty-five to forty servants of a great lord's household, some of whom had an allowance of up to three bottles a day, would come to only 6 livres.

There were no labels on early bottles; instead, many were embossed with the coat of arms of the buyer for whom they were destined. This practice tells us a great deal about the profile of the initial market for champagne. It quickly became known as the wine of kings: all the grand and wannabe grand courts and lords were determined to be able to get some of the status drink for their entertainments. England's long love affair with the bubbly began right away: the first surviving order from Dom Pérignon's cellars dates from November 14, 1711: the monks were asked to send six hundred bottles to England via Calais. (The savvy English merchant, aware of the breakage issue, specified that the bottles must be of "thick glass.") Champagne's prestige continued to grow throughout the eighteenth century. By midcentury, commentators on international trade routinely pointed out that among French wines, champagne and Burgundy were by far the most sought after by the rapidly growing international market for the new French luxury goods. They noted that demand had become strong from even as far away as India.

A huge demand, exorbitant prices, and a small, uncertain supply: the situation was an invitation to consumer fraud. There were reports of unscrupulous merchants and restaurateurs who were adding all manner of *drogues*, or mysterious ingredients, to vin gris to make it bubble—if only for the first seconds after the bottle was opened. Already in 1690, customers of Parisian cafés were warned that they were being cheated by the waiters who served them a glass of bubbly with panache: by pouring from high above the glass, they could make an inferior product foam up. Those concerned that they might have purchased a bad bottle were advised that they could get at least one glass with some sparkle out of it if they shook the bottle up a bit before popping the cork.

Those lucky enough to have obtained a bottle of the real thing were given careful instructions on how to serve the trendy luxury commodity, all of which were designed to preserve the frothiness that, in the early years, was never a sure thing. They were told to drink it in a new type of glass, invented in 1669, just as Dom Pérignon's reign was beginning: known as a *flûte,* the tall and narrow glass was absolutely necessary to preserve that precious fizz at a time when champagne's bubbles were often scarce and fleeting. In the late eighteenth century, the flute was replaced by the *coupe,* a short-stemmed wide glass said to intensify champagne's pleasure by affording the drinker's nose greater proximity to the tingling bubbles. By then, consumers could be sure that the bubbles would be around for a while, so they could afford to indulge in an expansive surface without fear of losing the fizz. Today, the flute, the original champagne drinker's glass, is once again getting the nod for "the wine that foams."

The list of suggestions for keeping the sparkle in champagne goes on and on. Hosts were instructed to bring the bottle up from their cellar only a few minutes before they planned to serve it, to uncork it before setting it in a wine cooler with two to three pounds of ice (at the time another hard-to-obtain item), and then to reinsert the cork just a bit so as not to lose all the bubbliness. (If a bottle was cooled before uncorking, it might break.) The bottle was to be cooled for about ten minutes; any more, and one might lose that precious foam. (The author of *The Art of Fine Entertaining,* however, railed against the practice of icing down champagne and declared that sparkling wine should be served at the barely chilled temperature at which it came out of the cellar.)

It's clear that so many things could go wrong that buying one of the early bottles of champagne was risky business indeed. Nevertheless, devotees of fine wine and haute cuisine all agreed that the experience was worth the risks. It was thus only logical that the greatest French dictionary of the late seventeenth century, produced by Antoine Furetière in 1690, featured the new bubbly to illustrate that quintessentially French verb *régaler* (to treat someone special to a perfect meal): "If you want to *régaler* someone, you have to serve champagne."

Ever since, party givers around the globe have followed Furetière's rule. Simply popping a cork evokes a world where elegance, sophistication, and style reign, so how could champagne fail to make guests feel special? And that first frothy glass, or so all the songs tell us, works its magic, and suddenly we think that champagne has just been invented all over again.

King of Diamonds

Diamonds, Diamonds, and
More Diamonds

When the phrase "crown jewels" is used today, the crown jewels of England come to mind. In the late seventeenth century, that collection barely existed. The only crown jewels in the world worthy of the name, the only truly great collection of royal jewelry, was the collection amassed by Louis XIV. When he inherited the throne in 1643, the French state possessed a stock of gemstones that was merely respectable. By the end of his reign, in 1715, the French crown jewels constituted by far the richest collection in the West.

Today, we say that diamonds are forever: for us, the flash of a solitaire signifies wealth, status, even emotional commitment.

Louis XIV understood the romance of the diamond in only slightly different terms. He realized that the diamond could be more effective than any other stone in demonstrating to the world the extent of his power, rank, and influence. He also saw that diamonds could serve as the perfect natural complement to the dazzling displays of style and opulence that he favored: the diamond was the precious stone of choice for a sparkly, effervescent reign, the champagne of gemstones. At the grandest soirées at Versailles, diamonds flashed as never before. And no man has ever dared show off more diamonds on his person than the Sun King: he was the original male peacock, the trailblazer on the path most recently followed by rock stars and rappers. The Versailles era was the first age to comprehend our commitment to the allure of diamonds: they owe their modern preeminence in the field of gemstones to the role Louis XIV crafted for them.

Cartier, Van Cleef & Arpels, Chaumet, Boucheron: for anyone who visits Paris today, the sight of the extraordinary concentration of the world's richest jewelers around Paris's ultrachic Place Vendôme may well be the experience most evocative of Paris's role as world capital of luxury and luxurious shopping. The very name by which these establishments refer to themselves says it all. They are *joailleries,* not to be confused with the far humbler *bijouteries.* French-English dictionaries translate both terms as "jewelers" because the English language has no such class distinction—for good reason, since Tiffany and Harry Winston may well be the Anglo-Saxon world's only joailleries worthy of the name. French requires two words to distinguish *joailliers,* the great artists of the world of jewelry, from *bijoutiers,* mere craftsmen.

Joailliers invent the designs that revolutionize the way jewelry is made and transform the way jewels are worn; they create works of art rather than mass-produced ornaments. Most of all, the joaillier is little concerned with metals, no matter how precious; he (few women have ever played a major role in this domain) works with stones, the finest and the most precious gems imaginable. The great joaillier demonstrates his artistry by imagining the settings in which the world's most beautiful gems can show off their size and their brilliance. Joaillerie, jewelry making raised to the status of a fine art, came of age during Louis XIV's reign. As a result, in the late seventeenth century, for the first time, shopping for fine jewelry became an integral part of the Parisian experience. The finest jewelers in the world began to think of Paris as their natural home as soon as Louis XIV's extravagant passion for the diamond had revolutionized the manner in which jewelry was created and enjoyed.

Before Louis XIV, no one would have ever conceived of diamonds as anyone's best friend. In France and during his reign, however, and largely as a result of his personal intervention, the diamond was catapulted from relative obscurity to the position it still holds today: the most precious of all precious stones, the ultimate gift. The Sun King taught an audience that was virtually worldwide how diamonds could pack a big punch in a small package and why they should become the best friend of kings and of anyone who could afford them.

Before the seventeenth century, few people thought very much of diamonds at all. In some Renaissance treatises on precious stones, they were ranked only eighteenth in importance, well behind rubies, sapphires, and, of course, the gem that displaced all stones during the Renaissance, the pearl. The pearl was *the* Renaissance status symbol. As Renaissance portraits demonstrate, when courtiers and princesses all over Europe wanted to appear powerful or wealthy, they showed off outfits with pearls (some of them fake) embroidered literally all over them. At the turn of the seventeenth century, Gabrielle d'Estrées, Henri IV's mistress, loved jewels, but she amassed only pearls—thirty-five hundred of them, to be exact. The most celebrated piece of jewelry owned by Anne of Austria, Louis XIV's mother, early in the seventeenth century, was a much coveted pearl necklace. By the end of her son's reign, the diamond rivière (a necklace composed of a single row of graduated stones) had replaced the string of pearls as the definitive trophy necklace. The Sun King limited his use of pearls to days when the court was in deep mourning. For all other occasions, he made sure that he and his courtiers glittered with all the diamonds the French treasury could afford.

It took two centuries, beginning at the end of the fifteenth century, and voyages to the four corners of the earth before the diamond supplanted the pearl as the ultimate object of desire. When Columbus first set sail, pearls figured at the top of the wish list drawn up by Ferdinand and Isabella, ahead of gold, silver, and spices. It was only on his third voyage, in 1498, that Columbus succeeded in fulfilling that wish. When he discovered oyster beds in the Gulf of Paria, in today's Venezuela, he set off a pearl rush that lasted for 150 years. Particularly during the first half of the sixteenth century, pearls flooded the European market: more pearls were put into circulation at that moment than ever before or since. Then, near the mid–seventeenth century, just when all known supplies of pearls had been depleted, diamonds began to reach the European market in significant quantities for the first time.

Until the eighteenth century, virtually all the diamonds in circulation in Europe came from India. Before Vasco da Gama opened a direct sea route to India, at the dawn of the sixteenth century, only insignificant numbers of diamonds ever left there. Even after his voyage, the diamond trade remained sluggish: the diamond was eclipsed by pearl mania; the stone never encountered the right combination of circumstances to create a market for it. In addition, unlike pearls, early diamonds were not at their best when they reached the West. Indians made only minimal transformations to rough stones; they valued size in a diamond rather than brilliance and believed that stones should be polished only when this was necessary to conceal flaws. (These preferences may also have been influenced by the fact that in India at that time, it was extremely difficult to polish stones.) In the West, polishing became much easier after the introduction of the rotating metal wheel, or scaife, in the fifteenth century. Until the seventeenth century, however, polishing technology remained fairly primitive: serious faceting procedures were first developed in the mid-seventeenth century.

It was only in Paris in the 1660s that all the factors responsible for the diamond's modern popularity came together: a diamond merchant willing to travel to India in search of the finest stones, stonecutters technically sophisticated enough to make those stones dazzle, joailliers who understood the stone's potential, and a public eager to use jewels in a new way. By the early 1660s, the craze for diamonds was finally able to take off.

In all the vast literature left by early voyagers, Jean-Baptiste Tavernier's accounts of his travels in the Orient stand out: no other adventurer was driven by a single-minded obsession with precious stones. A jeweler by profession, Tavernier not only knew stones but was willing to go to any length to purchase the world's finest gems. He was driven in particular by a passion for diamonds: to view the great collections amassed by Oriental rulers, to see where the stones were mined and how they were sold in local markets.

Tavernier characterized himself as "the first European to open the way to the mines that are the only place on earth where diamonds can be found." The Indian fortress of Golconda (now in ruins) was then the center of the world's diamond trade, and Tavernier visited all the mines in that area, especially the legendary Kollur mine, source of many of the greatest stones of all time. His account features scenes such as an epic vision of Kollur, teeming with humanity: sixty thousand men, women, and children alike were slaving to extract diamonds from the sediment in riverbeds. He describes workers, trying just as legions of diamond miners after them did, to smuggle out stones on their bodies—no mean feat since the men were naked "except for a little cloth that hid their shameful parts." One managed to embed a stone in the corner of his eye; when he was caught, his eye was gouged out along with the stone. Tavernier also describes the stones: he handled the biggest diamonds in the world—most impressively, a diamond that weighed 900 carats before it was broken by an inept polisher. (The carats in Louis XIV's day differ slightly in size from modern carats.) He even describes the market where the diamonds, still known as Golcondas, were sold, making it seem much like a truffle market in the south of France today: a few men milling around a square in a small town with little bags in their pockets, barely uttering a sound but instead scratching signals in one another's hands until somehow deals were done even though almost nothing had been visible to the outside observer.

Tavernier's account is that rare tale of flawless relations between foreign traveler and indigenous population. Indians, he says, were very partial to foreigners, "especially those they call Fringuis" (the French). He claims that when foreign merchants acquiring diamonds in India made their purchases in an official market, they were never cheated about the weight of stones; he describes being protected by servants who had been assigned to watch over his possessions.

And Tavernier's possessions were considerable: he crisscrossed northern India with a vast fortune stashed on his person. He brought with him quantities of the gold and enamel work for which European goldsmiths were then famous and which was highly prized by Indian rulers. He then exchanged the creations that had been until that time the most prized products of the jewelers' art for the stone that, with the help of his sovereign and the original royal joailliers, he was about to turn into a worldwide obsession.

Tavernier has been called the father of the modern diamond trade. It takes two to make a market, however, and Tavernier could not have pulled it off without the individual whose appetite for diamonds has never been surpassed.

Tavernier was buying gems throughout 1665 and 1666. He returned to France in December 1668 and lost no time in turning a profit from his travels. By February 1669, Louis XIV had already purchased everything Tavernier had brought back: forty-four large stones and nearly twelve hundred small ones—but when speaking of Louis XIV's diamonds, "small" is strictly a relative concept. He acquired only the kind of stones that cause you to whistle softly under your breath. He never owned anything really small; in fact, the average size of the smaller diamonds he added to the crown jewels was between 8 and 12 carats. And "large" could be truly large. His biggest initial purchase from Tavernier was a blue-tinged stone that weighed 111 carats, at that time larger than any white diamond in Europe.

That gem, which quickly became known simply as the Blue Diamond of the French crown, became the Sun King's signature stone. In 1673, he turned it over to one of the two polishers who were the King's official stonecutters, Jean Pitau, who recut it to conform to Western taste (a practice Tavernier deplored). The stone was thereby reduced to 69 carats, but it acquired both a distinctive shape, which some compared to a heart, and so much brillance that those who saw it never forgot its radiance. The King chose a minimalist setting, with just a few prongs to allow him to hang it from a ribbon around his neck. Until the end of his long reign, the Blue Diamond shone at all the ceremonies for which the French court became renowned.

The diamond became famous along with the court and was soon the best-known gem in Europe. It remained a treasure of the crown jewels until 1792 when, during the turmoil of the French Revolution, thieves got away with most of the former royal collection. It resurfaced in 1812 in London, where a diamond merchant named Daniel Eliason had had it recut to facilitate resale: the heart-shaped stone had become a 45-carat oval. By 1839, the Blue Diamond was the property of Henry Philip Hope. From then on, known as the Hope Diamond, it acquired a new type of celebrity because of the misfortunes that allegedly befell its owners. Its circulation finally ended in 1958, when a latter-day Tavernier, New York jeweler Harry Winston, presented it to the Smithsonian Institution.

The Blue Diamond doubled in value during the twenty years after its purchase, proof that Louis XIV had understood perfectly not only how best to transform that particular stone but also the criteria upon which the value of jewelry would henceforth be based. During the century before the King had his most-prized diamond reshaped, European polishers had been slowly abandoning cuts designed to give diamonds depth in favor of new cuts using an ever increasing number of facets and designed instead for maximum sparkle. The first of these cuts, the rose cut (sixteen facets above a flat bottom), was the favorite early in Louis's reign. By the turn of the eighteenth century, the most highly faceted of all cuts and the true triumph of the stone polisher's new sophistication—the brilliant, thirty-two facets above the girdle and twenty-four below—had been perfected and become all the rage, first in Paris and then throughout Europe.

Still today, the brilliant remains the most popular cut: the Sun King may be said to have invented our idea of a spectacular diamond, exactly the kind of glittering solitaire now considered the perfect engagement ring. The Blue Diamond was long held to be the first brilliant cut, though this was technically not the case. But this belief proves that the King instantly made maximum brilliance his primary concern. Not for the Sun King the discretion of the old cuts: he wanted his stones to dazzle. In his wake, French nobles rushed out to have all their old diamonds recut to give them added glitz.

When he chose to mount the huge diamond in the plainest possible way, the King inaugurated the glittering history of joaillerie. Until the seventeenth century, the setting was the thing. A rivalry existed among the greatest European courts to see which goldsmiths could produce the finest metalwork. The Sun King's preference for flash changed all that: he wanted nothing to distract from the stone. The future Hope Diamond's simple mount can be seen as the first step toward the perfectly invisible settings made famous in the twentieth century by Cartier and Van Cleef & Arpels, in which stones are set one up against the other without prongs to hold them in place. For Louis XIV and for the first time ever, the jeweler became the joaillier, the craftsman who demonstrated his artistry not with elaborately eye-catching settings, but with mounts intended to be as unobtrusive as possible, settings in which everything but the stone disappeared.

It was no accident that both the brilliant cut and the invisible setting were invented at the same time and in Paris. Because of the Sun King's hunger for diamonds, in the second half of the seventeenth century Paris became the only European capital with both polishers and designers able to realize the latest styles. (As late as the early eighteenth century, only one stonecutter in London was capable of carrying out the brilliant cut.) The area immediately adjacent to the Louvre and just minutes from the Place Vendôme, joaillerie's modern home, became, naturally enough, the first neighborhood in which joailliers congregated.

From the 1660s on, the royal commissions alone were extravagant enough to keep a number of premier designers busy. At least two of them—François Lefèbvre and Gilles Legaré—were important enough to be able to publish books that displayed the range of their designs. Legaré's 1663 collection is widely considered the most influential jewelry design book ever published. And Legaré was the ideal representative of the new French fashion for radically sparkling cuts: almost all of his designs require diamonds of at least sixteen facets (he used a cut, known as the *taille en seize*, that was the prototype for the brilliant); some feature stones with thirty-two facets. His collection was the first design book ever that did not show a single cabochon (nonfaceted) gem, as if to say that, from then on, Louis's taste would dictate to the world the manner in which stones were shown off. Indeed, the end of the seventeenth century inaugurated the age during which fashions in jewelry, just like fashions in dress, were decided by designers in Paris.

These French design books were also the first to be given a role rather like today's Neiman Marcus Christmas catalog. In the previous century, when the first such collections of prints had been published, they were intended to serve solely as models for jewelers and their clients. Even though their inventions were still copied, from the 1660s on, French design books were intended less for this purpose than to show off all the fabulous jewel creations that were actually for sale in shops in Paris. The collection of Lefèbvre's jewelry published in 1668 by the well-known engraver and merchant Balthasar Montcornet is by far the most carefully marketed of the early jewelry design books. The volume's title page indicates that the jewels depicted were all available "in Montcornet's shop on the rue Saint-Jacques."

At the same time, Montcornet was also advertising the new capital of luxury, Paris, and the newly luxurious French lifestyle in general. Print number 6 in the collection, for example, pairs a charming view of Notre-Dame with a ravishing diamond-studded portrait brooch. Number 9 features an idyllic vision of a "royal hunting party" along with a selection of elaborate pendants, each made up of a number of diamond dewdrops; it thereby suggests that there was no longer any occasion when diamonds were not appropriate and at the same time that the owner of a pendant purchased chez Montcornet would gain an intimate understanding of the lavish royal way of living luxe along with the bijous.

A radically expanded niche in the luxury market thus fed off Louis XIV's craving for diamonds. And no designer benefited more from the King's passion than Pierre Le Tessier de Montarsy. He sold precious gems out of a shop in his home near the Louvre and ran a workshop in which polishers experimented with increasing the number of facets on a stone. Above all, he made the King's glittering fantasies come true. Louis personally chose stones and discussed cuts and settings with Montarsy, who would then make a mold of the mount in wax, into which he fitted the stones, which he then presented for the King's approval. For his royal patron, Montarsy made *la parure,* a set of matching pieces of jewelry, into an art form. Parures are usually relatively modest affairs: say, earrings, a necklace, a brooch, and a bracelet or two. The Sun King's joailliers had a decidedly more expansive vision: the most fabled royal parures were made up of hundreds of pieces and cost millions of livres—many millions of dollars.

In 1691, Montarsy and Louis Alvarez, a diamond merchant through whose hands the finest stones in the world were said to have passed and one of the polishers the King kept busy refashioning his stones into brilliants, drew up at Louis's request an inventory of the crown jewels. From this description we learn exactly how much Louis spent on each stone he acquired and on each piece of his jewelry, as well as just how many pieces Montarsy had been able to cram into some of the grandest parures ever imagined. We also learn how much the joint efforts of King, jewelers, and diamond cutters had done to raise the diamond's commodity status.

In 1669 alone, Louis spent the truly princely sum of nearly 1,500,000 livres (nearly $75 million)—900,000 for Tavernier's haul and over 500,000 for that of a second merchant newly returned from India, Bazu. (The $24,500,000 sale arranged by Harry Winston in 1974 is reported to be the largest individual sale of diamonds of all time. The Sun King's purchases easily one-up that deal.) By 1683, the crown jewels had reached a value of over 7 million livres (more than $350 million)—and still the King went on buying. In 1685, he placed two orders with Montarsy, each for over a hundred diamond buttons worth more than a million livres. And when I speak of diamond buttons, I mean, not diamond-studded, but buttons each made from a single very large stone.

This was the part of his fortune evidently dearest to the King's heart. In the early 1690s, when Louis decreed that the magnificent solid silver furniture (all twenty-seven tons of it) and solid gold plate settings that had dazzled visitors to Versailles be melted down to get money to pay his troops in the interminable wars he was then waging, he refused to part with any of his diamonds. At the time of his death, in 1715, the crown jewels were worth 12 million livres ($600 million), then the equivalent of nearly nine thousand pounds of solid gold. In addition to the Blue Diamond, the collection included the Sancy, at 55 carats the biggest white diamond in the West; two other diamonds of more than 40 carats; two larger than 30; sixteen of between 20 and 30 carats; twenty-one of between 15 and 20 carats; and 132 of between 5 and 10 carats—the total came to nearly six thousand diamonds, none of which were tiny and almost all of which had been purchased by the Sun King. The inventory also demonstrates the extent to which the Sun King had made the crown jewels almost exclusively a collection of fabulous diamonds: he owned merely fifteen hundred other kinds of gemstones—and not even five hundred pearls.

This was clearly one investment for which, as we now say, Louis got a lot of bang for his buck. No man, and probably no one since, has ever dared indulge in such flamboyant displays of diamonds, displays that make it clear why, during his reign, the art of jewelry making was redefined as the pure showcasing of gems. Louis XIV was the first to understand that diamonds could convey as nothing else the message that their owner was the richest and the most powerful ruler in the world.

The King began experimenting with this idea in 1669, just after buying all of Tavernier's and Bazu's stones. Louis had made for himself the grandest outfit Europeans had ever seen. When he wore it, contemporary observers said that he "appeared to be surrounded by light," every inch the budding Sun King. His outfit was "absolutely covered" with every diamond in his possession—which meant that he had none left over to deck out his brother, whose garments were adorned "only" with lesser gemstones and pearls. This royal fashion show was staged to impress the Turkish ambassador (the ambassador whose visit proved key to the invention of the Parisian café). The Turkish visitor claimed, however, to have been decidedly underimpressed. When his interpreter was told to be sure to stress the number and the size of all the stones with which the King was adorned, the ambassador is said to have replied that on ceremonial occasions in his country, his master's horse wore many more diamonds. (This remark was omitted from the official account of the occasion given in the court newspaper, *La Gazette*.)

But the young Sun King was already the Sun King and naturally not to be deterred by any negative feedback on his attempts to outperform Eastern sovereigns (not to mention their horses). On February 19, 1715, at the last court function he was able to carry off before his death later that year, the reception for the Persian ambassador, Mehemet Riza Beg, the King demonstrated just how far he had taken the art of the diamond in the years since 1669 and proved to the entire world that no one would ever be more successful at playing the role of The King. He appeared with the Blue Diamond hanging around his neck; elsewhere on his person he displayed virtually the entire collection of crown jewels, all 12 million livres' worth. The outfit was so heavy that, royal chroniclers reported, the King had to rush away immediately after dinner to take it off.

During the long years of his rule, Louis and his jewelers had become highly imaginative about finding a place for astounding quantities of diamonds on one man's body. The King's hat was adorned with a pin made up of seven big stones, the largest of which weighed 44 carats. There were diamonds on the hilt of his sword, on his shoe buckles, even on his garter buckles. Above all, every item of his clothing sported diamond buttons, diamond-surrounded buttonholes, and sprays of diamonds extending from the buttonholes—up and down the front opening, along every pocket, all up the sleeves and the side slits, and even all down the back slit of his frock coat (Figure 8.1). In the 123 buttons on his

FIGURE 8.1. A seventeenth-century engraving depicts Louis XIV wearing one of his sets of diamond buttons. His outfit featured 125 buttons, each fashioned from a solid diamond; he also wore diamonds on his shoe buckles and on his garters. The King was showing off more than 1,500 carats of diamonds—and this was for day wear!

overgarment alone, the King showed off at least 1,500 carats of diamonds. Because his clothes had been turned into a sort of pretext for the display of diamonds, Louis's person must have been at least as dazzling as the Hall of Mirrors at Versailles, in which the Persian ambassador was received. No other ruler has ever matched the caratage worn by Louis XIV. Of this final reception of his reign, the Duc de Saint-Simon remarked that "the King was bursting with diamonds; he sagged under their weight." Today, we love words such as "glitz" and "bling": they might have been invented with this man in mind.

Because of the King's passion for sparkle, in the late seventeenth century diamonds were featured on clothing as at no other time. The King's taste also integrated the process of buying stones and jewelry into the Parisian experience. Indeed, in the work often considered the first modern novel, the Comtesse de Lafayette's *La Princesse de Clèves* (The Princess of Cleves, 1678), the hero falls in love with his future wife when he observes her selecting stones in the shop of a prominent jeweler. The scene points to a radical change in women's lives brought about by the new passion for luxury goods: for the first time it was acceptable for a young woman of noble birth to go shopping on her own.

Their encounter also indicates the extent to which the royal diamond mania had succeeded in making the display of glittering gems an inherent part of physical attractiveness. It is said that at the candlelit dinners at Versailles in the century's final decades, women's hairdos seemed to be virtually on fire with diamonds. The fashion was for a swept-up style, the better to contain a dozen or more aigrettes, plumelike hair ornaments in which invisible settings let the brilliants steal the show. Briolettes, highly faceted diamond drops, dangled from each curve like miniature chandeliers. At every turn of the head, hundreds of carats would be reflected in the mirrors positioned all around the rooms.

At the beginning of the seventeenth century, the English crown jewels were the richest collection in Europe, whereas by the beginning of the following century, the French owned nearly all the greatest stones in Europe, and the English collection was so impoverished that for the coronation of George II, in 1727, many of the diamonds adorning the crowns had been rented. In less than half a century, the Sun King had transformed the diamond from a rather insignificant stone into what the seventeenth-century jeweler Robert de Berquen called "the true sun of all precious stones." The French seventeenth century had ushered in what was being referred to only decades later as "the age of the diamond," during which, all over Europe, rich men fought over the greatest stones.

At first the pleasures of that new age were reserved only for the happy few on the guest lists for those lavish banquets at Versailles. But others naturally wanted to know what it was like to make a dazzling entrance. There was so much demand for the new favorite stone that by the late seventeenth century, paste had arrived on the scene. All over Europe, an industry developed to fashion imitation diamonds from rock crystal and from glass. The production of fakes increased dramatically when the Western diamond rush that Louis's example had inspired began quickly to deplete the riches of the Indian mines. Already in the early eighteenth century, Indian mines ceased production; it was only in 1730, when gems began arriving from the mines recently opened in Brazil, that the diamond mania could take off again.

The diamond did well by the individual who made that mania possible, Tavernier. His monarch was so pleased with his services that he ennobled the man who brought the Hope Diamond to the West. The official citation said that the honor was conferred "because of the services that Tavernier had rendered to the State." It was as if he had handed over the gems to the crown, rather than making what may have been the largest individual sale of diamonds of all time. Late in his life, Tavernier had himself depicted in all his prosperity by the noted court painter, Nicolas de Largillierre. Wearing a huge fan-topped turban and decked out in fur-trimmed flowing robes of gleaming silk brocades, Tavernier is a Western dream of an Indian nabob. The backdrop of rich velvets and still more brocade that seamlessly blends into the equally ornate Oriental carpet under his feet ostentatiously displays the goods gotten by Tavernier's trade. In this way, the portrait is over the top, yet it could also be seen as discreet, for it glows in the manner of Dutch Renaissance depictions of wealthy merchants, but it does not glitter, according to the new style of luxurious display that the Sun King had pioneered. In particular, Tavernier wears only one diamond, modestly placed on his little finger. In the Indian manner, it is a cabochon stone, with none of the faceting essential to the diamond's new life in the West. That stone seems to signal Tavernier's agreement with his colleague de Berquen's view that the new French passion for faceting was "ruining" the most beautiful diamonds in France, just as the French lust for sparkle had brought the world he had discovered in India to an end.

Tourists who stroll by the glittering displays of the grandest Parisian jewelers may never realize that the epicenter of today's trade in luxury parures, the Place Vendôme, was, until the Revolution, overtly linked to the Sun King. When it was inaugurated in 1699, the Place recognized the way in which Paris was developing around the new center for couture shopping, the rue Saint-Honoré. In 1699, in the central spot where in 1810 Napoleon placed a spiral column made from the cannon captured at the battle of Austerlitz, the Place, then known as the Place Louis XIV, featured a gigantic equestrian statue of the Sun King. It seems somehow fitting that the man who made the diamond what it is today and used the gem so brilliantly to help market his royal persona, the man who turned simple jewelers into grand joailliers, should still reign, even as only a flickering presence, over the industry that he created. In the geography of Paris, monumental statues have proved transient, but diamonds are truly forever.

THE ESSENCE OF STYLE

9

Power Mirrors

Technology in the Service of Glamour

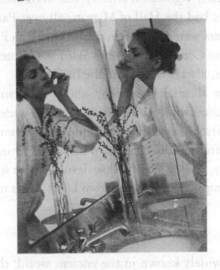

Mirrored ceilings, dressing rooms with floor-to-ceiling mirrors, mirror-lined elevators—mirrors are now so ubiquitous that very few people realize that they were once both fabulously expensive and immensely rare, the ultimate luxe commodity and power toy.

In the early 1660s, when Louis XIV first glimpsed the mirror's potential for transforming interior decoration, all mirrors were made in Venice, and the largest ever produced measured only about twenty-eight inches high. By the end of his reign, the Venetian mirror-making industry was in collapse: as a result of the first decidedly hostile takeover, the French had assumed control over this highly profitable sector of high-end commerce. Considerable state sponsorship and the personal supervision of Colbert, Louis XIV's finance minister, had created a mirror-making industry in France. French mirror makers first took existing technology to its limits. Then, when that wasn't enough to satisfy the monarch's prodigious appetite for sparkly surfaces, they invented a completely new technology that, by the end of Louis XIV's reign, enabled the French to make mirrors up to nine feet tall, nearly four times larger than those possible at the beginning of his reign. By the early eighteenth century, the world had gone mirror-mad: Versailles had the Hall of Mirrors; all over Paris, glittering candlelit suppers were reflected in mirrors made in France; palaces from Warsaw to Constantinople and Siam were lined with French looking glasses, always the bigger the better.

Mirrors are all around us today, and it is because of the Sun King and his decorators. They were the first to understand and to market the mirror's capacity to brighten up a room, to multiply the glitz of glittering surfaces, and to make everything seem larger than life. Today, catalog after catalog devotes lavish spreads to mirrors: they're simply taking a page from Louis XIV's recipe for interior design.

Mirrors were widely known in the ancient world: the Egyptians, the Greeks, and the Etruscans all had them. The first mirrors were made of highly polished metal; bronze was often chosen, but gold and silver were also used. The earliest surviving bits of mirrored glass date from the third century A.D. and are so small (one to three inches in diameter) that they were probably used as ornaments rather than for grooming. The Romans made the first transparent mirrors from rock crystal lined with a thin sheet of metal. Because they were so difficult to make, transparent glass mirrors were slow to break into the market. As a result, prior to the sixteenth century, very few people indeed had ever seen a glass mirror.

Glass mirrors were probably first made in the fourteenth century in the duchy of Lorraine (now in eastern France). By the early sixteenth century, Venetian glass workers had a stranglehold on their production. The Venetians ushered in the golden age of the mirror when, in the late fifteenth century, they discovered the art of making clear, colorless glass, rather than the green-hued glass that had been produced up till then. The Venetians were also the first to produce plates of glass in which both surfaces were perfectly flat and parallel, so that the images reflected in them would not be deformed. Flat, translucent glass was then backed with a silvery, reflecting metal, and voilà—the modern mirror had been invented.

Despite many attempts, for a long time French glassmakers were not able to duplicate the Italian production. This left the Venetians the undisputed masters of this sector of high-end commerce at a time when mirrors were among the costliest objects anyone could covet. During the Renaissance, a fine Venetian mirror cost more than an old master painting. Indeed, these early mirrors were treated exactly like great paintings: they were framed in the most extravagant fashion, sometimes with rare, exotic woods elaborately carved or inlaid with ivory and at others with precious metals studded with fabulous gems. And—in a style to which decorators today are returning—these glamorously framed mirrors were often hung in groupings on a wall, in the same way collectors displayed their paintings.

This star billing seems inconceivable when we think of just what was inside those magnificent frames. The most amazing thing about early Venetian mirrors is what puny affairs they were. For example, in the 1630s, Louis XIV's mother, Anne of Austria, performed her toilette in front of a mirror of which she was inordinately proud: it was all of eighteen inches high and fifteen inches wide. At the time, this was considered a mirror so big that it was worth going out of one's way to see. Factoids such as the tallest mirror in France or the largest mirror then known were common knowledge and readily exchanged, much as art and antiques buffs today evoke the highest price ever paid for a van Gogh or the most important Regency secretary still in private hands. In the 1650s, perhaps the most famous mirror in France, a mirror considered unimaginably huge, was owned by Nicolas Fouquet, Louis XIV's first finance minister: it was twenty-four inches square.

The phenomenon of celebrity mirrors naturally made others want to get into the act. Aristocratic ladies began to believe that they simply had to have their hair and makeup done in front of a mirror. (Louis XIV, never one to be outdone, owned twenty-nine of the original makeup mirrors.) And it was then that decorators first realized the showstopping potential of a highly public display of a great expanse—or what passed at the time for a great expanse—of glimmering glass. In the May 14, 1651, issue of his newsletter, celebrity journalist Jean Loret reported excitedly on the fabulous party held in honor of one of the age's legendary beauties, the Duchesse de Longueville: "Fifty Venetian mirrors reflected all the laughter, the allurements—the décolletages, the hands, the arms—of those being fêted." To our jaded eyes, fifty tiny mirrors in a huge room might not seem like much, but this was the moment that created today's desire for interior decoration's ultimate bling-bling: floor-to-ceiling mirrors.

A decade after this celebrated party, during the early years of Louis XIV's reign, the mirror craze was taking off in France. Hundreds of crates of mirrors arrived from Venice every year. And when I say crate, I have a formidable container in mind: the 216 crates sent from Venice in 1665 weighed over sixty-two thousand pounds. The young Sun King was naturally among the best clients. In the mid-1660s, he was spending upwards of 20,000 livres, or $1 million, every year—roughly the price of four hundred mirrors. In a single decorating gesture, he "covered" a room in mirrors (144 of them, to be precise) for his mistress of the moment, Louise de La Vallière. These purchases spelled, on the one hand, the beginning of a glittering new look in French interiors and, on the other, a steady money drain from French coffers—and this at the precise moment when the French government was most intensely preoccupied about a sudden monetary shortage.

When Colbert became the King's principal financial adviser, he immediately decided to stop dipping into France's scarce reserves of gold and silver to line Venetian pockets. The French would simply take over this highly profitable sector of the luxury trade. And not only would they make mirrors: they would make them bigger and better than ever before. Thus began, in the fall of 1664, one of the most incredible adventures in a reign that was always larger than life.

Colbert gave a mission to the French ambassador to Venice, Pierre de Bonzi: to identify highly skilled mirror makers and lure them to France. The enormity of this task should not be underestimated: in the seventeenth century, this was industrial espionage of the highest order. The Venetian government was well aware that to protect their cash cow, they had to prevent workers from sharing the secrets on which their monopoly was founded. Murano mirror makers all knew that any attempt to break out would be harshly punished. Venetian law stipulated that if any craftsman took his skills abroad, he would be ordered to return. If he refused to obey, all his close relatives would be imprisoned. And if this still failed to produce results, spies would be sent to murder him. No less an authority than the Venetian Inquisition, which normally policed domains touching on religious issues but which had the best network of informants in the republic, was assigned the task of keeping key workers in the flock. The inquisitors were so ruthless in their dealings with the mirror makers that they seemed more like Don Corleone than men of the cloth.

Colbert and his operatives fully understood what they were up against. In his first letter to Paris, Bonzi warned the minister that if he were to go ahead with his plan, the Venetians "will toss us all into the sea." For the next two and a half years, French and Venetians were locked in pitched battle over the secrets of mirror making. Miraculously, all the correspondence on both sides has survived. It shows that from the moment in December 1664 when Colbert ordered the ambassador to proceed, each side never stopped trying to find ways of tossing the other into the sea.

Using a notions seller as an intermediary (notions sellers had a monopoly on the sale of mirrors, so this was a logical way into the community of skilled workers), Ambassador Bonzi managed to identify some likely candidates. Already in late April, he informed Colbert that it was a go. Colbert dispatched a shady character named Jouan to Italy to bring the precious talent back alive. By late June, Jouan had managed to smuggle past the inquisitors a master mirror maker, La Motta, and his helpers, Pietro Rigo and Zuane Dandolo. (La Motta was still another unsavory fellow; he was rumored to have killed a priest and may have left because he felt that he had nothing to lose.)

The Venetians did not remain in the dark for long. In early July they searched the notions seller's shop and found proof of the deal. They began interrogating the relatives of the men who had gotten away. They gave the Venetian ambassador to France, Alvise Sagredo, the task of finding the craftsmen. On July 21, Sagredo reported that the ovens to fire the glass had already been built with the objective of making "mirrors more beautiful than Venetian ones." He reassured the inquisitors by adding that the initial results were most disappointing: miserable little looking glasses, "only ten inches high" and "giving off a black light."

But Colbert was well ahead of the game. While the inquisitors were on the trail of the first workers to leave, he was already preparing a second escape. On July 19, 1665—two days *before* Sagredo fired off his put-down of the first French mirrors— Colbert learned that he had hit pay dirt in the form of four master mirror makers: Antonio della Rivetta, Geronimo Barbini, Giovanni Civrano, and Domenico Morasse. Colbert's men had acted quickly after one of them happened to overhear during a gondola ride one Venetian giving another a detailed description of "the French spy" (none other than the man listening in) who was trying "to entice away" Italian mirror makers. "More dead than alive," the spy rushed off to rustle up his enticees. They left that very evening "at midnight, in a boat watched over by twenty-four valiant men armed to the teeth. . . . By four in the morning, they were fifty leagues out to sea"—outside, therefore, the jurisdiction of the republic of Venice. They reached Ferrara at daybreak and immediately continued their journey by carriage. When they finally arrived in Paris, Colbert was given assurances that, in no time at all, they would be making mirrors "six to seven feet high" and that the new French glassworks would be "the finest in the world."

For Colbert, those grandiose promises were enough. In December 1665, the Manufacture Royale des Glaces de Miroir, the Royal Mirror Manufactory, was established in handsome quarters on the rue de Reuilly in the Faubourg Saint-Antoine, the Parisian center for furniture making since the Middle Ages. The official royal company was assigned a mission as clear as it was daunting: to produce "for the decoration of the royal palaces and for the public's pleasure mirrors as transparent and perfect as those made in Murano." On January 22, 1666, the new company's letters patent were registered with the Parlement of Paris. A group of Parisian bourgeois led by Nicolas Dunoyer became its first directors. They were given an extraordinary total monopoly over mirror making in France. Anyone found trying to make mirrors would have his equipment and his production confiscated and be subjected to stiff fines.

The royal mirror works continued to enjoy this monopoly for some 125 years, far longer than any of the other royal manufactories—lace, tapestry, and so forth—founded in the 1660s. And the company that was created in 1665 still exists. Now known as Saint-Gobain (after a château in eastern France where it moved part of its operations in 1692), it is today the oldest continually operating business in Europe. Saint-Gobain's production is now diversified—it makes everything from insulation to glass fibers for fiber-optic cables—but it continues to make mirrors, and it continues to enhance the prestige of the French state: the glass panels that compose the I. M. Pei–designed pyramids through which tourists now enter the Louvre Museum were produced by Saint-Gobain. In 1665, however, such glory was a long way off.

To begin with, the Venetian ambassador started threatening the workers. Colbert only managed to keep della Rivetta in France by promising him a handsome yearly bonus. Louis XIV personally signed the document that granted him 1,200 livres, nearly $60,000, a year—more than either Molière (1,000 livres) or Racine (600 livres) was receiving at the time. His purse and his ego thus properly inflated, della Rivetta signed a four-year contract. Meanwhile, in the republic of Venice panic was spreading. A new ambassador, Marco Antonio Giustiniani, hastened to Paris with full powers to do anything necessary to stop the transmission of those precious secrets.

From then on, it was tit for tat: the ambassador threatened the craftsmen with the blackest of fates; the French stroked their egos and showered them with largesse. For example: two of the mirror makers were bachelors, so Colbert offered them fabulous dowries (75,000 livres, or well over three and a half million dollars) to take French brides. (This was a dowry comparable to those the wealthiest Parisian merchants of the time settled on their daughters.) Louis XIV even made a personal visit to rally the morale of his troops. On April 29, 1666, he went to the fledgling glassworks and observed the making of a mirror. While he circulated, talking with the workers and asking questions, Colbert followed him around handing out gold coins as though they were party favors.

The two sides changed tactics in May 1666, when Venetian officials forged letters from the wives left behind, pleading with their husbands to return home; the mirror makers didn't fall for the ploy, saying that the missives had been written by someone "much more intelligent than their wives." They were undoubtedly somewhat less than thrilled at the prospect of having their wives in Paris: the glassworks were open to the public, and glassmaking had become the hottest ticket in town; chic Parisiennes in particular loved to watch the spectacle their King had found so entertaining—the sight of so many able-bodied young men stripped to the waist might have had something to do with the visit's popularity. Ambassador Giustiniani fretted in a dispatch to the inquisitors that "the constant presence of so many pretty women is a very powerful attraction" for the Venetian workers.

Colbert retaliated in June 1666 by using a master forger to invent letters from the husbands begging their wives to join them in Paris. When they didn't fall for the ploy, he sent thugs to Venice to kidnap the wives. On August 7, the Venetians learned of his gambit and tried to put the wives under surveillance, but they angrily protested that "they were not about to leave their native nest." This appeal to patriotism was really a trick: the inquisitors' men returned two days later, only to learn that the wives had flown the nest they claimed to love. A warrant was issued for their arrest, but like their husbands before them, they slipped across the border ahead of the police.

The stage was now set for the long-running soap opera's final episode. The Venetian ambassador learned that the first master mirror maker to be lured to France, the alleged murderer La Motta, had not been on the receiving end of royal largesse and thus was wildly jealous of his colleagues. He convinced La Motta that the only proper way to avenge such injustice was by killing his rival, della Rivetta. One December day in 1666, La Motta and several friends, all armed, arrived at the mirror works; della Rivetta's buddies quickly pulled out their own guns. During the ensuing shoot-out, La Motta took a bullet in the shoulder, and two workers lost fingers. (Who knows how many costly mirrors were shattered in the melee?) It took a regiment of the Royal Guard, passing through the neighborhood on their way back to their base in Vincennes, to separate the warring mirror makers.

The Venetians next turned to that time-honored solution: poison. In early January 1667, the most talented mirror polisher in Paris died after a long agony. The ambassador's dispatch is coy: "The worker is now in another world; I don't know if he died from natural causes or artificial means." When, on January 25, one of the best glassblowers, Morasse, also died suddenly and after several days of "violent" suffering, Colbert ordered an autopsy. It proved inconclusive, to the evident relief of the ambassador, who proudly recounted to the inquisitors that the deaths had been achieved "with dexterity and in a tidy manner."

By mid-February, Colbert's spies in Venice had already found new recruits. This time, however, the inquisitors got wind of the plan in time to stop it. They locked the "villainous" mirror makers up in conditions so terrible that two committed suicide; the other two were sent to the galleys. By this time, the Venetians still alive in Paris had clearly gotten the message that mirror making was a high-risk profession. They wrote home asking for a formal pardon from the inquisition's tribunal and for money for the return trip. On April 5, 1667, they were given all they asked for and more: permission to open their own factory in Venice.

Colbert, as usual, got there first: he knew all about their intentions, and after learning that the directors of the French mirror works felt they had learned all they could from the Italians and that they were, in addition, sick of all the Wild West ways that the Venetians had brought along with them, he did his best to hurry their departure along by cutting their wages. In early April 1667, nearly two years after the first Venetian craftsmen had reached Paris, the surviving mirror makers and their crafty wives went home to their "native nest."

The King and his secretary of state were surely expecting rapid and dramatic returns on their considerable investment. The fledgling company did quickly produce its first flawless mirror; on February 26, 1666, the director presented it to Colbert. But this was merely a flash in the pan. For the first half dozen years of its existence, the Royal Manufactory lived up to the assessment of Sagredo, the original Venetian ambassador on the case: it was not up to much good. Colbert had planned to go on importing mirrors from Venice until 1667, to give the new operation start-up time. In point of fact, the French continued to rely on the Murano glassworks until 1671, and this despite the fact that Louis XIV was becoming ever more dependent on the mirror's potential for decorating dazzle. So, year after year, Colbert signed the purchase orders for roughly 20,000 livres (in the neighborhood of $1 million) to cover the King's annual fix. The manufactory founded to stem the outflow of precious metal had not gotten off to a good start. Only in 1672 did the situation change: from then on, Venetian imports were banned, and all the mirrors purchased in France were produced by the Royal Manufactory.

It was just in the nick of time, for work was heating up on Versailles. In 1672 alone, the crown nearly doubled its annual order, to more than seven hundred mirrors. And from then on, Louis's passion for the glass that added sparkle to already glittering occasions never abated. Over the course of the next quarter century, he purchased some 350,000 livres' worth of luxe looking glasses: that is roughly seventeen and a half million dollars' worth of power mirrors. By 1676, Louis had even begun to make mirrors an integral part of *outdoor* decoration: he unveiled the first grotto entirely lined with mirrors. And all the while, the Sun King was building up to what is surely the most famous outlay on mirrors of all time: the Hall of Mirrors that he intended as the centerpiece of the most monumental architectural project of his reign, the château at Versailles.

On May 6, 1682, the official announcement came that the seat of the French government was now at Versailles. However, no one, not even the Sun King, ever succeeds in building a dream house on schedule: in this case, thirty-six thousand men and six thousand horses were still deployed on the construction site. Nevertheless, Louis proceeded to move there, with his family, his ministers, and the entire court in tow. On December 1, 1682, he threw a typically grand housewarming party by opening the Galerie des Glaces to the public. The fabulous display of drop-dead interior design, whose total cost ran to the equally drop-dead sum of 654,000 livres, nearly $33 million, had not yet been completed. (Louis's architect, Jules Hardouin Mansart, and his official painter, Charles Le Brun, finished their jobs only on November 15, 1684.) But the mirrors that gave Versailles's most famous room its name were ready; the last ones had been put into place just the night before. Louis and Colbert could finally show the world that their grandiose scheme to take over the mirror-making industry had been worth it.

Jean Donneau de Visé devoted the lead article in the December 1682 issue of his newspaper, *Le Mercure galant,* to the new wonder. He described the mirrors as "pseudo-windows placed opposite the real ones" and reported, with a healthy dose of hyperbole, that they "multiplied a million times over the gallery's size, so that it seems to have no end." The Duc de Saint-Aignan contributed a long narrative poem about the festivities in which he claimed that "because of the reflection of so many mirrors, / The fire of all the diamonds with which the court was adorned / Made the dead of night as bright as day." The Sun King presented to the world a new brand of palace, the first château with nonstop, night-and-day glitter.

The Hall of Mirrors offered far more than design razzle-dazzle: it was also a monumental billboard advertising the French takeover of the mirror industry. Fifteen years after the royal mirror works had produced the first flawless French looking glass, it had pulled off a display of mirrored glass on a scale never before imagined. Seventeen extravagantly huge expanses of mirrored glass (each measuring nearly eighteen feet high and over six and a half feet wide) with rounded tops turned the gallery into an extended arcade of light, which has been from the beginning the highlight of any visit to the Sun King's palace. Directly across from each mirror stood an equally huge window through which visitors had a view directly onto the gardens that were André Le Nôtre's masterpiece.

Only about ten of the mirrored panes that visitors now admire are the original products of the first French master mirror makers. But modern tourists do still see themselves in some of the same looking glasses that originally reflected the images of Louis XIV and his court. When they do so, they might remember that for the original visitors in 1682, this was the first time they had been able to get a full-length view of themselves.

The minute Louis XIV declared Versailles officially open, the château became a must-see attraction. The first English-language guide devoted exclusively to the palace, Combes's *An Historical Explanation of What There Is Most Remarkable in That Wonder of the World, the French King's Royal House at Versailles,* was already available in London bookstores in 1684. That same year, Claude Saugrain's guide similarly pronounced Versailles "the eighth wonder of the world"—and the Hall of Mirrors "the most enchanting sight known to man." Saugrain also told visitors how to get there from Paris (a coach that cost one and a quarter livres, or a little over $60, made two round trips a day; four people could get together and hire a carriage for 3 livres, a bit less than $150, per person).

Versailles may well have been the original theme park. Far from being the exclusive preserve of the court and official visitors, the château and its gardens were always open to the public: visitors had to be suitably dressed, and they had to get an entrance pass before leaving Paris. Once there, they could make a day of it: see the sights, stroll and picnic in the park, buy picture postcards (or their seventeenth-century equivalent at least, small engravings of the major attractions, which, according to John Locke, could be purchased for 2 to 5 sous, roughly $5 to $12), and even go for a ride on the first roller coaster any visitor had seen. (Contemporary novelist Madeleine de Scudéry described it as "a painted and gilded mechanical contrivance called *roulette* [roller] in which you glide with extreme rapidity straight down the hill in a precipitous manner, and which isn't dangerous if you are careful.") Disney World it may not have been, but Louis XIV had created a concept with a big future. And it all centered on that in-your-face display of expensive French-made glass.

The Hall of Mirrors immediately became the setting for every occasion that Louis XIV wished to turn into a demonstration of the power of his monarchy and the superiority of the new French style. For example, the almanac for 1687 (Figure 9.1) featured one of the emblematic scenes of the previous year. The king of Siam, Phra Narai, hoping to open his country to the

FIGURE 9.1. The almanac for 1687 shows Louis XIV and the members of his court in full regalia gathered in the recently completed Hall of Mirrors at Versailles for just the type of event for which power mirrors had been created, a reception for the first ambassador from Siam. Several large arcades of glass are depicted.

West, had sent an embassy of important nobles and high-ranking civil servants. On September 1, 1686, the King received them at Versailles in one of the most carefully staged state visits of his reign. Decked out in his finest garb, with his court assembled around him and his throne installed at one end of the new mirrored gallery, Louis was every inch the Sun King, the only truly fabled monarch of his age. Officially, the ambassadors were paying homage to the King, but they took careful note of the wonders worked by French technology as well. When they returned to Siam in 1687 with tales of the shimmering new way to decorate, their king promptly honored the Royal Manufactory with an order—for four thousand mirrors to add glitz to the walls and doors of his residences. The order couldn't have come at a better time: the French East Indies Company was desperately trying to take business away from the English and the Dutch trading companies, both of which had been implanted in the Orient long before it.

In January 1689, James II arrived in France in exile. He was soon taken to Versailles for the obligatory power visit. Queen Mary of Modena pronounced herself "stunned, especially by the Grand Gallery," which she called "the most beautiful thing of its kind in the universe." In her case, the standard reaction seems strange, for the English had been trying for some time to break into the new luxury industry and end their dependence on French mirror makers. The English royal couple would thus have been among the few early tourists who should have been able to tell at a glance that the reflecting magic at the heart of Versailles's mystique was, in fact, a great big shiny game of smoke and mirrors.

For a piece of mirrored glass to become famous and worth more than an old master painting, two things were necessary: quality of workmanship and size—hence the grand promise made to Colbert upon the arrival of the master mirror makers in the fall of 1665, that they would soon produce mirrors "six to seven feet tall." Anyone familiar with the annals of mirror making would have expected the testimony to the French victory over the Venetians installed at Versailles seventeen years after the founding of the mirror works in Paris to be an illustration of how gloriously that promise had been fulfilled. To serve as a proper ad for the French takeover of the mirror industry, the huge reflecting panels in the Grand Gallery should have been composed of no more than four individual panes, sheets of mirrored glass of a size never before produced.

The reality unveiled in November 1682 was a far cry from Colbert's dreams. Each of the seventeen mirrored panels contains not four, but twenty-one panes: on the top, three rounded ones; next, three small rectangles; and below, fifteen additional panes, each measuring twenty-six by thirty-four inches, for a grand total of 357 individual panes. The Hall of Mirrors, in other words, is flaunting mirrors hardly larger than those treasured in 1650, before the Franco-Venetian mirror war had been launched. The Grand Gallery may be the greatest con job in decorating history.

In point of fact, the promises Colbert had believed in 1665 could never have come true. By 1682, France had yet to outperform the Venetians in any way, precisely because they had learned to make mirrors exactly as the Venetians did—from glass that was blown and then flattened and cut. Mirrors produced this way could never be bigger than about thirty-five to forty inches high, and even this size was rarely attained. To begin with, few glassblowers had the necessary lung capacity. More important, blown glass exceeding these dimensions was uneven, too thin in spots to withstand the foiling process. To cover up the failure of Colbert's grand dream, Louis XIV dazzled visitors from the four corners of the globe with glitzy window dressing.

There are two great ironies in the mirror saga. First: a major breakthrough was just around the corner; had the Galerie des Glaces been delayed by only a few years, it would have stood as glowing proof that under French control, the modern age for the mirror had begun. Second: on September 6, 1683, Colbert died; he was never to know just how spectacularly right his instincts had been.

Virtually as soon as the French love affair with the mirror began, Bernard Perrot, an Italian naturalized by Louis XIV, became known as one of the finest practitioners of the art. As early as the 1670s, there were rumors that Perrot was working on a new technology. The first public confirmation of his breakthrough came in early 1687, just three years after the completion of the Hall of Mirrors. In March 1687, Donneau de Visé excitedly announced to his newspaper's readers that Perrot was no longer blowing glass, but "pouring it onto metal tables of any size that he chooses." At the end of the April 2 meeting of the Royal Academy of Science, during which Perrot had formally presented his discovery, "the Academy gave him a certificate."

Of all the inventors of this extraordinarily fertile age, Perrot alone lacked entrepreneurial instincts: he proudly accepted the certificate, a purely honorific document that in no way protected his invention, and went back to his experiments. In fact, Perrot was so slow at staking a legal claim to his discovery that he lost control over it. In 1688, another master glassmaker, Abraham Thévart, obtained a license to make mirrors using a completely new technique "that no one in Europe has heard of before"—that is, by pouring them. And in 1691, still another master of the art, Louis de Nehou, presented the King with what seem to have been the first four mirrors to have been successfully produced using the technique Perrot had invented. From then on, there was no looking back. The Royal Manufactory hired Nehou; he was on Saint-Gobain's payroll as of 1692. With his help, the royal company commercialized Perrot's invention; it was the springboard that catapulted Saint-Gobain to world dominance. Perrot took the royal company to court but was awarded only a small annual stipend of 500 livres, not even $25,000—small change indeed in such a high-stakes game.

Without the revolutionary technique, the mirror could never have become a central element in interior decoration. Perrot's breakthrough, which consisted of pouring molten glass just as one casts metals, was the step forward that the King had been waiting for. At last the French had something to brag about, and brag about it they did. In 1696, Jean Haudicquer de Blancourt published *L'Art de la verrerie* (The Art of Glassmaking), the first comprehensive study in print of both glassmaking and mirror making, in which mirrors are referred to as "the most glorious of all works of art."

Haudicquer reserves his highest praise for the mirrors "whose extraordinary size surpasses anything ever seen before," now being made in France. In a revised edition of his guide to Paris, Germain Brice proudly told tourists that "it is in France that the art of casting glass and pouring it like metal was discovered. Formerly, mirrors were blown, as they still do in Venice, and consequently they could never attain the prodigious size of those now made by the Royal Manufactory." The English physician Martin Lister described as a highlight of his 1698 trip to Paris his visit to what he called the Glass House and especially the chance to watch workers polish "a looking glass 88 inches long and 48 inches broad." Because of the new technology, the size of the largest mirrors possible had more than doubled since the beginning of Louis XIV's reign. Next to this, those twenty-six-by-thirty-four-inch mirrors in the Hall of Mirrors must have seemed insignificant.

Lister was a lucky man, for such mirrors, the largest yet produced, were a rare sight indeed: between 1688, when the new technology was first exploited, and 1699, probably no more than three of this size had been successfully made—many others had been attempted; all had shattered before completion. Around 1700, the new procedure was stabilized, and soon the ceiling on glass was raised again: mirrors one hundred inches high—nearly as tall as each of the composite mirrors at Versailles—became possible. In the course of the eighteenth century, the ceiling was raised to 120 inches—a height that was not surpassed until 1884. And until about 1920, all mirrors made anywhere in the world were produced using the technique invented by Perrot in the 1680s.

In 1690, as soon as mirrors began to be produced using the new technique, engraver Jean Dieu de Saint-Jean became the first artist to depict the moment at which one of the largest mirrors ever seen entered a private home (Figure 9.2). A fashionista has just acquired one of the trendy-looking glasses and has had it framed in a manner befitting its exorbitant price tag. She has perched it rather awkwardly on top of a dresser not quite big enough to show it off properly—the French design books that would soon teach people how to use large mirrors had not yet begun to appear. She is enchanted with her purchase: she touches her face as if to ask, "Is this really me?" She can be forgiven for this gesture that now seems naïve: no one before could have imagined a looking glass that could belong in our category of a full-length mirror. The full-length mirror arrived just in time for the fashion queens of the French fashion industry's first golden age, the 1690s, to be able to check out every detail of the ensembles they were putting together.

Once the long-impossible dream of creating truly large looking glasses had at last become a reality, the entire culture of mirrors was quickly revolutionized. The Venetians were resistant to change; they

Femme de Qualité en deshabillé.

FIGURE 9.2. In 1690, French mirror makers were bringing the original full-length mirrors into the home. The earliest depiction of someone able to get a view of more than just her face in a mirror portrays a woman touching her cheek in wonder at the amazing new experience.

continued to blow their mirrors. On June 24, 1697, the French ambassador to Venice triumphantly announced to Colbert's successor, the Marquis de Louvois, that Murano workers had given up trying to make large mirrors. As a result, by the mid–eighteenth century, their industry had practically disappeared. This meant that the industry's founders never enjoyed a share of the truly spectacular profits that began in the final years of the seventeenth century.

The years 1698–1700, the moment that marked the conquest of the size barrier, were banner years for the royal mirror works. Sales quadrupled; in 1700 alone, the company took in nearly a million livres, somewhere in the neighborhood of $50 million, or far more than the entire cost of the Hall of Mirrors. Foreign sales skyrocketed: French mirrors were exported all over Europe, and as far away as Constantinople, China, and Latin America. And the mirror became no longer an object reserved exclusively for princes and their wealthiest subjects, but accessible to far more average consumers. Size was the crucial factor in pricing; once the big mirrors had arrived to occupy the luxury niche, the prices of small mirrors tumbled. While in 1700, one of the newly available hundred-inch-high mirrors cost well over 3,000 livres, about $150,000, a twelve-by-ten-inch one could be purchased for a mere 3 livres, less than $150. On June 13, 1685, the Marquise de Sévigné begged her daughter, who was then redecorating her bedroom, not to buy a second small mirror to put in it: "You can't indulge in decoration to such an extent that you buy things that you can't afford." A decade later, the purchase would no longer have been an indulgence. In the last two decades of the seventeenth century, half the households in Paris bought a mirror from the royal company.

Already in 1697, in his commentary on Parisian life, Marana pronounced that "ribbons, mirrors, and lace are the three things without which the French cannot survive." In less than half a century, a great many people in France had seen the formerly extremely rare experience of looking at themselves in a mirror become part of their daily lives. Prior to this time, only a few, wealthy ladies had owned the kind of tiny mirror women today always have in their purses. By the seventeenth century's closing decades, such mirrors began popping up everywhere—in England, where they were all the rage, they were known as pocket *miroirs,* since everyone knew them as still another French fashion trend. Many of the fashion plates designed to teach women how to pull off the latest looks from Parisian couturieres featured pocket mirrors as a very basic luxe accessory. For example, artist Jean Dieu de Saint-Jean (Figure 9.3) issued a print that taught fashionistas the most elegant way of using one of the trendy small mirrors to make sure that every detail of one's makeup and every curl was exactly as it should be. Today, whenever we try to camouflage this same gesture—sneaking a peak at our lipstick, furtively checking that our hair is not too messy on

Dame en habit de ville.

FIGURE 9.3. A fashion print shows women the right way to check out their makeup and hairdo using a trendy new designer accessory, the pocket mirror.

a windy day—we might think of the seventeenth-century women who inaugurated it, and, like them, happily flaunt one of the most practical of the Versailles era's legacies.

But it was with the ways in which the French used mirrored glass to bring the look of Versailles into their homes that they truly proved that they "could not survive" without mirrors. It was in this manner that still another gesture that we take for granted today, being able to check out an outfit's overall effect in a full-length mirror, first began to spread beyond court society. The minute the royal style began to spill over into private homes, expanses of glittering glass became a staple of interior decoration. The mirror's new role was first evident in some of the most extravagant private parties ever thrown.

In some cases, a rather slavish imitation of the royal style was the rule—and never more gloriously so than at one of the great society weddings of the late seventeenth century, that of the Duc de Saint-Simon, celebrated today for his voluminous (and absolutely scathing) memoirs of daily life at Versailles. Saint-Simon's marriage had a *Bonfire of the Vanities* style all its own. The ceremony took place on April 8, 1695, in the private chapel of the groom's father-in-law, the Maréchal de Lorge, at midnight—an hour whose blackness provided the perfect foil for such a glittering event. In the detailed coverage of the festivities that Donneau de Visé featured in the April issue of his newspaper, readers learned that "all the distinguished personages at the court and in Paris" were assembled in a miniature version of the Hall of Mirrors. Huge "arcades of mirrors" reflected not only all the beautiful people but also the splendid gardens seen through the equally enormous windows positioned across from the looking glasses—with the closure de rigueur for all perspectives in the gardens at Versailles provided by "the mountain of Montmartre," visible in the distance.

In June 1704, the Baron de Breteuil threw a grand dinner for the Duke of Mantua. When the guests entered "the supper room," the garden filled (also shades of Versailles) with orange trees was "suddenly illuminated." The duke was placed opposite a door that gave onto a walkway at the center of the orange grove: the instant he sat down, the door opened, and the path suddenly lit up, revealing at the end "a gigantic arcade of lights, which was reflected in mirrors placed behind the table."

By the end of Louis's reign, the Versailles mode of entertaining had spread all over Europe. On June 6, 1715, the king of Poland opened the carnival season in Warsaw with a grand ball. The central rule of the Versailles style was evident in every room: "Opposite each door, mirrors had been placed, so that all the decoration was multiplied with a marvelous symmetry." Naturally, all the mirrors had been purchased from the French royal company.

At the turn of the eighteenth century, France was in the grips of mirror madness: people were desperate to own one of those gigantic new mirrors that the Royal Manufactory had just begun to market at an equally gigantic price. Saint-Simon—apparently having forgotten the mirrored excess featured at his wedding—positively oozes sarcasm as he recounts the tale of the Comtesse de Fiesque, who bought one the minute they became available in the late 1690s. "Countess, her friends inquired, however did you get that? Oh, she replied, I had a worthless bit of land that was only being used to grow wheat, so I sold it, and got this fabulous mirror in exchange. Didn't I do a wonderful thing? Just think: wheat or this gorgeous mirror!"

By 1704, the fever had spread to the bourgeoisie. In his guidebook, Germain Brice urged visitors to Paris to get a glimpse of the McMansion just completed for Jean Thévenin, a financier who had amassed his vast fortune the way certain individuals have ever since, via somewhat shady military subcontracting to the government. It featured a gallery built at a cost of over 200,000 livres, more than $10 million, money largely spent on "exceptionally large mirrors that were its most striking feature."

Of the many ways in which the craze for large French mirrors changed the lives of those who lived in the age of Versailles, one of them is still very much evident all around us today. In 1699, Robert de Cotte, then one of the chief architects of Versailles, made a giant leap forward for interior decoration: he hung a mirror measuring eighty-four by forty-two inches over a fireplace at the King's latest palace, Marly. By the early eighteenth century, de Cotte was the principal design force behind the grandest mansions being built in Paris's chic neighborhood of the moment, the Faubourg Saint-Germain. In every one of them, he put the largest mirrors available over fireplaces, advertising at the same time the trend he had started and the wares of the French royal company. De Cotte's reputation spread quickly: soon he was traveling all over Europe to redesign and redecorate royal and wannabe royal residences. Everywhere he went, he left his signature: large mirrors over fireplaces. In no time at all, a half dozen design books had been published by de Cotte and other leading architects of the day, such as Claude Audran, featuring engravings that showed exactly how to achieve the new fireplace look, which was baptized "cheminées à la royale" or "à la française"—royal fireplaces or French fireplaces. A generation of trendsetting French designers thus showed an ever broader public how every home could have a touch of Versailles.

The early proponents of designer glass played a second role in creating the place for the mirror that it still occupies in our homes today. They started hanging large mirrors facing each other across the drawing room in the trendy mansions in the Faubourg Saint-Germain. Soon decorators were imitating this design trick and using mirrors to open up spaces, and not only in drawing rooms but first in bedrooms—and soon all over the house. Every time anyone today, from professional interior decorators to those of us who take our decorating cues from Crate and Barrel and Pottery Barn, gives mirrors a starring role in a home or apartment—whether arranging mirrors all over a wall or simply positioning a very large mirror over a fireplace—we prove that we are all still indebted to the vision unveiled in the Hall of Mirrors in 1682, and to those who risked life and lungs to make it possible.

I O

Bright Lights, Big City

From Streetlights to Nightlife

Low do cities get their pet names? Chicago *is* the Windy City; anyone who has ever spent a few wintry days experiencing lake effect in all its glory can see that. And Philadelphia's Quaker origins make the City of Brotherly Love another natural. But city names are not always easy to decode. Is it immediately clear to everyone why New York became known as the Big Apple? And Paris, Ville Lumière, City of Light—where does that one come from? Since the phrase "City of Light" means both a brightly lit, sparkling city and an exciting, modern city, it's easy to see why it would have been applied to Paris. But when and why did this usage start? We may never be certain, but one thing is clear: the lights of Paris first attracted attention because of Louis XIV's direct intervention. To people all over Europe in the final decades of the seventeenth century, Paris became celebrated as a city of light because it was the first city anywhere ever to illuminate its streets after dark on a regular, permanent basis.

Today, we think of cities as hubs of light, places where darkness is never really complete. The East Coast blackout of August 2003 became infamous precisely because it changed all that, if only for one night. Reports focused on the overwhelming blackness of that exceptional night: the total absence of all kinds of lighting—from traffic lights to neon signs and huge motion picture screens—upon which we've come to rely brought New York, one of the world's most resourceful cities, virtually to a halt. In the city as we know it, nighttime is the time for nightlife, that sparkling and appealing term we use to designate all the varieties of entertainment and sociability that cause city dwellers to leave their homes after dark—and sometimes to stay away from them all through the night. This is, however, a decidedly modern view of the city.

Prior to Louis XIV's reign, no cities glittered after sunset. Instead, they were plunged into a darkness so absolute that city streets could hardly be associated with any form of entertainment. In seventeenth-century Paris, performances began at three in the afternoon so that theaters could let out at the latest at seven—after dark during the winter months, it's true, but still far from the moment at which the night truly became a time to be feared. The dead of night, it was felt, began already at nine. If honest citizens were forced for any reason to leave their homes at night, they were legally obliged to carry a lantern or a torch to light their way; after nine, anyone found on the streets without a light could be arrested on the spot. All agreed that the only forms of activity with which the dark streets of Europe's capitals were associated were illegitimate: Parisians, for example, were justifiably terrified of the gangs of robbers who roamed their city's streets virtually at will.

Louis XIV instantly understood that Paris could never live up to his ambitions and become the new capital of luxury and glamour until the stylishness that reigned by day began to exist after dark as well. Thus he came up with one of the most innovative of all his ideas right at the beginning of his reign: in 1662, he proclaimed the need for what he termed "a convenience," a form of lighting as a result of which, he argued, Paris's "streets will become much busier at night . . . and people involved in business and trade will go about more freely." Upon royal decree, Paris quickly came to be the original *ville lumière,* the only city in the world whose streets could be said to glitter after dark. And before the end of Louis XIV's reign, people were feeling so comfortable in the capital's newly brightened passageways that Paris turned into the first city anywhere where public life did not stop at sundown but carried on both outside and after dark. Paris had become "La Ville Lumière," the first city that seemed never to sleep.

There had been earlier attempts to light up the night. For centuries, on official holidays and in times of danger, Parisian authorities had asked homeowners to keep a candle burning all night long in a window. In the sixteenth century, the idea of making this practice permanent was first discussed. In 1504, Parlement ordered all Parisians whose windows faced onto a street to keep a candle lit in them after nine in the evening. Similar laws were passed throughout the century, but none of them had much impact. Until the 1660s, when Louis XIV decided that his capital had to become busy both night and day, it was only on special occasions that Paris after dark was anything but pitch-black.

The Sun King initially decided to let private enterprise deal with the problem. On October 14, 1662, at the spot where the rue Saint-Honoré opens off from the city's traditional market area, Les Halles, the head office of a new venture opened for business: the Center for Torch and Lantern Bearers of Paris, run by a man of the cloth who was very much a man of the world, Abbé Laudati-Caraffa. Like all the great modern entrepreneurs, Laudati-Caraffa knew that any truly innovative concept is only as good as its marketing campaign. He sent out a flyer—the earliest use of this strategy that I know of—detailing just how the new system for ending the reign of darkness would function.

Uniformed torchbearers equipped with substantial torches (a pound and a half of "the best yellow wax") and uniformed lantern bearers carrying oil lamps were to be stationed at strategic points in the most frequented areas of the city (near the Louvre, on the major squares); like cabdrivers today, they had to register and be assigned a number. (The abbé aimed high: he planned to employ over fifteen hundred light bearers.) All you had to do was to show up at one of the designated locations, and for a set fee, a torchbearer would light your way to any spot in Paris. Attached to their belts was an hourglass marked with the arms of the city of Paris that timed fifteen-minute intervals. The new service was not cheap. Pedestrians paid 3 sols, about $7.25, a little more than the price of a cup of coffee in the first chic café, for each quarter hour during which they were accompanied by a torchbearer. And for 5 sols ($12.50) per quarter hour, a torchbearer would pop up onto your carriage and act as human headlights while you drove across town. (The flyer claimed that "in the space of a quarter hour one can get to any destination" in Paris.)

Parisians went wild over the new "convenience"—a popular song of the day praised Laudati-Caraffa for having "lit up all of France." Yet despite its popularity, his system was short-lived, and the monarch who was beginning to be known as the Sun King found himself once again with a capital that could not sparkle after sundown. This time, he decided to take matters into his own hands, and in October 1666, he created a high-profile commission, each of whose members was given responsibility for two of the city's districts (today's arrondissements). The task assigned them was one now all too familiar to mayors of major cities: that of cleaning up the streets of Paris and making them safer, so that business would improve.

The following March, the King decided to follow up on the commission's ideas, and for the first time ever, he put one individual in charge of running the city of Paris. The position he created, lieutenant general of the Parisian police, was a combination of mayor and police commissioner—in the seventeenth century, the primary meaning of "police" was municipal administration, but the word was beginning to take on its modern meaning. The man Louis chose for the new job, Nicolas de La Reynie, proved to be a brilliant administrator who governed Paris for over thirty years. During that time, La Reynie presided over some of the most politically sensitive police investigations in French history (notably the Poison Affair, in which the King's reigning mistress, the Marquise de Montespan, was accused of having had recourse to everything from aphrodisiacs to poison to black masses in her attempts to hold on to the monarch's affections; the true story will never be told for, once it became clear that the accusations were serious indeed, Louis ordered La Reynie to organize a massive cover-up). He also oversaw one of the greatest transformations in the history of the city of Paris.

The minute La Reynie assumed his new office, he devoted his energy to the unfinished business of the dark and dangerous streets: he decided that stationary, rather than portable, lighting was the way of the future. On September 7, 1667, barely six months after La Reynie took office, Paris's town crier, Charles Canto, and the King's official trumpeter, Hiérosme Tronsson, paraded through the city's streets proclaiming with all due pomp that street lighting was about to begin: 2,736 lanterns made from glass panels about two feet square were being positioned throughout the 912 streets of Paris. Small streets were allotted one lantern at each end, while a third one was added in the middle of longer passageways. The lighting was scheduled to begin functioning the following month—amazingly, this draconian timetable was met: the October 29, 1667, issue of Charles Robinet's newsletter proudly announced that in Paris "it is now as bright at night as at high noon." That bit of journalistic swagger seems only justified. It was an amazingly quick plunge into an entirely new concept of city life—and from the minute those nearly three thousand lanterns were lit in October 1667, the world never looked back.

For the city of Paris, however, street lighting was first of all an administrative nightmare. Different methods for suspending the lanterns were tried out. At first, some were hung about twenty feet off the ground in the middle of the street. Then it was decided to attach them to the side of houses about a story off the ground; they were raised and lowered by means of a pulley system. The cord that maneuvered the lanterns was enclosed in a metal tube attached to the wall of the nearest house; the handle that controlled the pulley was locked in a small box at the bottom of that tube. The system was both visually and spatially discreet, perfect for a city where the buildings were the center of attention and where the streets were often narrow.

The lighting was highly expensive, so the King proclaimed a new tax, "the mud and lanterns tax," allegedly to cover the cost of both street cleaning and lighting; just the lanterns, however, more than ate up the additional revenues raised by the tax. At the end of the century, when the tax brought in 275,000 livres, or well over thirteen and a half million dollars, each year, the city spent over 200,000 livres, $10 million, for the candles alone—for they were huge, designed to burn for eight to ten hours. (The city consumed 1,625 pounds of candle every night.) By this time, a quarter century after lighting had begun, the system had proved so successful that the number of lanterns had been more than doubled, to nearly sixty-five hundred.

In addition, there was the headache of maintenance. Home owners were assigned on a yearly basis responsibility for a certain number of streets. Those appointed lantern lighters for their neighborhoods were issued keys to the pulley boxes and a basket large enough to contain ten to fifteen of those giant candles, and were reminded by a nightly bell that it was time to set off on their rounds. The schedule for lighting went through many changes. At first, lanterns were lit from late October to early April; in 1708, the season was extended from September 1 to the end of May. From then on, the lanterns were lit at seven in September, at six-thirty in October, at six in November, at five in December and

January, at six in February, and so forth. (With a bit of fine-tuning, since we now measure time with far more precision, street lighting in Paris today still follows this timetable.)

The costly convenience was carefully watched over. Each neighborhood had an official glazier to keep the lanterns clean and in good repair. Each neighborhood had as well an official snuffer, assigned the task of maintaining their wicks; for if the wicks became too long and "charred," the candles "smoked, and the lighting was greatly reduced." This meant that the wick minder had to devote most of his evening to snuffing the smoking lanterns, cutting back their wicks, and relighting the candles.

And woe to those who failed to carry out their duties properly or who damaged the precious lanterns in any way. On February 17, 1698, for example, an officer on the beat, François Trivelin, noted that one of the lanterns was out in the heavily patrolled area near city hall, on the rue de la Mortellerie—today the rue de l'Hôtel de Ville. He sent for the lantern lighter, Antoine Pailleux, a grain merchant by day. Pailleux sent over his maid; she lowered the lantern and announced that it was broken. When the officer asked if it had been out of commission for a long time, "she replied that she had no idea and that she didn't give a damn about the rules." La Reynie hit the grain merchant with a hefty fine of thirty livres, nearly $1,500.

Even though it was quickly evident that the original system had many flaws, change was slow in coming. Would-be innovators were up against the Royal Academy of Science, founded in 1666, which had been given the right to approve any modifications. It was only in December 1745 that a patent was issued for the first *réverbère* (literally a "reflector," and now the generic term in French for a streetlamp). The original réverbères were oil lamps with metal reflecting plates; the first one was installed near Saint-Germain-des-Prés, in the rue Dauphine. The new lamps provided much better lighting; however, since they were also far more expensive, candlelight still reigned supreme. It was only in 1812 that a lantern was patented with a wick long enough to burn all through the night, thus ending the long suffering of generations of snuffers. It was only in 1818 that Paris got its first gas-lit lamps. And in 1843, the Place de la Concorde was finally lit up by electricity.

All the early technology, from pulleys to smoking wicks, seems unbelievably primitive today. At the period, however, it was both cutting edge and one of those giant steps forward that, once taken, make people wonder how they ever got on before. The budding Sun King understood all too well the role lanterns could play in his plans for Paris. He said that they "made his reign glitter," and in 1669, two years after the glittering began, the King issued a commemorative medal. One side featured the royal profile, the other the allegorical figure of a woman surrounded by a Latin inscription: *URBIS SECURITAS ET NITOR,* security and light for the city. In her left hand, the woman holds a lantern, and in her right, what is clearly a very well-lined purse—to represent both the money that robbers would no longer steal from Parisian merchants out and about at night and the prosperity that, Louis trusted, would come along with the gleaming lights.

Rulers elsewhere in Europe clearly saw the French king's pride in his accomplishment as fully justified. In 1670, Amsterdam became the second capital to introduce public street lighting. In Berlin in 1680, the Prussian government began to erect posts on which to hang lanterns. Vienna was first lit at night in 1687. Central London was so widely destroyed by the Great Fire of 1666 that afterward street lighting was hardly the city's top priority: only in 1694 did the institution get off the ground. Even then, London was lit only on moonless nights.

From the beginning, lanterns were seen both as a quintessentially Parisian invention and, for better and for worse, as the mark of a modern city. When, for example, after decades of resistance on the part of its citizens afraid that street lighting would ruin their city's calm, Geneva finally installed public lighting in 1793, one of those who went about smashing the new lanterns was heard to cry out that "this is not Paris and people want nothing to do with its lanterns."

Historians who contend that Louis XIV turned his back on Paris and lavished all his attention on his palace at Versailles are forgetting the spectacular transformation of the French capital that took place during his reign. It was then that Paris first became the glamorously public city that it has remained ever since, the first truly stylish and truly public modern city. From the beginning, a belief in the exciting possibilities for spending an evening there was essential to Paris's glamorous image. The minute those lanterns were lit all over the city in October 1667, Paris by night came into existence and, with it, a completely new way of experiencing cityscapes.

Parisians immediately thrilled at the uncharted territory that had suddenly become available to them. On December 4, 1673, for example, in the dead of winter when the city was at its darkest, the Marquise de Sévigné had dinner with a number of her closest friends. The conversation was animated, and the party broke up only after midnight. Before the new convenience, the guests would have scurried home separately, each in their own direction. Now they made a second party of the return trip: "We thought it was great fun to be able to go, after midnight, to the opposite end of the Faubourg Saint-Germain"—Sévigné lived just off the Place des Vosges, in the Marais; the trip thus took her to what was then the opposite end of the city—"just to bring someone home. . . . We came home merrily, all because of the new lanterns." In one fell swoop, from a brush with a fearful, threatening environment, the experience of being out and about in Paris late at night had become an extension of the evening's entertainment, even a form of entertainment in and of itself. In Paris in the final decades of the seventeenth century, nightlife first became seen as the essence of fun and glamour.

The King and his mayor–cum–police commissioner initiated other reforms that helped change the face of Paris. In 1669, the use of that most basic form of advertising, the shop sign, was completely overhauled in Paris. Until then, shops had identified themselves by means of huge paintings, often so wide—they frequently extended fully into the middle of the street—and hung so low that they largely obstructed all traffic, and also prevented the new street lighting from functioning effectively. The King decreed that all shop signs were to be taken down, redesigned to the same, much smaller dimensions, and rehung so that they were high, at least three and a half feet off the ground, and extended no more than two feet into the street.

Until then, those streets themselves were humble affairs, made only of dirt, which, in a damp climate, meant that they often turned to pure mud. The King ordered them covered over with the cobblestones that have been ever since essential to the romance of Paris. Immediately, foreign visitors began to write home about them. In 1698, for example, the noted English physician Martin Lister exclaimed over how clean the streets had become since they had been paved, over how beautifully they were paved ("with a very hard stone, about eight inches square"), and about what an elegant look this gave the city. Lister had first traveled to Paris forty years earlier, just before Louis XIV had begun his reforms. In 1698, he felt that the city he was visiting had been reborn. "Paris is a new city within this forty years. 'Tis certain," Lister concluded, "since this King came to the crown, [Paris is] so much altered for the better, that 'tis quite another thing." And it had all begun with those streetlights.

At the end of the century, engraver Nicolas Guérard II portrayed (Figure 10.1) for the first time a scene of what has been known ever since as nightlife, a city continuing to function without interruption after sundown. To this end, he showed first of all how street lighting operated in Paris. On the right, we see a well-dressed man who has just rung the bell to announce that it is time to light the lanterns. Right on schedule, the designated lantern lighter has begun to perform her task: she is inserting a lit candle into the lantern, while her child is bent over the official basket preparing a candle for the next lantern. The man who lowered the lantern is waiting by the side of the adjacent building to raise it again once the candle is in place.

FIGURE 10.1. The earliest portrayal of nightlife. This late-seventeenth-century engraving shows both how the original system of street lighting worked and the ways in which life at night in Paris had been transformed once its streets began to be illuminated.

Guérard's engraving depicts at the same time the effects of the new system on Paris and its citizens. Note the street itself: it's both spotless and neatly paved with those famous cobblestones. And the shop shown on the left is flourishing under the newly possible extended business hours. It is brightly lit and stylishly decorated, prosperous and inviting, proof that street lighting and good business went hand in hand. Guérard shows the establishment of a *traiteur,* a new type of professional cook, one of the businesses that began to thrive with the advent of street lighting. This traiteur's specialty is roast meats: he is preparing leg of lamb both to take out and eat at home, as the couple in the street is doing, or to be enjoyed on the spot in one of the plates that adorn the shop's walls. For Louis XIV's capital, the image tells us, street lighting was synonymous with the good life.

Bright lights, big city, or so the saying goes. In the case of Paris, this was certainly true—at least in the way that surely counted most as far as its monarch was concerned: in people's minds. The minute Paris had been established as a ville lumière in the sense of a brightly lit city, people suddenly began to think of it as much bigger than it actually was. Although Paris had grown spectacularly in size in the course of the seventeenth century, by the end of Louis XIV's reign it was being outstripped by London, which was experiencing even more spectacular growth. And yet guidebooks to Paris constantly overestimated its size—even going so far as to claim that Paris "is a world unto itself. . . . There is no city in the world with a bigger population than Paris."

Paris may have given the impression of being so heavily populated because of a phenomenon remarked upon by foreign observers such as Lister—what he called "the great curiosity of the Parisians, who are much more delighted in fine shows than the people of London." This Parisian curiosity meant that the minute there were new reasons to be out and about, as well as new times at which to gallivant, Parisians never hesitated to throng those newly paved streets. To help them do just that, Louis ordered that the crumbling remains of the walls built between the late twelfth and the early fifteenth centuries to mark the city's limits be leveled.

Once "downtown" Paris (still known in French as "Paris between the walls," despite the fact that the walls are long gone) had been opened up, the King added to the cityscape the first of the majestic long straight thoroughfares that soon came to be known as "boulevards" and that ever since have been considered one of the signatures of French urban planning. After they had been lined with shade trees and magnificent town houses, the original "grands boulevards" became a favorite place for Parisians to stroll and to enjoy those "fine shows." Perhaps the most famous boulevard in the world, the Champs-Elysées was originally laid out in 1667, the year that street lighting began. All these urban reforms helped Paris become a city of light in the term's second meaning: an exciting, a modern city. As Lady Mary Wortley Montagu—one seventeenth-century commentator who had her facts right—concluded, by the end of Louis XIV's reign, London was a

larger city than Paris—"and when I have said that, I know nothing else we surpass it in."

During the same period when the Sun King was making Paris
a thoroughly modern capital, he was also shoring up the city's
monumentality. He had a new façade built for the Louvre; he had
many of Paris's older landmarks similarly "reedified," as Lister put
it; he added new sites to the cityscape. In all these projects, the
monarch was driven by a single guiding principle: he wanted to
leave behind works that would fulfill the meaning of an adjective
first used in the seventeenth century, "monumental." He wanted
to be remembered for buildings greater than the sum of their
parts, buildings so obviously significant that they were certain to
remain conspicuous for posterity, landmarks that simply had to be
seen, so fabled that someone from a foreign city would believe that
they simply had to come to Paris to take them in. By holding out
the promise of a capital with both matchless monuments and
completely new pleasures, Louis XIV gave the modern tourist
industry a raison d'être.

In antiquity—notably in ancient Rome—the wealthy had
taken vacations that involved travel. With the fall of the empire,
however, the practice died out. In the Middle Ages and the
Renaissance, very few people made journeys of any importance.
Princesses crossed Europe when they married, usually never to
return to their native lands; religion inspired pilgrims and Cru-
saders to travel long distances; ambassadors were sent off on diplomatic missions; a few great adventurers undertook fabled journeys
to distant lands; the most ambitious merchants traveled in search
of new goods and new markets. Almost no one, however, ever
imagined going to a foreign city just to see its sights and to enjoy
its entertainments. People did not travel for pleasure—until, that
is, the Sun King created an "unsurpassable" capital and made possible a phenomenon that has had an ever greater impact on people's lives since that time: tourism.

The 1680s and the 1690s in particular witnessed a surge in
travel to Paris. One contemporary chronicler claimed that, in

1697, more than fifteen thousand foreign visitors descended on the newly fashionable Saint-Germain neighborhood alone and that, by the following year, the number of foreigners strolling through Saint-Germain had more than doubled. Foreign visitors naturally wrote home comparing the French capital with their native cities: they sent back reports of the first glittering cityscape ever. When Lister visited Paris in 1698, he marveled at its street lighting and grumbled about "the impertinent usage of our people in London to take away the lights for half of the month as though the moon was certain to shine and light the streets." Lister's countrywoman Lady Mary Wortley Montagu agreed with his assessment: "Paris has the advantage of London in . . . the regular lighting of [its streets] at night." In the letter to a friend in which Lady Mary praised Paris's street lighting, she added that her sister had joined her there and that they were "running about together." Her letter indicates that the new lighting was at the same time an attraction, one of many sights that one "ran about" to see when in Paris, and a convenience that encouraged foreign visitors to take advantage of all the city had to offer.

The first modern guidebooks confirmed Lady Mary's assessment. Nemeitz's 1718 proto-Baedeker for German visitors prepared them for a "dazzling" new experience: arriving in Paris was like "suddenly coming out of the shadows and into bright daylight." In order to appreciate the new attraction properly, Nemeitz suggested that visitors position themselves at an intersection where several streets crossed: they could thus admire "the rare sight" of lights suspended at fixed distances from one another and extending out in all directions. Marana's 1692 guide rates steet lighting as one of the wonders of the modern world: "This invention alone is worth the trip, no matter how far away you live. Everyone must come and see something that neither the Greeks nor the Romans ever dreamed of. . . . This spectacle is so wondrous that even Archimedes, if he were alive today, could not improve on it."

Once they got there, of course, visitors quickly realized that those bright lights influenced their stay in more concrete ways as well. Colletet's 1689 guide to Paris stressed that its streets were then so well lit that until two or three in the morning, "it was almost as bright as in daytime." For this reason, Nemeitz added, there were now "almost as many people out and about at night as during the day." And just what were the first nocturnal crowds ever up to? More or less what people are out doing after dark in any big city today. "Many shops, as well as most cafés, also grill-rooms [such as the one depicted in Figure I] and bars are open until 10 or 11," Nemeitz proudly informed his foreign readers, whose more provincial hometowns could in no way have prepared them for this astounding new way of spending nocturnal hours. And for the first time ever, travel now included an activity today widely considered basic to any vacation: it had become possible to shop till one dropped.

In 1669, on the medal Louis XIV had struck to commemorate street lighting's inception, the allegorical figure held up a fat purse as if to express the crown's hope that the money saved from robbers would be spent on French luxury goods. Several decades later, Nemeitz confirmed that intuition when he instructed Germans preparing to visit Paris to take a lot of money with them, since street lighting had made Paris the ultimate shopping city: "You spend your money with so much more pleasure and contentment than in cities where you live almost in complete solitude, surrounded by your wealth but deprived of all amusement." London and Amsterdam were fine cities, he concluded, but only in Paris would a visitor truly have a fun time, and in particular only in Paris would a visitor have so much fun being parted from his money. As soon as Paris had begun to sparkle by night, the beautiful people began to indulge in high-end shopping after dark. And foreign visitors naturally began to do as trendy Parisians did.

The words we now use to describe this new kind of travel, "tourism" and "tourist," came into existence only in the early nineteenth century. But the experience they were created to designate, the phenomenon of traveling to enjoy a particular mix of pleasures, has its origins in the late seventeenth century. The 1690 spoof of the tyranny of la mode, *The Ladies Dressing Room Unlocked*, begins by discussing a new fashion: young English lords were traveling abroad, in the company of their tutors, to make "le petit tour," an extended sojourn on the continent designed, rather like today's junior year abroad, to combine education and pleasure. "Le petit tour" was soon superseded by "le grand tour" as those stays became more and more extended.

It is fitting that the phrases that are at the origin of our vocabulary of tourism were originally cited in French, for from the beginning, Paris was the jewel in modern tourism's crown, the centerpiece of every tour, "petit" as well as "grand." (In fact, the "petit tour" was essentially a prolonged stay in Paris.) Armed with the first true tourist guides—volumes that, according to Lister, could be purchased in every bookstore in London—the original tourists began to explore the now spectacularly monumental, great walking city that the Sun King and La Reynie had created. By night as well as by day, they shopped, they ate out, sat in cafés; they did just what tourists still do in Paris. Today, when we set out, by night as well as by day, guidebook in hand, to tour the sights and soak up the atmosphere of a foreign city, we are following in their footsteps.

There was, however, one major difference. The first tourists "ran about together," in Lady Mary's phrase, for lengthy periods unheard of today. Nemeitz informed visitors that they really should plan on staying for an entire year in order to take proper advantage of the joys of Paris. Since, however, the city's high life was so dear, if they couldn't afford an entire year, then six to eight months would have to do. Nemeitz's guide came with a warning to potential consumers of Parisian "abundance": they ran the risk of "falling so much under the spell of French ways that, after their visit, nothing else would be to their taste." Or as Joe Young and Sam M. Lewis put it in 1918—after the United States' entry into World War I had made another type of mass foreign travel a sudden reality—"How 'ya gonna keep 'em down on the farm? (After they've seen Paree.)"

11

Waterproofed Walking

The Original Folding Umbrella

The throngs of pedestrians who now march down city streets on rainy days surely are not enjoying the experience of being outdoors in a downpour. They are so well sheltered under their umbrellas and their raincoats, however, that for them, the rain is simply a minor inconvenience rather than something that could ever keep them from going where they want to go.

Prior to the late seventeenth century, no one could have understood the modern attitude toward a rainy day. Before the invention of waterproofed protection, and the umbrella in particular, people only dreamed of something we now take for granted: going out into the rain and arriving at one's destination with dry clothes. The umbrella was a liberating invention because it made it possible for pedestrians out on rainy days to get on with their normal activities in more or less normal fashion. In the beginning, however, umbrellas were immensely cumbersome: even though they helped their owners deal with the rain, their effectiveness was decidedly limited.

Then, at the turn of the eighteenth century, a brilliant inventor created the first umbrella that was convenient to use, the original folding umbrella. Jean Marius, the man who brought the umbrella into the modern age, fully understood the culture of luxury commerce that was then transforming Paris. Thus he designed the earliest modern umbrella as an accessory that was far more than practical: it was also elegant and chic. Marius's invention so perfectly realized the umbrella's potential to be both useful and trendy that for the next century, a folding umbrella was high on the list of must-have purchases for well-heeled tourists visiting Paris.

The folding umbrella was invented just in time to play a role in Paris's transformation into the international capital of style, luxury, and upscale shopping. Indeed, few luxury commodities had a greater impact on the way people lived their lives than the folding umbrella. It helped foster a new way of enjoying the city. The easily portable umbrella encouraged various activities associated with the stylish capital Paris was becoming—from strolling to sightseeing to shopping—all of which were dependent upon a degree of autonomy in the streets that had not previously been possible. Like the new streetlights that were making it possible for high-end Paris to carry on after dark, folding umbrellas extended the hours that could be devoted to the high life: rainy days no longer kept the fashionable set indoors. Instead, they provided them with an occasion for showing off the trendiest designer accessory of the first age to understand the craving for designer accessories: Jean Marius's elegant little "pocket umbrellas."

Umbrellas are now among our most disposable possessions. All over the world, they are the most commonly lost item, as well as the item least often returned to lost-and-found services. In Paris, the Lost and Found Department of the transit authority, the

RATP, explains their low rate of return by the fact that someone who finds an umbrella on the subway is far more likely to take it home than to turn it in. For city dwellers at the turn of the eighteenth century, however, the new breed of umbrella was a precious object. It was an exotic new idea—rare, chic, and cher.

The umbrella has a long history. Objects resembling modern umbrellas or parasols are depicted on Egyptian wall paintings and on Greek vases. These are known as royal or sacred parasols because they were purely honorific: to prove their rank, important personages had themselves depicted with servants holding one over their heads. Until late in the seventeenth century, such objects functioned above all as status symbols. Although a parasol held over your head by a servant did of course throw shade on your face, its chief purpose was to send the message that you could afford to employ someone just to shelter you from the sun.

There is no evidence that these objects were ever intended to afford protection from the rain. All the Greek and Latin vocabulary used to describe them is concerned with shade and never with rain. The same is true of the word we use now in English, "umbrella," which is derived from the Latin *umbraculum*, a diminutive of *umbra*, shade.

During the late sixteenth and the early seventeenth centuries, the nature of these objects began to change in two ways: first, parasols became appreciated more for their practical than for their symbolic function, and second, inventors began to experiment with something without which the parasol could never have been adopted to protect against the rain: waterproof fabric.

The first parasols to be appreciated as sun protection rather than as status symbols were an early example of ethnic chic. Travelers to the Orient or to major port cities returned with Chinese paper parasols. In his diary, for example, the English gentleman-scholar John Evelyn describes one that he purchased in Marseilles in October 1644. When travelers showed off these exotic souvenirs at European courts, fashionistas fell in love with them. Soon after, craftsmen—first in Italy and then in France—began to try their hand at a new game: in the sixteenth century's closing decades, we find the earliest references to European-made parasols.

Some of the original parasols produced in Europe may have been stylish, but it's clear that most were not. Of the first models he encountered, Montaigne quipped in his essay "On Vanity" that they "burden the arm more than they relieve the head." In fact, until the final decades of the seventeenth century parasols were generally impossibly cumbersome. Since they were often made of leather with a frame fashioned either from whalebone or from wood, they weighed in at roughly four pounds. They were also nearly four feet long. Early in the seventeenth century, a mechanism was created that made it possible to open and close parasols. They then became an item that, though still bulky and far too heavy to be held comfortably in the hand, could be carried under the arm—or at least could be carried by men; most women found them far too heavy even to try.

Men seeking protection from the rain at that time most often turned to wide-brimmed leather hats. Both men and women generally used heavy, broad-collared cloaks to give their clothing some protection, although some early parasols could function as umbrellas for those who didn't mind their weight. Beginning in the late sixteenth century, inventors, particularly in Italy, were experimenting with various ways of waxing, oiling, and gumming ordinary fabric. We have no evidence, however, that any of the early waterproofed fabric lived up to its billing: there is no record of the sale of waterproofed clothing prior to the reign of Louis XIV. After about a century of trial and error, the marketing of objects made from specially treated fabric began in France, in 1677, just after the earliest experiment with water-resistant fabric to have received scientific documentation.

In the summer of 1677, two men jumped into Paris's Seine River. One of them was nude and was carrying his clothes in a backpack made from waterproofed leather. The other wore what could be called the original wet suit, waterproofed pants, over his street clothes. A delegation from the French Royal Academy of Science (still another institution founded by Louis XIV) had gathered on the riverbank to observe the experiment: the academicians were thus able to certify that both men walked away from the dunking with dry outfits. This was such big news that John Locke recorded it in his journal on September 16, 1677. The experiment is the earliest definitive proof that the time was right to inaugurate the umbrella's modern age: by 1677, just as the original fashion industry was taking shape, Parisians clearly wanted to be able to walk in the rain and get to their destination with dry clothes. Soon after the men jumped into the river that fine summer day, the earliest ads for waterproof pants, coats, and boots began to appear. And other inventors turned their attention to an object for which a word had just been invented in French—*parapluie* (literally: protection against the rain). French thus became the first language ever to have a rain-specific term.

It's hard to know exactly when the first functional umbrella was produced. This difficulty stems largely from the fact that most languages created a new word to designate umbrellas only well after the new objects designed to protect from the rain were developed. English, which never bothered to imagine a rain-specific word, is the most difficult case of all. In English, it was only near the mid–eighteenth century that a distinction began to be made between two words that until then had been interchangeable, "umbrella" and "parasol." Until then, it's often difficult to be sure that an object being referred to as an umbrella really was what we know as an umbrella.

French was undoubtedly the first language to recognize the umbrella's existence because the umbrella was originally marketed in France. At the time when the new word, *parapluie,* made its initial appearance in a dictionary in 1680, we know from Samuel Pepys's diary and John Locke's journal that umbrellas were not yet in use in England. The new French word for an umbrella became commonly accepted in Paris only during the seventeenth century's final decades. This was exactly the moment when Jean Marius, one of the visionary inventors of Louis XIV's reign, transformed the decidedly primitive original protection from the rain into a decidedly modern umbrella.

Marius was by trade a *maître boursier,* a master purse maker. He was thus an expert in the intricate metal mechanisms needed to open and close the increasingly elaborate bags fancied by ladies of the court. He applied his expertise to the umbrella, and in one fell swoop, by 1705 he had turned the massive, primitive object into something so thoroughly modern that, if today's sophisticated pedestrians were to pick up one of his creations, they could easily confuse it with the tiny, sleek folding umbrellas they slip into their briefcases on cloudy days. Three centuries later, two of Marius's umbrellas still survive, one of which even still retains its original green taffeta covering (Figure 11.1). The fabric was oiled or gummed to make it water-resistant.

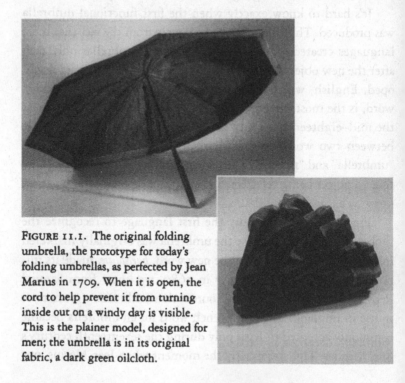

FIGURE 11.1. The original folding umbrella, the prototype for today's folding umbrellas, as perfected by Jean Marius in 1709. When it is open, the cord to help prevent it from turning inside out on a windy day is visible. This is the plainer model, designed for men; the umbrella is in its original fabric, a dark green oilcloth.

Marius clearly understood that in order to create a market for the umbrella, he had to make it completely portable. Thanks to a steel frame virtually indistinguishable from those found in modern folding umbrellas, his invention could not only be closed easily but also collapsed (Figure 11.2). This was the umbrella that created our definition of a folding umbrella, the first umbrella ever able to be held effortlessly in one's hand, or hung from a belt, or slipped into a bag, the first umbrella ever that someone would not have hesitated to carry all day long just in case of rain.

By the time Marius had perfected his invention in 1709, it weighed a mere five or six ounces and could be folded down to a length of 7 1/2 to 9 inches, depending on the model, with a diameter when closed of only 1 1/2 inches. Yet Marius's umbrella unfolded to quite respectable dimensions and became 22 1/2 inches long and 17 1/2 inches wide when open. To close it, one pushed a button at the top; to open it, one simply extended the

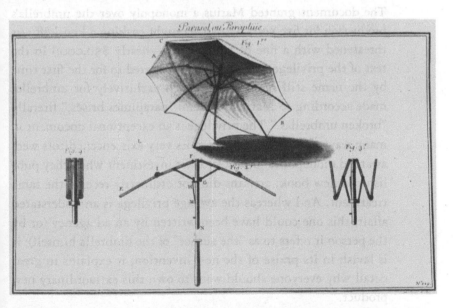

FIGURE 11.2. The diagram Marius used to explain his umbrella's construction to the members of the Royal Academy of Science.

handle fully. (The extensible part of the handle is made of steel; the end is turned wood with a copper tip.) Marius stretched a cord across the frame to help prevent the umbrella from turning inside out on a windy day. He even created a little case, from matching fabric, in which the folded umbrella could be stored.

Furthermore, Marius realized that without an advertising campaign, this object whose function had yet to be widely understood could very easily have been lost in the shuffle. He therefore set about creating a market for pocket umbrellas, teaching the public that parasols offered protection against the sun, while umbrellas sheltered from the rain—and in particular that his invention, depending on the fabric with which it was covered, could be used for both purposes. To this end, he staged one of the first true publicity campaigns.

Louis XIV was so impressed with the invention that in 1710 he issued a royal privilege, the ancestor of the modern patent, the contents of which would have been known to professionals in the field. The document granted Marius a monopoly over the umbrella's production for five years. (Anyone caught making a knockoff was threatened with a fine of 1,000 livres—nearly $50,000.) In the text of the privilege, the invention is referred to for the first time by the name still reserved in French exclusively for umbrellas made according to Marius's system: "parapluies brisés," literally "broken umbrellas." The privilege is an exceptional document in many ways, first of all because of its very existence: editors were awarded monopolies to protect their investment when they published a new book; artisans did not ordinarily receive the same treatment. And whereas the average privilege is an understated affair, this one could have been written by an ad agency (or by the person it refers to as "the author" of the umbrella himself): it is lavish in its praise of the new invention; it explains in great detail why everyone should want to own this extraordinary new product.

The fashionable newspaper of the day, *Le Mercure galant,* soon weighed in with an article in which its editor, Jean Donneau de

Visé, announced that he already carried one of the umbrellas in his pocket. He encouraged all his readers to buy one at Marius's shop, which was located on the rue des Fossés Saint-Germain, at the sign of the Three Funnels, near what was beginning to be known as the most fashionable shopping street in Paris, the rue Saint Honoré.

The Royal Academy of Science on several occasions showered still more free publicity on Marius. The academicians, who normally gathered to discuss more weighty scientific matters (for instance, advances in instruments of calculation such as the barometer), in the public record of their deliberations hailed the new umbrella as "far lighter than any other," "easily carried in one's pocket," and yet "just as sturdy as any of the larger models." They confirmed that it "weighed only five to six ounces" and even announced that "it is being widely used." The Royal Academy's assessment was just the message Marius wanted to get across. In June 1715, with the permission of the head of the Parisian police, the Marquis d'Argenson, he had a poster pasted up in the streets of the capital advertising "umbrellas and parasols to carry in one's pocket" (Figure 11.3).

The Royal Academy of Science, the head of the Parisian police, the King himself: the highest authorities in the land all worked together to make Marius a household name. Indeed, both the royal patent and the poster announced that Marius had been authorized to do something previously unheard of for a fashion accessory: "Each umbrella will be stamped with his mark." Jean Marius, in other words, became one of the earliest brand names in fashion history.

The poster advertising his wares was most unusual for the period. Broadsheets, then the standard form of publicly posted advertising, featured only text without images. The ad for the original folding umbrella, which uses both text and image, was surely among the earliest ancestors of today's billboards. It was also the beginning of a new kind of fashion advertising, the first time that the fashion industry had been able to make this type of highly visible impact on a city's streets.

PARAPLUYES
ET PARASOLS
A PORTER DANS LA POCHE.

LES Parapluyes dont Mr Marius a trouvé le secret, ne pesent que 5 à 6 onces : ils ne tiennent pas plus de place qu'une petite Ecritoire, & n'embaraffent point la poche ; ainfi chacun peut fans s'incommoder en avoir un fur foy par précaution contre le mauvais temps. Ils font cependant auffi grands, plus folides, refiftent mieux aux grands vents, & fe tendent auffi vite que ceux qui fonten ufage.

C'eft le témoignage que Meffieurs de l'Académie Royale des Sciences en ont rendu.

Cette nouvelle Invention a paru avoir été bien reçue du Public par le grand debit qui s'en eft fait, ce qui a excité l'Auteur à la perfectionner, au point qu'il ne laiffe plus rien à fouhaiter du côté de la folidité.

A l'égard de ceux qui font ornez, l'on conviendra qu'il ne s'eft encore rien vû en Paraffols de plus agréable pour le goût & la légereté, & que l'on peut contenter en ce genre les Curieux les plus difficiles, pour la richeffe des montures & des ornemens. *Ils auront tous fa marque.*

Ils fe font & fe vendent à Paris chez Mr MARIUS, demeurant ruë des Foffez Saint Germain, aux trois Entonnoirs.

Par l'autorité d'un Privilege du Roy, portant deffenfe par toute l'étenduë du Royaume de les contrefaire, à peine de mille livres d'amende.

Il ne faut pas confondre cet Invention avec celle des Parapluyes dont les branches fe mettent dans une Sarbacanne. Ces fortes de Parapluyes ont déplû par leur petiteffe & leur peu de folidité ; d'ailleurs il falloit trop de temps pour les rendre.

De l'Imp. de J. C.

Permis d'imprimer & d'afficher.
Fait à Paris ce 12 Juin 1715.
M. R. de V. D'ARGENSON.

FIGURE 11.3. The poster that Marius had printed in June 1715 to advertise his umbrella. He included the drawings to prove that the umbrella could be used by both men and women and to show how small it became when folded and stored in its matching case. The advertising copy sings the praises of the new invention. The lower right-hand corner contains the permission to put up the poster in the streets of Paris given by the head of the Parisian police.

The ad campaign that Marius took to the streets of Paris spelled out just the niche in which he positioned his invention. The text explains at length how practical and sturdy the pocket umbrellas are; to emphasize their compactness, the image depicts what it tells us is "the umbrella in its case." The ad copy also made Marius's second big point: these are "the most stylish umbrellas that have ever been seen"; "their trimming and their frames are so richly detailed that even the most difficult consumers are sure to be satisfied."

The image reinforces the ad copy by depicting two elegant Parisians positively beaming with satisfaction now that they own the trendiest umbrella in town. On the left, we see a woman holding a very frilly model, and on the right a young man or a boy with a far more sober one. Sturdy *and* chic: the pocket umbrella had something for everyone. The double image thus sought to counter the gendering that threatened the sales potential of Marius's invention: early commentators had been quick to declare that the umbrella was more suitable for women; Marius wanted to stop this notion dead in its tracks. And his marketing campaign evidently paid off for, when Benjamin Franklin arrived in Paris for the first time, in September 1767, one of the details about the Parisian street scene that immediately impressed him was the fact that everyone he saw there seemed to be equipped with a folding umbrella: "Men as well as women carry umbrellas in their hands, which they extend in case of rain."

The poster's ad copy cites "the testimony of the Gentlemen of the Royal Academy of Science" to back up its claims that the new invention would work just as well as its far larger precursors and yet was so easily portable that "everyone can with no inconvenience have one on their person as a precaution against bad weather." Indeed, Marius suggests that the umbrella had already found its niche: "This new invention appears to have been well received by the public, judging by the way it has been selling."

We have to wonder about the accuracy of Marius's claim that "everyone" would have been able to own one of his "broken umbrellas." We don't know how much the first ones cost, but they were surely beyond the reach of all but the very wealthiest customers. Indeed, in 1754, the first time the price of "broken umbrellas" is quoted, they still sold for between 15 and 22 livres—somewhere between $750 and $1,100—far more than a nonfolding umbrella from the same shop, which could be had for a mere 9 livres. Those prices tell us that the chic pedestrians who caught Benjamin Franklin's eye had been willing to pay a small fortune for the special combination of practicality and high style offered by the umbrella Marius had invented.

The fact that "broken umbrellas" were still a sought-after luxury commodity well into the eighteenth century proves the staying power of Marius's influence. Perhaps his most important legacy was the increasingly widespread perception that umbrellas were indispensable accessories. Ads for umbrellas started appearing in German newspapers in the 1730s, just at the moment when umbrellas began to become fashionable in England. In all cases, they were known as something best acquired in Paris.

In 1769, the Parisian police established a system of "public umbrellas," that is, umbrellas made available day and night at such highly visible locations as the Louvre and the Place Louis XV (today's Place de la Concorde) for rent by the hour. This was an early step on the road to the umbrella's spread beyond the luxury market, a process finally completed in the nineteenth century. By then the French umbrella industry had a powerful rival across the channel. Until the twentieth century, however, the French reigned supreme over the territory that Marius had staked out: the luxury trade remained firmly under French control, while the English dominated the mass production of inexpensive umbrellas.

At the end of the seventeenth century, during the early decades of the fashion industry's existence, stylish Parisiennes were wearing increasingly elaborate and costly ensembles that made them ever more vulnerable to the vagaries of France's constantly changing climate. Marius's little umbrellas gave these women the chance to acquire a degree of independence they had not previously known: they no longer needed to be accompanied by a servant holding something over their heads to protect them from the elements. In the city, they surely took advantage of this autonomy to visit the first celebrity coiffeurs and coiffeuses, as well as the couturieres of the moment, to shop for antiques and trendy mules.

Little testimony has survived from three centuries ago concerning the ways in which newly created objects changed the daily lives of those who were the first to own them. In the case of the folding umbrella, we have letters from some of the female consumers who were its most enthusiastic proponents. Thus, on June 12, 1712, Louis XIV's Bavarian sister-in-law, the Princesse Palatine, described for her relations in Germany the new umbrella "that one can easily take everywhere, in case rain would happen to surprise you just as you are in the middle of a walk."

The princess's letter shows us that the folding umbrella performed what may have been its most significant initial function outside the urban setting in which its creator had advertised it. The princess makes plain that she considered the umbrella newsworthy mainly because it gave women for the first time ever the chance to do something we now take for granted: to be, whenever they felt like it, on their own outdoors, alone with their thoughts while they explored the gardens and landscapes of their country estates.

In France during the last decades of Louis XIV's reign, women writers were already promoting the idea that we come to know ourselves more fully as a result of an introspective communion with nature, a belief that much later became one of the founding tenets of Romanticism. Perhaps the earliest detailed evidence of the desire for a new way of being in nature is found in the correspondence of the Marquise de Sévigné. She complained bitterly about how often she risked "drowning" when she walked in unsettled weather with only a coat and hat for protection. On June 21, 1680, she described her plan to have little shelters, which she called "umbrellas" (this is one of the earliest uses of the word *parapluie*), put up in strategic spots on her estate. Thus protected, she would be free to spend time looking out "upon infinity." Sévigné decided that her invention was so important that she should announce it to the relentlessly trendy readers of *Le Mercure galant*. Because of Marius's invention, women of the next generation were able to walk about completely on their own in the country whenever and wherever they liked. They were able to gaze out "upon infinity" and then to record what they found there in their letters and their novels.

Design is sometimes defined as the union of form and function. We know that Marius got the style right since, three centuries later, the folding umbrellas we own today are little changed from his creation. And if we stop to consider all the different functions performed by his pocket invention, we might be tempted to call the umbrellas branded with the name of Jean Marius the most significant design of his very design-conscious age. How many designs have an impact on the history of literature as well as the history of shopping?

I 2

A New Kind of Shopping

Antiques, Fine Furniture, and Interior Decoration

Photograph courtesy Ann Margaret Calhoun

The collecting lifestyle is no longer the exclusive preserve of America's bluebloods: it's all around us now. Although most people will never lift a paddle at Christie's or Sotheby's and very few will ever venture into the posh establishments of the country's premier antiques dealers, as *Antiques Roadshow* continues to demonstrate season after season and week after week, today people all over the country can't get enough of antiques. They are into provenance; they want to know all there is to know about the

231

objects that have been handed down in their families; they are fanatical about their collections; they love buying things at auction and on eBay. And above all, they are addicted to the most primal of all the pleasures of collecting: the thrill of the hunt. All over the country today, antiques fairs and antiques flea markets continue to proliferate. And whenever they pop up, there are hordes of fanatics fighting to troop by the tables and the stands in search of a bargain, or a treasure, or just a quick fix.

It makes perfect sense that the attitudes toward collecting and decorating that made today's passion for antiques possible also began to take shape in the last decades of the seventeenth century. After all, the craze for the designer of the moment and for the must-have accessory is directly related to the passion for furniture produced by one particular genius or pottery from one specific workshop. Neither the hunt for antiques nor shopping for luxury goods could have taken off without the same craving: for brand names. In addition, both shopping experiences are quests for just the right style: antiques bring the standards of couture into the home.

Prior to the 1660s, the world of collecting was tiny and private. Then, in the middle of that decade, shopping was revolutionized. Because of the new ways in which merchandise began to be displayed and because of the new kinds of wares that began to be offered for sale, consumers began literally to see things differently. Their attitudes toward both shopping and to the activity that we now know as interior decorating were transformed. Collecting began on a larger scale and the antique emerged as a category when people began to shop for antiques as they shopped for designer clothes.

This meant first of all that those who developed a passion for antiques enjoyed the type of shopping theater that came into existence in Louis XIV's Paris: new types of shops, new marketing experiences, sparkly nighttime shopping. This also meant that the new collectors, like the original fashion queens, wanted to go public with their passion: they wanted to be the first to discover the next great potter or painter of the moment, to become the first private individual to buy the same kind of vase the King had been seen snapping up the day before. A very public notion of competitive shopping was essential in order for the world of a few great collectors to become today's world of antiques fairs and flea markets. Finally, the new collectors no longer exhibited their treasures separately, in a sort of private museum; they saw antiques and collectible objects as part of decorating, essential to the look they wanted for their homes. They therefore shopped for their treasures in contexts, such as a fair, in which many different types of high-end goods—from luxe fabrics to fine tableware—were laid out side by side. It was in that context that the thrill of the hunt moved for the first time ever out of the private museum and into living rooms all over Europe.

It was also logical that antiques and antiquing should have begun their modern life in Paris: ever since the 1660s, no other city has been more visibly identified with the acquisition of all the categories of luxury goods that people collect and display. When they visit Paris today, any tourists who have ever hunted for antiques before—and even many who wouldn't be caught dead doing such a thing anywhere else—make the pilgrimage to the biggest and the most famous flea market in the world, on the northern edge of the city, at the Porte de Clignancourt. And many others take in one of the dozens of antiques fairs that are an established part of Parisian tourism.

My personal favorite takes place twice a year just outside of Paris at Chatou. For ten days each September and March, over four hundred dealers from all over France create a bit of antiques theater. In an idyllic setting near the banks of the Seine, they pitch a stage set designed to evoke simultaneously the elegance of Parisian shopping and the simple pleasures of village life.

The urban pleasures first. The central part of this antiques fair is made into a little shopping city. The Chatou market is laid out on a geometric grid in a flawless example of the classic French urban planning that influenced the design of many American cities—downtown Philadelphia, for example. Each street is lined with always soigné and often downright elegant shops or booths; some streets have roofs like a covered market. Thus, those who go antiquing at Chatou, just like those who shop in a city, are continually moving back and forth from indoors to outdoors. Visitors who know Paris well realize that Chatou's streets—which are marked with the same blue signs with white lettering that one finds on every corner in Paris today—are named for actual streets in Paris's eleventh arrondissement (the area just north of the Bastille): Boulevard Richard Lenoir, rue du Chemin Vert, rue Oberkampf, and so on.

Chatou's staging of a Parisian neighborhood opens onto an equally theatrical version of a French village: the northern edge of the market is devoted to booths offering food and wine rather than fancy vases and chairs. Visitors can thus take a break from fretting over a particularly tempting purchase that they can't really afford but find impossible to resist by sitting at communal tables and eating hearty fare, just as if they had suddenly been transported to a village deep in the French countryside celebrating its annual fête. Some merchants in this area stand in their booths shucking oysters, others cook sausages, while still others carve the truly gigantic smoked hams that give the event its name: the antiques fair at Chatou is officially known as a *foire aux jambons,* a ham fair.

The brand of antiques theater now staged at Chatou, the pairing of upmarket glitz and countrified entertainment that tourists today love to encounter when they shop for antiques, is still another product of the 1660s. It was then that a centuries-old Parisian institution was transformed from one type of fair, a form of popular entertainment that had been a tradition all over Europe since the Middle Ages, into a completely novel form of entertainment. At the new-style fair, the first modern collectors began to hunt for different kinds of treasures that they intended to use just as collectors use the finds they make at an antiques fair today, to give their dining tables or their living rooms a special look.

As early as the twelfth century, Parisians began to look forward to an annual event, known as the Foire Saint-Germain: it took place outdoors during the three weeks after Easter. In the early sixteenth century, the abbot of the Saint-Germain Abbey (the monument that gives its name to today's trendy neighborhood, Saint-Germain-des-Prés) had a vast covered market built specifically to house it. From then on, the fair had a fixed location.

All over Europe until the seventeenth century, the medieval tradition of fairs continued to flourish. Among the best-known were the Frost Fairs held in London on those rare occasions when the Thames froze over. The frost fairs, like all traditional fairs, offered mass-audience popular entertainment. Londoners skated and even roasted animals on the ice; they shopped for souvenirs at rather primitive booths constructed mainly with blankets. At the grandest frost fair of them all, in 1683, the most exotic shop was devoted to highly practical pedagogical entertainment for the masses: it displayed a printing press, where fairgoers paid sixpence to have their names printed as a souvenir.

Until Louis XIV's reign, the Saint-Germain Fair was different from events like the frost fairs only because it was always held at the same time and in the same place. Parisians went there for attractions such as jugglers, puppet shows, wild animals, and lots of low-end, practical shopping. Then, in the mid-1660s, the Foire Saint-Germain was radically redefined. Circus-style entertainment was still part of the mix; improvised farces in the Italian commedia dell'arte tradition even began to be performed on modest stages. A raucous, sprawling, haphazardly organized fair, however, could hardly continue to be a featured event in the stylish new capital that Louis XIV's Paris was becoming. Low-brow entertainment was thus moved to the periphery, displaced by the fair's new focus, a focus unimaginable in the context of a medieval fairgrounds: posh shopping in elegant surroundings. The new Foire Saint-Germain was a milestone in the history of shopping.

In this novel setting, a wealthy and stylish clientele became the first of a new breed of fairgoer. They went to the foire to laugh and be entertained, just like generations of fairgoers before and since. But they went above all in search of other pleasures. At the

Foire Saint-Germain in the mid-1660s, luxury shopping became for the first time ever a truly public event. Aristocrats attended the fair exactly as if they were going to an evening at the theater or a dinner party. They went in groups, dressed to the nines. While there, they shopped till they dropped, from the finest selection available in Paris of designer accessories, silverware and tableware, jewelry, and so forth. If it was high-end, you could find it at the fair. You could shop Paris under a single roof. And looking for respite after all that shopping, you could find elegant refreshments to pick you up for more luxe consumerism. And yes, it was at the fair that the merchants now called antiques dealers got their start.

By the mid-1660s, the annual event had grown spectacularly. It lasted for about two months, from early February to Palm Sunday. Its covered market housed some twenty pavilions containing roughly 350 booths. An engraving from the late seventeenth century (Figure 12.1) shows off the fair's structure, a model of classical urban planning. The engraver eliminated the roof that was considered, just the century before, the fair's most famous architectural feature: he wanted to highlight the elegantly precise layout of this early urban shopping arcade because that layout was the feature that set this fair apart from traditional gatherings. Inside those pavilions, an entirely new type of fair, the prototype for today's antiques fairs, had been created. The individual pavilions were separated by walkways, named for actual Parisian streets—rue de Normandie, rue de Picardie, and so on. And the fair's walkways were closely connected with the streets outside.

Virtually the minute that the area around the Saint-Germain Abbey began to become a hot new residential area for the fashionable set, the offerings at the annual fair started to reflect the surrounding neighborhood's new ambitions. We know exactly when the changeover took place and exactly what it involved, thanks to the journalistic acumen of early newshounds, who, like reporters today who track trends in the making, set out to make the original fashionistas aware of a major development on the Parisian shopping scene.

FIGURE 12.1. A late-seventeenth-century engraving of the annual Saint-Germain Fair in Paris, the setting in which shopping for antiques began. Contemporary commentators always praised the elegant layout of the fairgrounds.

Jean Loret was on the case first. The 1664 fair had barely opened when, on February 23, 1664, he gave readers of his gazette, *La Muse historique* (The Historical Muse), the news that the event was becoming a center for luxury commerce: they could shop there for silver, beautiful jewelry, linens, porcelain, mirrors, paintings—just the items that shoppers today are seeking when they visit an antiques fair. Loret made it clear that the new merchandise targeted exclusively a well-heeled clientele and added that the beautiful people had already turned the foire into a scene. They arrived late—the really chic set came after the theater—and shopped by the light of candles and torches, when "exquisite jewelry is at its most dazzling." Loret was probably referring as much

237

to the bijous on the shoppers as in the display cases: from then on, the Foire Saint-Germain was *the* place to go to be part of the Parisian luxury experience, to buy the latest goods, and to show off those already acquired.

In his coverage of the 1666 fair, La Gravette de Mayolas cites specific shops that were absolute musts for different wares: Mademoiselle Hutin had the finest silver; François Le Maître, on the rue Beaubourg, "the most limpid crystal and the most luminous chandeliers"; while in his *loge* (the first name used to designate dealers' stands; it's also the name for a box at the theater) Monsieur Forest displayed the finest paintings—and not just any banal canvases, mind you, but what we now term old masters, though some were then not yet very old. Our reporter singles out Poussin, who, even though he had died only the year before, was already among the most desirable French artists. And in his account of the 1666 foire, Charles Robinet focuses on its most famous visitor: the King had been spotted ogling paintings, furniture, and jewelry.

Such visible royal patronage could mean only one thing: trendy Parisians who did not already shop at the fair's elegant booths would have immediately begun doing so. Indeed, comedies by Jean-François Regnard and Florian Dancourt, both called *La Foire Saint-Germain* and staged in the mid-1690s, prove that once it was redefined as a haven for glitzy shopping, the fair only got bigger and better. They also indicate that its merchants had begun to deal in all the exotic goods first widely available in France after its East Indies trading company was established in 1664.

Both comedies open with dealers calling out to fairgoers to offer them "Chinese silks," "goods from the Levant," even "Siamese hats" (which had undoubtedly become fashionable after the first Siamese embassy to Louis XIV's court, in 1686). It was at the Foire Saint-Germain in 1672 that the Oriental import destined permanently to alter the Parisian landscape was originally marketed: coffee was first drunk in public in France at the stand of an Armenian named Harouthioun. Both plays commemorate this event by featuring *limonadiers* (as the owners of cafés were then called) dressed *en Arménien*—in the elegantly exotic flowing garments worn by those who served refreshments at the real-life fair and in the original posh cafés that became a fixture of the Saint-Germain neighborhood from the mid-1670s on.

The merchants who worked cheek by jowl in the vast covered market were eager to do away with the low-end ambiance of medieval fairs; in so doing, they invented a shopping experience unlike anything previously known, the prototype for boutique shopping. It was totally public—what could be more public than a fair?—and yet was still defined by elegance, sophistication, and luxury, the very qualities that aristocrats had traditionally sought to preserve by insisting on seeing merchants only in the privacy of their own homes. The foire's savvy merchants gave their sophisticated clientele the sophisticated shopping experience they required—with a twist. They made high-end shopping fun, shopping theater.

The frontispiece to Regnard's comedy (Figure 12.2) shows how the foire worked its shopping magic. It depicts several dealers awaiting customers in their boutiques. The booths are just as seductively stylized as the stands found at high-end antique fairs today. And the merchants themselves are every bit as fashionably garbed and coiffed as their affluent customers. Note also that one of the booths is manned by an attractive young woman; the gendering of the sales force was an essential part of the sexiness of the new shopping theater. An early-eighteenth-century guidebook to Paris explained this practice to German and continental tourists, obviously unaccustomed to this way of doing business: "In France, women mind most of the shops. They know their merchandise just as well as men and, besides, their beauty is often a very powerful way of attracting customers and making big sales."

In the foreground we see the figure of Harlequin, a character in Regnard's play, trying on an "Armenian" robe for size. Once Harlequin has been properly garbed, he'll be able to get down to the business of serving sophisticated nibbles like those shown on the tray, as well as that of pouring coffee and other beverages in the ele-

FIGURE 12.2. A well-heeled Parisian clientele having fun at the Saint-Germain Fair. The ladies are dressing Harlequin in the "Armenian" robe worn by waiters in stylish cafés. He will thus be ready to report for work in the booth shown in the background, a *maison du café*, or French-style coffeehouse. These refreshment stands allowed fashionistas to take a break from shopping for the luxury goods shown in the adjacent booths.

gant refreshment stand shown in the background. And properly refreshed, trendy Parisians will continue to ferret out treasures in adjacent booths. Harlequin's opening lines in Regnard's play express just the reactions echoed by consumers from all over Europe when first confronted by the quality and the quantity of the merchandise laid out at the foire: "Man's desire is insatiable! I hear everyone at the fair carrying on about everything that's beautiful and delicious in Paris; I want to buy everything that's for sale!" The Foire Saint-Germain, it seems, had invented retail therapy.

Foreign visitors who attended the new theater of posh consumerism left detailed accounts explaining why the Foire Saint-Germain was a fair in a class by itself. One of the things that impressed them most was the fact that, like brilliant directors all through the ages, the merchants had understood that lighting was essential to the spectacle they were putting on. Just as tourists were bowled over by the beauty of the street lighting that was introduced in Paris at the moment when the foire went high-end, so visitors never failed to stress, as Marana put it in his 1692 work, *Lettre d'un Sicilien* (Letter from a Sicilian), that "the enormous number of lights arranged in all the shops made the foire infinitely more brilliant and magnificent." And as late as 1718, world traveler Lady Mary Wortley Montagu still maintained that nothing in England could hold a candle to the experience of shopping at an upscale French fair and that the quality of the lighting was essential to the "spectacle" staged by merchants there. The Foire Saint-Germain resoundingly demonstrated the success of a phenomenon made possible by Louis XIV's program for urban reform: nighttime shopping.

The foire also brought for the first time the idea of shopping for antiques—and even the idea of the antique itself—to the attention of a broad public. Until then, the kinds of objects now known as antiques were lumped together in the category *curiosités*. (The category also included many natural marvels no longer sought after by collectors today: "unicorn" horns and exotic shells, freaks of nature, Egyptian mummies.) Curiosities were the exclusive preserve of a few elite collectors who wanted them not to serve as interior decoration but for display in their private museums, their *cabinets de curiosités* or *Kunstkammern*. In the sixteenth century, there were signs that the market for old and rare objects was beginning to open up. The first public auctions took place; the Frankfurt Fair created a section in which curiosities were sold. For the most part, however, these events were frequented by traditional collectors who hoped to acquire objects from one another. Before the second half of the seventeenth century, the trade in such objects was not yet either large enough or public enough for merchants to have shops in which they featured it.

Then, in the mid-1660s, as our man on the style beat, Loret, immediately noted, merchants appeared at the Foire Saint-Germain to deal, no longer in curiosities, but in high-end antiques. This is the earliest indication that everything about the trade in old and rare objects was beginning to change. In the seventeenth century's closing decades, both the nature and the purpose of the objects in this category were in flux. In addition, these objects began to be acquired by a new type of customer: the public for high fashion began purchasing them.

Once the foire had helped create a stylish public eager to indulge in shopping theater, a new type of merchant appeared to cater to its desires for all things haute. Today we would call them antiques dealers, but in the seventeenth century theirs was a profession too new to have a fixed name. They worked out of elegant surroundings, and their shops featured what might be called couture for the home, a range of drop-dead objects—upmarket furniture, paintings, fine porcelain—that beautiful people wanted to display in their elegant interiors. Louis XIV's favorite jeweler, Pierre de Montarsy, was best known for his bijoux, but he also handled old master paintings and sculpture, rare porcelain, crystal vases. In addition, almost all these merchants also sold the exotic wares from the Orient that were widely marketed for the first time in France at the Foire Saint-Germain.

Indeed, the craze for an Oriental look in décor that took off all over Europe at the seventeenth century's end is key to understanding how and why the trade in rare and curious objects was radically redefined in France, as well as to understanding what came to be included in the new category of antiques. First at the Foire Saint-Germain and then in Parisian shops, merchants displayed old master paintings and bronzes and a wide range of newly available goods (initially referred to simply with a mere descriptive label, *ouvrages et meubles de la Chine*—Chinese articles and furniture) side by side, as part of the same style of interior decorating.

All these Oriental wares were quite obviously foreign, and some of them were old. Thus, new-style collectors would visit the same stylish shop to purchase something legitimately antique (an old master painting) and to shop for a fashionable object that may or may not have been antique (an end table made in Japan). In no time at all, the same shops also featured trendy objects with no claim whatsoever to age and only a precarious claim to foreignness: French craftsmen had begun to turn out furniture and objects decorated in what was considered a Chinese style (usually lacquered and often decorated with pseudo-Chinese figures and fantastic animals cavorting about in exotic settings). Soon, a catchy term had been invented to cover this trendy decorating territory. In the 1692 edition of his insider's guide to Paris, Nicolas de Blégny referred to all such Oriental-style objects, whether imported or made in France, whether old or new, as *lachinage*, which is a made-up word, a bit like "Chinesing" or "Chinesed." In the late seventeenth century, lachinage was all the rage; it was said of certain rooms in Versailles that they were "more Oriental than the Orient itself." This decorating mania inaugurated an era during which Oriental-style goods made in France were avidly sought after all over Europe.

The market for lachinage sparked a period of extraordinary creativity among French craftsmen. The prospect of a mass market for porcelain was first glimpsed in the early 1650s when a few extremely rare and extremely dear pieces of Chinese porcelain made an appearance as serving dishes on European tables. From that moment on, Europeans had longed to break into this luxury market. In the mid-1690s, Pierre Chicaneau and other French ceramists fulfilled the dream of producing a ceramic substance that lived up to the standards set by Chinese porcelain. By 1698, when the English physician Martin Lister visited the pottery of Saint-Cloud, which had just begun regular production, he admitted that he "could not distinguish between the pots made there and the finest China Ware I ever saw." And by 1709 Louis XIV believed that French ceramists could now satisfy the demands of their national market, so he banned the import of foreign porcelain.

No craftsmen did more to fuel the craze for lachinage than the Martin dynasty of *vernisseurs* ("varnishers," that is, those who work the magic of putting multilayered varnished finishes on furniture, an art that even today guarantees that French antiques have an unequalled glow). Blégny's 1692 guide to the best shops in Paris contains the first ads for artisans able to lacquer furniture "in the Chinese manner." The Martins turned what is now called japanning (in seventeenth-century English, it was known as "China polish") into a fine art—and a cash cow.

Guillaume Martin, founder of the dynasty, was among the first to profit from the lachinage mania. By 1714, he had obtained a royal privilege, official recognition of the superiority of the process of decorating and lacquering that he had developed. His heirs continued his tradition all through the eighteenth century. The royal seal of approval notwithstanding, their techniques may not have been inherently different from those of other well known japanners. But their mastery of these techniques became so renowned that their name became the first, and surely one of the few, brand names in furniture finishing. Even today, regardless of whether or not the Martin family had any hand in the finish, dealers and collectors use the term *vernis martin* to signify any object painted or engraved with Oriental scenes and japanned with an extremely high-gloss, transparent varnish. The Martins' production so thoroughly dominated this sector of the luxury trade that—like

"Kleenex" or "Band-Aid"—the brand name became synonymous with the process itself.

These new techniques for decorating encouraged the design of innovative objects whose surfaces would show them off. The minute japanning was developed, for example, a new piece of furniture began to be marketed: the first four *commodes* (chests of drawers) on record were delivered to Versailles in May 1692. Like the armoire (wardrobe), which also appeared on the scene in the 1690s, the commode fulfilled the need for more compartmentalized storage, which was created by the proliferation of high-fashion garments and accessories. Until then, clothes were simply put away folded in large chests. Such rudimentary storage was no longer adequate once haute couture had begun to change the very conception of clothing. (Can you imagine just piling Saint-Laurent and Lacroix dresses and Chanel bags into the same big box and closing the lid on it?) The original elegant Parisiennes' reliance on these new forms of storage was given official recognition when one of the hot hairstyles of the 1690s was named the commode. Commodes and armoires performed an essential new function, and they also provided large surfaces that could show off the new varnishing techniques.

Louis XIV's reign inaugurated the golden age of French furniture, 150 years during which the wealthiest international clientele wanted only furniture made in France and those a little less wealthy wanted only copies of that furniture. During that period, the great French *ébénistes* (cabinetmakers or furniture makers) dictated furniture style to much of the world. In 1550, when the first public auction in French history took place, mainly furniture brought over from England was offered for sale. This was never again the case after Louis XIV raised the status of furniture making in France. Louis XIV helped determine the preeminence of French furniture in many ways, most prominently perhaps because of his patronage of André Charles Boulle, the man he named royal ébéniste and to whom he awarded a vast three-story workshop in the high-profile space in the Louvre where the *Winged Victory* now stands. In that privileged space Boulle invented still another adornment for the furniture styles of the day, the intricate marquetry of brass and tortoiseshell known as boulle marquetry. Boulle was the original brand name in furniture making and design, the first cabinetmaker whose pieces were instantly recognized by all those who hoped to re-create the look of Versailles in their own homes: from the start, owning a Boulle was considered essential to achieving that look.

Even more than exquisitely applied varnishes, even more than intricate marquetry, a third finishing technique has come to be synonymous with the classic French look in decorating: gilding. Before Louis XIV's reign, furniture simply did not glitter: no one attempted to give wood a jewel-like look. Then, in 1669, Philippe Caffiéri, another of the King's ébénistes, crafted an extraordinary base for an equally extraordinary slab of antique porphyry (the reddish purple stone that can be polished to a dazzling sheen). He thus created a table that illustrated perfectly the way in which collecting and decorating became entwined during Louis XIV's reign.

The richly glowing porphyry had previously been part of the celebrated collection of strange and beautiful things amassed by Louis XIV's original finance minister, Nicolas Fouquet. The King acquired it after he had had Fouquet imprisoned on embezzlement charges. Rather than displaying the stone as Fouquet had, simply as a fabulous curiosity, Louis XIV turned it into a table, but of course not just any table. Caffiéri's base almost one-ups the stone: it features cupids frolicking in a lavishly ornate setting. And it is one of the earliest pieces of furniture in *bois doré*, gilded wood. Louis XIV and his royal cabinetmakers thus invented the quintessential French look in home furnishing, sparkly furniture that could hold its own when surrounded by the caratage of diamonds, the wattage of candles, and the acreage of mirrors that dazzled at a grand soirée at Versailles. Louis's style of collecting also had a big future. He wanted the extraordinary curiosity to be functional, and he wanted it to function as part of a decorative ensemble.

Observers of French style immediately sensed how the world of collecting was changing and tried to find words to characterize the new developments. In his coverage of the 1664 Foire Saint-Germain, just five years before Louis XIV commissioned that gilded table, Loret announced that people were beginning to shop for "antiquailles," a word meaning worthless old furniture; to show he was not using it in the usual way, Loret added that these "antiquailles ne sont pas pour des canailles"—are not for riffraff. The used furniture for sale at the foire, Loret explained, was resolutely high-end.

Now, of course, we would simply say that at the Foire Saint-Germain in 1664, people began an activity with a big future: they shopped for antiques. At the time, no one would have ever thought of using that word because it was already taken, and referred to the collection of Greek and Roman sculpture housed in the Louvre. It was only near the end of the French monarchy that the word "antiques" was freed up from its original meaning and our modern usage began. In fact, another vocabulary, one still very much alive in French today, began during the golden age of the original antiques fair, the Foire Saint-Germain. The verb *brocanter* began to be used to describe the activity we call antiquing and the noun *brocanteurs* began to designate the merchants who took the formula developed in the artificial streets of the Foire Saint-Germain into the streets of Paris, where they became the original antiques dealers.

In his 1715 Paris guidebook, Louis Liger describes a category of merchants he calls brocanteurs. We know a great deal about their commerce thanks to the fact that the leading brocanteur of that age, Edme-François Gersaint, asked his friend, the greatest painter of the end of Louis XIV's reign, Antoine Watteau, to paint a shop sign for his commerce near Notre-Dame. Watteau's painting is among the earliest depictions of luxury shopping and the first representation of shopping for antiques. In this work, the men are attracted to Gersaint's impressive display of fine painting; one of the women spends her time admiring a makeup mirror and various luxe toilet articles lacquered in vernis martin, and the shop is crammed with all sorts of dazzling objects, all of which are decorative and perfect for display in anyone's living room or bedroom. Some of the objects are old, some are new, and some have undoubtedly been artificially aged.

As the antiques vocabulary evolved, the word contemporary guidebooks used to describe merchants like Gersaint, brocanteur, lost its status. At present, a big-ticket dealer is known as an *antiquaire,* while a brocanteur deals in merchandise closer to what in the seventeenth century was referred to as antiquailles, worthless used furniture. Of course, as reporter Jean Loret was trying to indicate in 1664 by speaking of "upscale antiquailles," in this domain high-end and low-end are constantly being redefined. Once you jumble together in the same context objects both old and new, goods that are authentic, fake, and artificially enhanced, all sorts of things can happen. For instance, one person's discarded junk will become the centerpiece of a chic living room. And that's the lesson that *Antiques Roadshow* continues to teach us every week. One period's worthless old furniture becomes the next generation's fine antiques—especially if the merchants at an antiques fair get their hands on it.

1 3

"The Most Sweetly Flowered King"

Perfume, Cosmetics, and la Toilette

Haute cuisine, haute couture, joaillerie, champagne—the roll call of sectors of the luxury economy in which, from the 1660s on, France has never ceased to play a defining role is long indeed. On the list of all the French-made luxuries that are now seen as indispensable complements to a stylish life, an obvious one has not yet been mentioned here: perfume. And yet few upmarket products are more closely associated with France than the tantalizing scents of fine perfume. "French perfume" was long a set phrase, used to refer to the magical, mysterious scents that, the phrase implied, only the French could produce, fragrances so seductive that they were guaranteed to make any woman more alluring and to add a touch of glamour to any occasion. And though the high end of the perfume industry is no longer as completely under French control as it once was, even today most still believe that only perfumes made in France possess that elusive je ne sais quoi that makes a scent truly magical. This is the story of how France nearly failed to understand perfume's importance to style and sophistication and almost missed out on an association with the perfume industry that has proved to be as enduring as it was lucrative. The story of French perfume begins during the reign of Louis XIV.

Throughout the Renaissance and until the early seventeenth century, Italy led the way in perfumery. All over Europe, the most powerful princes and the most stylish queens relied on Italian perfumers to initiate them into the art of sweet scents. Then in the 1660s and 1670s, there were indications that France was assuming supremacy over this sector of the luxury trade. Just as had happened shortly before in the world of fine cuisine, just as was happening at the same moment with the art of mirror making, as soon as the practice of perfumery began to open up to a broader audience, the French quickly became more visible than the Italians merchants who had formerly dominated the profession.

Seventeenth-century French perfumers sold a wide range of goods: the word "perfume" was then used to refer to any substance that emitted an appealing odor. When someone spoke of making or buying perfume, they could be thinking of anything from pastilles that gave off a sweet smell when they were burned, to potpourris, to aromatic powder or soap, to scented gloves. None of these goods was a seventeenth-century invention; all were already in use in the Renaissance. In the seventeenth century, however, modern methods were used for the first time to market scented goods. And when that happened, the French were there. For the first time, a series of influential books made available in print information on perfumery by professionals whose products were also available for purchase. There was, in addition, extensive coverage in newspapers and in contemporary guidebooks, always trumpeting the news that the finest practitioners of the arts of perfume and cosmetics, as well as the most magical beauty products and the most enticing fragrances, were all now to be found in Paris.

All these sources promoted a vision of Paris as the new world capital of stylish ways of making people and their environment smell good. From then on, sweet scents became both increasingly widely available and increasingly widely used. And when the market opened up, French merchants received a hefty share of the profits. By about 1680, to any observer of the world of high style, France must have seemed destined soon to become the exclusive center of the highly prized trade in fragrant goods.

One institution was key to the marketing of perfume: it was known all over Europe by its French name, *la toilette*. That phrase came into use about 1680 and was used to designate the process by which aristocrats prepared themselves every morning to face the world. The ritual was as complex as it was extended: it was necessary to set aside a full three hours for la toilette, according to one estimate (and the estimate was given for a *man's* toilette). Every step of the process—from coiffure to the preparation of the skin to the application of makeup to perfuming—required costly products sold by perfumers. And each and every one of those products was used as much or nearly as much by noblemen as by their female counterparts. The notion of a metrosexual was in full force in Louis XIV's Paris. All this meant, of course, that the beauty game was very big business indeed.

Aristocratic women, and sometimes noblemen as well, had always gone through elaborate beauty rituals. From the late 1660s to the early 1680s, however, the process changed in very basic ways. Change was brought about above all because of the availability for the first time ever of mirrors large enough to allow someone to perform a toilette on their own, without requiring the presence of a servant at every moment to be certain that all was in place. From then on, the person being groomed had greater control over the process. From that moment, many aristocrats began to stage la toilette as still another scene in their highly theatrical lives.

During the Versailles era, the time devoted to personal care was much like a small private party. One "frequented les toilettes," the Duc de Saint-Simon quipped, as though visiting a museum or attending a performance. The most stylish citizens of Versailles adored showing themselves off while they were in the process of being dressed, while they were being turned out. At the end of the 1670s, the desire on the part of French nobles for a casual look made the state of undress fashionable for the first time and launched boudoir fashion. Couturieres created the déshabillé and the déshabillé négligé. La toilette was the theater on which fashion queens could try out the most négligés of déshabillés. People gathered during a toilette: they talked business and politics; they gossiped and they flirted. And the burgeoning cosmetics and perfume industry thus acquired an enviable showcase for its goods. A fashion trendsetter could pass around to her friends the divine new cream that gave her skin a satiny glow; everyone could have a whiff of the seductive new scent that had just been made up for her.

The grooming ritual created trends just as the marketing of high fashion had invented the concepts of the fashion season and the accessory of the moment. I got there first; you'll want this, too—in a flash, the new cream became a must-have. The contemporary press helped the process along by featuring the earliest newspaper ads for cosmetics. In the August 13, 1667, issue of his newsletter, for example, Charles Robinet reported on a precursor of today's dermabrasion that, he claimed, was able to turn "prune skin" into "a complexion as fair as lilies and roses." Opponents of the new procedure had nicknamed those who had undergone it "les écorchées" (the skinned alive) since their faces at first looked so raw. Robinet advocated the new procedure and encouraged his readers to "rush off" to the cosmetologist's—"Just look for her shop sign." The popularity of la toilette thus had the capacity to generate increased revenue for French beauty professionals. It also created the desire for a stable setting in which to act out this moment of cosmetics theater.

La toilette's name is related to the growing contemporary tendency to carve out niche spaces within previously multipurpose rooms. Before the invention of the new French style, there were no dressing rooms and no dressing tables, for no space was devoted exclusively to grooming. The word toilette originally referred to the piece of fabric (*toile* = cloth; *toilette* = a little cloth) that was laid out on an ordinary table or chest so that all the accessories necessary for hair and facial care could be arranged upon it; nobles groomed wherever the toilette was spread out. And as long as personal care was spatially defined only by a piece of fabric, it failed to live up to its potential. Then, in 1682, Louis XIV moved his court to Versailles. The King's grooming ritual became one of the hottest tickets in town. The blueblood fashion plates who were living together under Versailles's gigantic roof outdid one another to make their toilettes the next most popular act. The golden age of la toilette had been launched. The ceremony known by the humble name of "the little cloth" quickly took on grandiose proportions.

By the century's final decades, people had come to believe that grooming deserved a place all its own. The *table de toilette* (dressing table) was invented, as was the dressing room, a space reserved for la toilette that opened off from a bedroom. Throughout Europe, the new dressing rooms were crammed to the gills with French luxury goods of all kinds. Remember the Comtesse de Mailly (Figure 3.5, page 73), the hayseed turned fashion queen, proudly positioned in front of that newly invented piece of furniture, a dressing table (covered with the requisite cloth, here in a luxe brocade), in the apartment at Versailles that she was constantly having redecorated, always at Louis XIV's expense? Well, the comtesse was a model for the type of conspicuous consumption that la toilette inspired: she's surrounded by mirrors, and perfume containers, and the jars that held *pommades,* or face creams.

And across the channel, French merchants had a powerful ally in the woman often known simply as Charles II's French mistress, Louise de Kéroualle, Duchess of Portsmouth. In his diary entry for October 4, 1683, gentleman scholar John Evelyn recounts a visit to the royal palace, Whitehall. Along with the king and his attendants, he attended the duchess's toilette. His account makes it clear that Louise de Kéroualle was one-upping the fashion queens back home. She had turned her dressing room into a showcase for luxury goods—and for French-born Louise de Kéroualle, true luxury goods could only be French.

By 1683, Evelyn tells us, she had already had her dressing room "pulled down and rebuilt" at least twice "to satisfy her prodigal and expensive pleasures"—and to keep up with the latest standards in toilette luxury. The version visited by Evelyn was a tribute to the interior decorating style then being promoted at the Foire Saint-Germain and by the original French antiques dealers. The room contained early examples of what the French were calling "lachinage" and what Evelyn refers to as "Japon cabinets and screens." There were trendy tables and clocks and silver objects galore.

And then, covering the walls, there was the pièce de résistance, a magnificent suite of Gobelins tapestries, straight from the royal manufactory that Louis had founded in 1662. "For design, tenderness of work," Evelyn pronounced, they were "beyond anything I had ever beheld." (And to think that today Dennis Kozlowski's $6,000 shower curtain is considered the most scandalous grooming-space expense possible.) The tapestries depicted "Versailles, St. Germans and other palaces of the French king." For Evelyn, who viewed the love of luxury as the darkness at the heart of Charles II's monarchy, the king's French mistress was doubly corrupt. Not only was she proud to show herself off surrounded by the most luxurious goods possible but she showed one and all that the standards for decorating to which she aspired were being set by the court at Versailles.

One element was missing from such a scene as we now conceive it: water. And with good reason—in the seventeenth century, water was not considered essential to la toilette. While washing one's hands and one's face was advised on a daily basis, bathing was an activity indulged in only very, very occasionally. In the late 1670s, Louis XIV had the first *cabinet des bains* (bathing cabinet) built at Versailles; it featured two marble bathtubs. There is, however, no evidence that he ever put it to much use. Prior to the late eighteenth century, Europeans—unlike the ancient Greeks and Romans, unlike their contemporaries in the Muslim world, in China, in Japan—considered bathing not an indulgence but a trial.

In seventeenth-century Paris, when one absolutely had to bathe, one put oneself in the hands of *les baigneurs*, the "bathers": that is, the barber-bathers who ran bathhouses. Some of these establishments were places of ill repute, where one could get cleaned up and indulge one's sexual preferences, allegedly in utmost secrecy. In the finest bathhouses, various services, rather like today's spa treatments, were available. There were perfumed baths and even depilatory baths.

For the seventeenth-century French, male and female alike, a perfectly smooth, hairless state rather than frequent bathing may have been the hallmark of cleanliness. In his 1691 dictionary, Antoine Furetière admonishes with an unusually moralizing tone that "les gens propres vont chez les baigneurs pour se faire dépiler" (clean people go to the bathers to have hair removed). Dr. Louis Guyon's *Cours de médecine* (Course in Medicine), first published in 1664 and frequently reedited till the end of the century, gives a good idea of the essential importance of hair removal and of all the places from which hair absolutely had to be removed.

The opening chapter of this popular medical advice book for a lay audience is devoted to illnesses concerning the head. Before he discussed migraines, before he turned to tooth-related problems, however, Dr. Guyon concentrated at length on a subject evidently of more burning concern in his day: "how to get rid of hair from places where it is indecent to have any." Some spots are predictable—facial hair in women, for example. But who knew that neither women nor men should have hair on their hands or on their chests, that this is "against nature's laws," "a deformity" that "spoils a person's beauty and health"? Now, those who want to be satiny smooth all over have such high-tech means as laser and ultrasound at their disposal. Seventeenth-century practitioners, however, were not exactly slouches: they used plasters, waxed strips, and depilatory creams and ointments containing ingredients ranging from turtles' blood to the urine of female dogs to quicklime.

The most famous bathing and depilatory establishment in Louis XIV's Paris was run by François Quentin, known to all as La Vienne. The King was so devoted to him that he appointed him first valet de chambre; La Vienne was living at Versailles when he died in 1710. In his tell-all memoirs, the seventeenth century's premier gossipmonger, the Duc de Saint-Simon, had, as usual, an indiscreet explanation for the King's great loyalty to his bather. "Du temps de ses amours" (that is, during the period before and after his marriage when the Sun King went through a prodigious quantity of mistresses), the King frequented La Vienne's bathhouse "to have himself bathed." And here's the zinger: the King, "who didn't have the capacity to lavish his favors upon every object of his desire, found at La Vienne's establishment the fortifiers necessary to make him more satisfied with himself." If Saint-Simon is to be believed, the Sun King, whose appetite for sex was as legendary as was his appetite for food, signed up for a rather particular spa service when he visited les baigneurs, the aphrodisiacs, or proto-Viagra, necessary to keep up his self-esteem and his reputation. (No contemporary perfumer's manual contains a formula for what Saint-Simon euphemistically terms *comfortatifs*, or comforters.)

Saint-Simon's naughty little anecdote makes it plain that for Louis XIV, bathing was intimately linked to womanizing. He bathed as a turn-on for a new woman; no one would have bothered to go to all that trouble for a wife. And after he was bathed and smooth, Saint-Simon concludes, he had the bathers cover him with sweet scents, "for no man ever loved fragrances as much as he did." The young King may have loved fragrance partly because he was so used to it. In a world where, on a daily basis, bathing played almost no role, where people limited their ablutions to their hands and faces, body odors were either allowed to flourish in peace or camouflaged with hefty doses of scents. Such a context naturally encouraged merchants to develop new ways of using scented goods.

Until the mid-sixteenth century, "perfume" referred exclusively to the fumes (not necessarily aromatic) given off when any substance was burned. It was at that point that "perfume" began to designate all the sweet-smelling goods, from soap to powder, that the French were beginning to use to disguise body odor. At the turn of the seventeenth century, those who made these fragrant wares were finally given the title *parfumeurs* (perfumers). In 1624, the makers of scented gloves won the right to be known as *gantiers-parfumeurs* (glove makers–perfumers). This was the earliest official recognition of French perfume professionals.

In March 1656, Louis XIV issued the letters patent that conferred legal status on the first guild licensed to make sweet scents, and the French fragrance industry was officially born. The King's desire to recognize the status of perfumers made good economic sense, for during the first half of the seventeenth century the French had become Europe's greatest consumers of aromatics, using and abusing essences and quintessences as never before. As usual, Louis XIV and Colbert did not look kindly upon a major drain of revenue from French coffers: they were determined to put France at the center of the perfume trade.

Under the direction of the French East Indies Company, plantings of aromatics were begun on the French islands in the Indian Ocean, Ile-de-France and Ile Bourbon (now Mauritius and Réunion). The quality of their production became legendary: perfume professionals still speak of patchouli Bourbon and oil of vetiver Bourbon. In 1673, Colbert's Ordinance of

Commerce, an attempt to regulate the luxury trades that he was so busily fostering, made the guild of glove maker–perfumers one of the six most powerful business societies, thus guaranteeing them tax-free access to foreign products such as those new aromatics from the Indian Ocean. Finally, Colbert chose the town of Grasse, in Provence, as a sort of capital for the production of fragrant substances. In the mid–sixteenth century, Grasse first rose to perfume prominence as a manufacturing center for what was long the sector's bestselling product, scented leather gloves. With Colbert's sponsorship, by the end of the seventeenth century, the Grasse region had assumed the role it still plays: it was producing oils from flowers such as jasmine, initially grown in Grasse in the sixteenth century, violet, orange blossom, and the highly fragrant tuberose, newly (1670) introduced into Europe from Mexico.

Under official patronage, the smells of France were transformed. In the early seventeenth century, perfumed goods made in France, like those made elsewhere in Europe, were dominated by scents produced by exotic animals: civet (the musky fluid secreted by a catlike mammal native to Africa and Asia), ambergris (a substance formed in the intestines of sperm whales), and the musk secreted by the male musk deer native to the mountains of central and northeast Asia. By the century's end, French fragrance makers increasingly favored indigenous aromatics such as lavender and orange blossom. Thus, at the same time as French chefs were breaking free from their dependence on foreign ingredients, French perfumers were also developing a Eurocentric national style.

In the second half of the seventeenth century, perfume merchants were setting up shop all over Paris. Nicolas de Blégny's insider's guides to Paris include all the trendiest establishments. Naturally enough, there was a cluster of shops near couture's nerve center, the rue Saint-Honoré. Each store featured specific scented products. The merchants near the Saint-Michel bridge specialized in fragrant powders and soaps. The perfumer Jobert on the rue

Croix-des-Petits-Champs was famous for his potpourris. The place to go for orange blossom water was "A l'Orangerie" on the rue de l'Arbre Sec near the Louvre. To avoid the middleman and get the finest flower oils (jasmine was the must-have scent), you looked for the merchants who brought them straight from Provence and set up a stand near the Louvre, around the corner from the Church of Saint-Germain-l'Auxerrois. Or you could go to Grasse itself and buy directly from the best-known wholesaler in France, Antoine Artaud. By the turn of the eighteenth century, another Artaud, Jean, had founded the new industry's first institution, a distillery that changed hands many times but remained in Grasse until 1996.

The century's most celebrated perfumer, Simon Barbe, did more than market fragrant goods and primary ingredients: he published the most complete early compendium of the art of perfumery. Barbe sold his products from his shop on the rue des Gravilliers; customers looked for the shop sign La Toison d'Or (The Golden Fleece). The publication of Barbe's *Le Parfumeur français* (The French Perfumer) in 1693 was surely intended to sound a rallying cry in the manner of *The French Cook* and *The French Pastry Chef*, to proclaim the existence of a French national tradition of perfumery. Also in the manner of those original modern cookbooks, *The French Perfumer* made its claim to fame through codification: "This art has been brought to its utmost perfection by the use of infallible rules."

In *The French Perfumer* and its follow-up, *The Royal Perfumer* (1699), Barbe taught readers many different ways of perfuming the body, first of all with fragrant soaps. (Colbert had recently raided the Italian soap industry; with the promise of higher wages, he had managed to lure enough workers to Provence to establish soap making there.) Barbe also instructed them in the art of perfuming fashion accessories: gloves, handkerchiefs, and even fans could be scented. He included numerous potpourri formulas and explained how to fashion small bags of potpourri that, when worn on one's person, were known as "sweet bags." For ladies, there were even little perfumed cushions to be tucked into their under-garments: they provided the additional benefit of a bit of uplift ("correcting imperfections," as one manual put it).

And then there were perfumed powders for hair and wigs, one of the most profitable sectors of the fragrance industry, so much so that, in 1689, the glove makers–perfumers added a third term to their guild's title: *poudriers* (powderers). This sector was a money-maker by virtue of the vast quantities of powder required—in this case, the powder did a double duty: it added another camouflag-ing, sweet smell, and at the same time, it tinted one's hair. (Women of the seventeenth century also used pastes or pomades for hair coloring.) Many women chose powders that added blond or red highlights to their hair.

By far the favorite hair color of the late seventeenth century, however, was the gray-white color familiar to us from countless portraits of European aristocrats. The fashion for silver hair created a dilemma for fashionistas: they had to choose between the trendy hair color and the fashion for wigs. Contemporary wig makers complained that it was virtually impossible to find high-quality gray hair, so silvery-white wigs were prohibitively expensive. Most women who wanted to go prematurely gray chose therefore to do so by turning to a silvery powder known as "argentine."

To achieve a flawless gray-white look, it was necessary to blan-ket the head with argentine. A perfumer-powderer threw an enor-mous quantity of powder up at the ceiling. Newly coiffed nobles then positioned themselves so that the falling cloud landed on their heads. (In the eighteenth century, powderers turned to huge puffs mounted on long sticks and even to bellows to help with the process.) To avoid repeating the ritual every day, women began sleeping with a new kind of coiffe, a white taffeta hair covering designed to "imprison" their hair and all that precious, sweet-scented silvery whiteness.

For readers today, the introduction to the world of perfume that Barbe offers is surprising: the method for using scents about which he speaks least is exactly what we now think using perfume means, that is, spraying or pouring a liquid fragrance onto the skin. But Barbe's books were not visionary volumes; they did not play for perfumery the role that *The French Cook* and *The French Pastry Chef* played for cookery or *The Art of Glassmaking* for mirror making. They did not announce a new age for fragrance technique. Perfume—unlike all the other sectors of the luxury trade, from champagne making to shoe making to café making—was not blessed in the golden decades of Louis XIV's reign with a marketing and technological genius to bring it into modernity. The well-heeled tourists who shopped late-seventeenth-century Paris never exclaimed that French perfumers were making them understand fragrance for the first time. Visitors simply had a wider choice of the same perfumed goods that they could have purchased a half century before. Perfume did not become modern in the final decades of the seventeenth century, and the fault should be laid at Louis XIV's feet. At some point in the 1670s, the Sun King began to go off perfume.

The Duc de Saint-Simon said that early in his reign, "no man had ever loved sweet smells as much as he did." Louis XIV was then known as "le roi le plus doux fleurant" (the most sweetly flowered King). The King's favorite perfumer, Martial, had so much influence with his royal client that he became an instant celebrity and the A-list scentmeister of the moment, whose doings were recorded in the press as though he were on an equal footing with the aristocrats who paid handsomely for his services. Molière quipped that when French aristocrats heard the name Martial, they thought automatically of the perfumer rather than the Latin poet. ("Martial makes poems? I thought he only made scented gloves.")

The first indications that all was not well in the land of sweet flowers date from the early 1670s. On August 19, 1671, the Marquise de Sévigné lamented that even a sheet of perfumed stationery made her daughter (one of the trendiest creatures imaginable) ill. In the June 1673 issue of the newspaper that served as a barometer of French style, *Le Mercure galant,* Donneau de Visé categorically informed his readership that "perfumes have lost all credit; their smell is so excessive that it gives a headache. People of quality now use only little bags filled with fragrant herbs, known as sachets à la royale." That name, "in the royal manner," proved that "people of quality" knew which way the wind was blowing. By the end of the century, it had only gone from bad to worse. In 1699, the *Satire nouvelle sur les rues* (New Satire on Street Life) pointed out that because so "many men are now subject to the vapors and can't abide the smell of flowers," entertaining in Paris had changed in a major way: hostesses with the mostest now made sure that there were no flowers in their homes.

All the noblemen who fainted at the sight of a rosebud, all the fashion queens who got migraines at the faintest whiff of perfume were simply doing what the ladies and gentlemen of the court did all through the Versailles era: they were following their monarch's lead. In 1692, when Gian-Paolo Marana composed his guide to Parisian high life, *Lettre d'un Sicilien* (Letter from a Sicilian), he was among the first to reveal why fragrance phobia had become de rigueur. In Paris, he warned, foreigners "enjoy pleasures that flatter all the senses, except that of smell. Since the King does not like fragrances, everyone is compelled to hate them. Ladies pretend to faint at the very sight of a flower." The "sweetly flowered King" was no more. Once again according to Saint-Simon, "in the end" of his reign, no man had ever "feared [fragrances] as much as he did."

We know a great deal about the ways in which the King's fear of perfume manifested itself because of the *Journal de la santé du roi* (Diary of the King's Health), an extraordinary blow-by-blow account of every single health-related "event" of the King's life from 1647 to 1711. Everything from enemas to tumors is noted, often in overly graphic detail. In early December 1705, the doctors made an eye-catching entry: each time that the King "had leafed through highly perfumed old papers, he had been seized by strong vapors accompanied by dizzy spells." A 1713 letter from the King's sister-in-law provides confirmation of the doctors' analysis and reveals the only remedy that had been discovered: if ever the King got wind of a perfume, "paper was immediately burned," and this put an end to his migraine. Looking back in 1715 at the end of Louis XIV's long reign, Saint-Simon noted that during its final decades the King had "suffered from headaches and vapors, . . . he couldn't stand any fragrance and everyone had to be careful never to wear any in case they had to go near him."

Saint-Simon blamed the King's migraines and his fainting spells on the perfume mania of his youth: "He had used fragrances to excess *du temps de ses amours*," in his heyday as a lover. During the golden age of the monarch's lovemaking, Saint-Simon explained, the young King had allowed the bather-perfumer La Vienne to cover him with scent before he took the "drugs" that allowed him to continue performing "to his satisfaction" for a dizzying succession of mistresses. Were the "highly perfumed old papers" that gave the aging sovereign migraines reminders of the exhausting loves of his youth? Were the King's vapors provoked by the memory of all the drugs and all the overexertion that had obliged him to turn to them?

Migraines and vapors are frequently dismissed as hysterical maladies. The Sun King's malady, however, had consequences for the French perfume industry that were all too real. Without official encouragement, the perfumers of Louis XIV's France failed to make the kinds of technical breakthroughs that their counterparts in other sectors of the luxury trade were accomplishing at the turn of the eighteenth century. As a result, the French almost lost control over the world of sweet scents: they were not the first to distill the highly concentrated alcohol necessary to make perfume in a modern way or to master the technique by which this highly concentrated alcohol was brought into contact with flowers. They thus fell behind in the race to invent the product around which the modern perfume industry took shape, fluids containing the essence of flowers or other sweet-smelling substances. What is now known as eau de cologne was invented by Gian Paolo Feminis, an Italian who immigrated to Germany and began to market his Aqua Admirabilis in Cologne in 1709. The modern perfume industry as a *German* idea? Just think of the blow to French national pride.

Rest assured, this unfortunate situation was quickly remedied. Under Louis XV, perfumes staged a comeback—with a vengeance. Soon Versailles was known as the perfumed court, "la cour parfumée." The last facet of the style ever since considered quintessentially French was finally in place. In 1759, new taxes on leather made scented gloves, the cash cow of the seventeenth-century French perfume industry, prohibitively expensive and sales plummeted. From this point on, French perfume makers were known, no longer as glove maker–perfumers or bather-perfumers, or powderer-perfumers, but simply as perfumers. At long last they began to focus their efforts on the production of bottles of sweet-scented fluids, perfume in the word's modern meaning.

The first perfume dynasty was founded by the Fargeon family in the early eighteenth century. Jean-Louis Fargeon was one of the royal family's favorite perfumers; he continued to supply the royal children with lavender water even when they were in prison during the Revolution of 1789. And in 1775, Jean-François Houbigant opened a boutique named A la Corbeille de Fleurs (The Flower Basket)—where else but in the rue Saint-Honoré? When the royal family tried to flee France in 1791, one of Marie-Antoinette's last gestures was to send her perfume flacons to Houbigant to have them refilled for the road. Houbigant is now the oldest continually operating perfume manufacturer in France. The Comité Colbert, a trade association for some seventy French firms, all at the highest end of the luxury trade, today counts among its members numerous Maisons de Parfum: the oldest of them, Guerlain, was founded in 1828.

Meanwhile, back in Cologne, Giovanni Maria Farina took over from his uncle in 1732; he presided over a vast expansion of the family business. The French firm Roger & Gallet acquired the Feminis-Farina concern in 1884. They have marketed the original eau de cologne—comfortably Gallicized as Eau Jean-Marie Farina—ever since. In similar fashion, Louis XIV's initial misstep has long since been repaired, and the perfume industry has been as thoroughly Gallicized as the original eau de cologne. By now, haute parfumerie seems just as characteristically French as haute couture or haute cuisine.

Remember those classic fragrances with wonderfully evocative names: Jolie Madame, or Soir de Paris, Evening in Paris? They held out the promise of all the elegance of the chic Parisienne, all the glamour and romance of Parisian nightlife, distilled and captured in a bottle, like a genie ready to pop out and work its magic. The look of Paris *and* the essence of style, all for sale in a little violet blue flacon. How would the modern perfume industry have marketed its mythical scents without the mystique of Paris to back them up?

CODA

"The Most Magnificent Party Possible"

Entertaining Versailles Style

Imagine a grand party staged at the Metropolitan Museum of Art. Luxe antique dealers have stands displaying a selection of their finest goods. New York City's most renowned chefs prepare their signature dishes in miniature versions of their restaurants, and Broadway divas then perform a number to invite hundreds of glamorously attired guests to step up and taste the cuisine. Throw in for good measure several million dollars' worth of jaw-dropping décor, and you begin to get an idea of the kinds of parties haut-monde notables were attending in Paris in January and February 1700.

* * *

For the carnival season of 1700, trendsetters were vying to come up with the most novel and the most stylish concepts for parties. In the words of the original society reporter, Jean Donneau de Visé, "the court had never had as much fun as at that moment." The King kicked off the festivities on January 7 with a ball on the theme of "le roi de la Chine" (the king of China). Versailles's pseudo-Chinese décor formed the perfect backdrop for a soirée during which an actor dressed as the emperor of China was paraded around on a covered litter and actors in Chinese costumes mingled with the guests.

Then the Duchesse de Bourgogne, whose marriage to the King's grandson had been lavishly celebrated only three years before, got into the act. On January 21, she threw a masked ball at which ladies costumed as goddesses and nymphs arrived in couture masterpieces, many of them in black velvet, considered the ideal fabric to set off elaborate designs in diamond-studded embroidery. (One masked guest pranced about with a hairdo so high that it was a showstopper, even in that age of big hair; the coiffure was topped with a pair of stag's antlers, which made for a creation so tall that it kept getting caught in chandeliers.) The next night, country came to Versailles, and the ladies who had been goddesses the evening before appeared garbed in a style that was pure Marie-Antoinette avant la lettre, as "elegant country wenches."

On January 27, the King was host once again. That evening, the Duchesse de Bourgogne actually managed to pull off two complete costume changes: she appeared first as the goddess Flora, then as a milkmaid, and finally as an old woman. (Since she was only fifteen at the time, this could have meant that she tried to look twenty-five.) The baby duchess was the era's Lady Di; she was adored by the aging King, who felt she brought a breath of fresh air to his court. She was clearly positioning herself on the cutting edge of the new French style and as the premier hostess of Versailles's millennial generation.

At the end of January, the duchess threw down the gauntlet to one of the few women both influential and stylish enough to rival her. She "asked Madame la Chancelière to give a ball in her honor." Marie de Maupeou was the wife of the newly appointed chancellor, the head of the French justice system and the most powerful man in France after the King. (Her husband, the Comte de Pontchartrain, was also Colbert's successor as finance minister; it was as if one man were Chief Justice William Rehnquist and Alan Greenspan combined.) The chancelloress decided to prove her mettle as the perfect political wife and agreed to hold the party in only eight days' time. This was an act of sheer hostess bravado.

To make her mark, Madame la Chancelière invented a soirée that rolled several different forms of entertainment into one. The result was so extraordinary that even one of the guests who was no fan of her husband, the Duc de Saint-Simon, pronounced it "the most stylish and magnificent party possible." Donneau de Visé lingered over every detail of her triumph, from its razzle-dazzle kickoff, in which guests entered the chancellor's official residence via a room "completely covered with mirrors and vast quantities of lights," to the play staged in the mansion's private theater. This was followed by the pièce de résistance, dinner theater and shopping theater Versailles style.

The guests left the formal theater and moved on to a room completely transformed for the occasion. It was as if they had entered a Hollywood film studio's miniaturization of the Foire Saint-Germain. In his account of the first great party of the new century, Saint-Simon stressed the experience of shopping theater, the chic boutiques re-created there and the lavish spread of lachinage, or Chineselike wares on display in the room: "There were Chinese shops, Japanese shops, and so forth, selling all manner of the most refined, beautiful, and unusual goods. And the shop-keepers would take no money: all the merchandise was presented as gifts to the Duchesse de Bourgogne and the other ladies." Party favors or goody bags indeed.

Then there was the evening's dinner theater component: five

of the kinds of stands at which fairgoers paused for refreshment while shopping the Foire Saint-Germain had been faithfully reconstructed. Each establishment was presided over by an actor playing the role of its owner, a purveyor of elegant food and drink. There was a pastry chef—a French pastry chef, but of course. There was a merchant newly arrived from Provence with a glorious assortment of citrus fruits. A *confiseur* (confectioner) presided over a luxe candy shop, filled with candied fruits, sugared nuts, caramels, and every sweet treat then known. The café was naturally manned by an actor dressed as an Armenian, while the *limonadier*, or soft drink merchant, had an Italian accent. He proposed the same array of cocktails, hard as well as soft, featured at the world's original chic café. In this case, the actor was playing the part of a real-life limonadier, the first celebrity on the Parisian café scene: above this shop hung a sign with PROCOPE spelled out in golden letters.

The décor was easily worthy of the lavish spread. The exotic treats were laid out on long gilded tables and were presented in containers made of crystal, silver, and vermeil. All these bright, shiny things were made brighter still by the lighting expertly planned by the chief designer for the Paris Opera, Jean Bérain. Chandeliers hung from each shop's ceiling. But the master's touch was most evident in the indirect lighting. The columns that separated the shops from one another also camouflaged several hundred candles positioned to create a shimmering interplay among the many glittery surfaces. A final hefty dose of sparkle was provided by the enormous mirrors, the biggest that that French royal mirror works could produce, that covered each shop's rear wall. The resulting scene was, according to Donneau de Visé's account, so bright that "your eyes could hardly bear the dazzling brilliance that came at you from all sides."

Next, the merchants (who were all members of the King's choral group) issued an invitation in song to the guests to come taste all that was on display in their gilded shops. That's how the Versailles glitterati learned that the grand set was Madame la

Chancelière's way of introducing the light meal, the *collation*, traditional at grand Parisian soirées. She made the collation, too, into
a shopping experience, for guests received their snacks in adorable
little ribbon-tied packages. After they had spent time on the set
grazing in the re-creation of places, such as Procope's café, that
they frequented in their daily lives, the ladies and gentlemen of
the court went on to the evening's final entertainment, a ball.
They literally danced the night away, leaving, as one of the last to
depart, Saint-Simon, reported, only when it was past eight the
next morning. (They didn't have to go far to get home, since the
chancellor's residence in Versailles was only a stone's throw from
the château.)

Needless to say, the evening sealed the Comtesse de Pontchartrain's reputation as a fabled hostess and a great political wife.
Who else but the spouse of Colbert's successor could have imagined turning a midnight snack into a Broadway-style extravaganza
that showcased French cafés, Paris's chic eateries, its pastry and its
bonbons, the royal mirror works, the capital's trendy shops and the
experience of shopping in luxurious surroundings, and the sparkly
nightlife in such settings for which Paris was now famous—with
the entire scene illuminated by a miniature version of the street
lighting that had made the first nighttime capital possible?

The many provincial and foreign readers of the period's equivalent of *The New York Times* or *The Washington Post,* Donneau de
Visé's *Le Mercure galant,* must have devoured the paper's extended
coverage of the glittering festivities that chased the February
gloom from the chancellor's mansion. Just like them, readers
today are avid for accounts of the latest celebrity wedding or the
most recent extravaganza staged at the Isabella Stewart Gardner
Museum in Boston or the Art Institute of Chicago. Because of the
theme that Madame la Chancelière had chosen for her glam soirée,
however, accounts of this party also read like an extended ad for
Paris, for the new French style, and for French luxury goods in
general. This high-concept entertainment absolutely cried out for
imitation. Come see the new kind of capital that Paris has become;

come shop and enjoy a coffee and the world's most delicious pastry in surroundings so stylish that they have to be seen to be believed. You'll be doing just what high society's darling, the Duchesse de Bourgogne, does. And if that isn't possible, then you can always bring Versailles to your city: invest all you can in French mirrors, French-made Chineselike goods, diamond-embroidered French gowns, and a French pastry chef.

Donneau de Visé ended his coverage by stressing that Madame la Chancelière "had received much praise because of her party." Louis XIV was undoubtedly one of those who commended her. The evening was, after all, a performance worthy of the man who had always turned his person into a living billboard for French couture and French joailliers and France's haute cobblers. The miniature Foire Saint-Germain laid on in February 1700 proved that thirty-five years of royal spending had paid off. By now, the Sun King's subjects were so well trained that they could participate actively and effectively in the marketing of France's new image. It was an interpretation of the duties of France's finance minister of which Colbert would have been proud.

It was also a display of elegance, glamour, and sophisticated style that would be the envy of any hostess today, proof that the standards for luxury living set during the Versailles era are still alive and well.

Acknowledgments

Some help is easy to acknowledge, so that's where I'll begin. I am grateful to the staffs of the many libraries and museums where I did research for this project. No collection proved more valuable than that of Paris's Arsenal Library, where several curators consistently went out of their way to help me solve problems. Sabine Coron provided invaluable assistance with culinary questions and late-seventeenth-century engravings. Paule Tourniac worked miracles with the library's cataloging system. In similar fashion, everyone on the sixth floor of the University of Pennsylvania's Van Pelt Library did all they could to make this project easier. Many thanks in particular to John Pollack for problem solving with a smile and to Greg Bear for photographic wizardry.

Nicole Hechberg of the Musée International de la Chaussure in Romans-sur-Isère answered many questions about the history of shoe making. Barbara Spadaccini-Day of Paris's Musée des Arts Décoratifs helped me track down information about subjects ranging from fashion dolls to the culinary arts. Annette Bordeau, the late Secrétaire Général of the Musée National de Monaco, was a rich source of information about the history of fashion dolls. Her successor, Béatrice Blanchy, continued Madame Bordeau's tradition of generosity to scholars. Mary Guyatt, curator of the Victoria and Albert's Designs and Images Department, set new standards for efficient and generous help to a scholar in distress. Fabienne Falluel and Annie Sagalow of the Musée de la Mode de la Ville de Paris gave me one of the great thrills of this project when they opened an umbrella made by Jean Marius for me. Beth Dincuff Charleston and Jessa Krick of the Metropolitan Museum of Art's

Costume Institute also gave me extraordinarily moving hands-on experience with fragile survivors from Louis XIV's reign. I am grateful to Colin Bailey, chief curator of the Frick Collection, for having made that experience possible. Gill Huggins of the Bath Museum of Costume and Bianca DuMortier of Amsterdam's Rijksmuseum helped me retrace the history of fashion dolls.

I bothered many friends and colleagues with questions and requests for information. A few, however, were bothered far more than should be allowed: Herb Blau, Ann Jones, Christian Jouhaud, and Peter Stallybrass dealt cheerfully with questions about everything from the most beautiful women in Renaissance Europe to the most significant fashion photographers of the 1990s. Judd Hubert generously arranged for a photocopy of a rare book from his collection. Thanks for help with fact checking are owed to Roger Chartier, Robert Descimon, Joe Farrell, Burt Malkiel, and Babette Momesso, as well as to Didier Bondue at Saint-Gobain. JoAnne Dubil helped me think about all manner of questions.

I am grateful to those who read early versions of parts of this study and helped me along with their reactions and questions: Lance and Mary Donaldson-Evans, Gwen Edelman, Ursula Hobson, Maria Menocal, Jerry Singerman. No friend—and here begins the category of help so overwhelmingly generous that it's hard to imagine how it could be adequately acknowledged—no friend was a more careful or a more demanding reader than Alan Chimacoff. Others might let things slip by, but Alan would confront me with questions like "You don't know how x is made, do you?" And when I admitted that I wasn't entirely sure, he would pile books on a long table and sit me down for what I thought of as culinary boot camp. And then he read my revised pages to make sure I'd gotten it straight. To Alan also go thanks for the inordinate amount of time and attention he devoted to my photographic woes. Ava Margaret Calhoun and Alain Damlamian also got out their cameras and worked for that cause. Peter Gaffney worked miracles with digital images. June Hines makes it possible for me to go on writing. And no one can top Fannie Lucile Genin, David

Hult, Joan Girgus, Ralph and Ellen Rosen, Jeanne Damlamian, and Ron Sribnik for unflagging support.

Cary Hollinshead-Strick and Martin Pokorny were the perfect research assistants. I can't imagine that research assistants are often confronted with so many bizarre requests; both of them always tried to crack the codes, all the while acting as if it were perfectly normal to be asked one day to look into the cost of living in New York City today and the next to try to verify a claim about the invention of waterproofing. I am grateful to Fred Hills for believing in this book early on and for shepherding it through the publication process. Isolde Sauer was both constantly reassuring and always watchful. My thanks to Dana Sloan for her careful handling of the book's design. Dean Sam Preston and the University of Pennsylvania made it possible for me to complete the research for this project.

Maria Menocal, a good friend as always, began the chain of events that shaped this book when she introduced me to Alice Martell. Right from the start, Alice was a miracle worker. To begin with, she helped me redefine my project on the invention of luxury. She also knew how to get the most out of me, just how to make an argument clear, and even the right word I'd spent hours searching for and never managed to find. Alice was both the most attentive and the most demanding reader I have ever encountered. No one could have been more enthusiastically committed to this book. And no one could have been more fun to work with.

Sources and Bibliography

Since it's not always possible to indicate one's sources clearly in a book written without footnotes, what follows is a brief guide to the seventeenth-century works on which this study of the luxury trade is based.

I found that of all the material published during Louis XIV's reign, the following kinds of works were most likely to include information on the topics of interest to me here: seventeenth-century newspapers, newsletters, and gazettes; late-seventeenth- and early-eighteenth-century guidebooks to Paris; accounts of their travels to France left by voyagers of the period; late-seventeenth- and early-eighteenth-century French comedies; and contemporary correspondences and memoirs. The authors of these types of works tried in various ways to identify what was changing at the period; they were unusually sensitive to objects and developments that were seen as new and important by Louis XIV's subjects. Accounts by foreign visitors to Paris are invaluable sources of information on the kinds of merchandise and experiences that did not yet exist in other countries and that were thus seen at the time as French inventions.

Newspapers and gazettes are essential to understanding how the new French style came to be and how it was able quickly to establish market dominance. Prior to Louis XIV's reign, very little news circulated publicly in France. Prior to the 1650s, much of the coverage that did exist circulated only in manuscript. During the years between 1652 and 1672, the French press underwent a period of significant expansion. Newsletters that had initially circulated in manuscript began to be printed; more journalists began to publish their accounts of contemporary events. Once this happened, news began to circulate far more rapidly than when it was handed about essentially by word of mouth; new ideas could spread virtually instantly over the country. The French press developed when it did because the French language was then taking on the role of international lingua franca that English plays today; the French-language press circulated all over Europe and brought news of changes in French fashion to a wide readership.

From the start, the early French journalists emphasized far more than their counterparts in other European countries what is now called style reporting: the press actively reported on all aspects of the new style being created and marketed in France; French journalists were at least as likely to include a description of a banquet as an account of a battle. Newspapers were in effect selling French fashions in food, dress, interior decoration, and so forth. The early newsletters and gazettes published by Edme Boursault, La Gravette de Mayolas, Jean Loret, and Charles Robinet show how style was shaped in the late 1650s and in the 1660s. Then, from 1672 to the end of Louis XIV's reign, one of the most remarkable of all early newspapers, Jean Donneau de Visé's *Le Mercure galant*, not only provided far more detailed coverage of Parisian styles than ever before but also helped aggressively to market those styles and to shape fashion. Every month, Donneau de Visé published several hundred pages that are a mine of information on almost all the topics discussed in this book. Finally, for the last years of Louis XIV's reign, Addison and Steele's *Spectator* helps pinpoint fashions and inventions that the English saw as quintessentially French.

The accounts of foreign voyagers to France also play this role. The journals composed by John Evelyn, Martin Lister, and John Locke, as well as the letters written during her Parisian sojourn by Lady Mary Wortley Montagu, show us all that a visitor determined to take in what was thought to be most remarkable about France would try to see and try to purchase. Evelyn's diary during the years he lived in London is informative about the French goods most desired by English consumers, as is that of Samuel Pepys. Gian-Paolo Marana's book-length *Letter About Paris by a Sicilian to One of His Friends,* composed in 1692 and published in 1700 in Italian and then translated into several languages, is directly related to the guidebooks about Paris that were appearing at the time: Marana explains how Paris was different from other European capitals and tells foreign visitors about must-see sights and experiences.

The period from the late 1670s to the early eighteenth century was the first golden age of guidebooks to the city of Paris. (After this, the genre went into steep decline until well into the nineteenth century.) The volumes by François Colletet (1676, 1677) and Germain Brice (1684) and Claude Saugrain's 1716 guide to the city's monuments are an excellent introduction to the ways in which the cityscape of Paris was reshaped during Louis XIV's reign. Joachim Christoph Nemeitz's guide, first published in German in 1718 and translated into French in 1727, set out to give young foreigners planning a trip to Paris the kind of practical information any tourist requires: where to stay and where to eat, where to shop and what to buy. Nemeitz's guide and the volumes their authors call "address books" (Saugrain in 1708 and, above all, Nicolas de Blégny in 1691 and 1692) are the most detailed sources of information on the functioning of luxury commerce in Paris. Blégny's volumes list the best-known purveyors of everything from toilet water to jewelry and pastry; he explains what's different about each cobbler's production; he tells how to find merchants and what their goods cost. Taken together, these guides give a sense of the commercial vibrancy of Louis XIV's Paris and of the manner in which luxury shopping was mapping itself on the city.

Memoirs—in particular the Duc de Saint-Simon's inimitable insider's view of the Sun King's court, but also the less flamboyant account left by the Marquis de Dangeau—and correspondences (the Marquise de Sévigné gives information on virtually every subject discussed in these pages; the Princesse Palatine is always attuned to what she saw as the strange goings-on of the French court) testify to the presence of luxury goods in the daily lives of the elite consumers who kept the Parisian shopping scene going. They also reveal the ways in which new inventions and institutions changed the lives of Parisians.

I describe a number of seventeenth-century paintings without reproducing them. The reason for this is simple: the details that interest me don't come across in black-and-white. However, when they are seen in living color, the portraits of several of the outstanding artists of the final decades of Louis XIV's reign, in particular those of Nicolas de Largillierre, have a great deal to teach us about the look of luxury then favored at the French and English courts.

By far the most detailed evidence of the ways in which new luxury goods and new styles changed the look of the French court is provided by the *gravures de mode*, fashion plates, that were produced by the thousands at the turn of the eighteenth century. (Some fashion plates, such as the depiction of the Comtesse d'Olonne that I discuss in chapters 2 and 4, were hand-tinted. These are not reproduced since the important details can't be appreciated in black-and-white.) Like newspapers, fashion plates were all about advertising: they were intended to show off the latest styles available in Paris. These engravings are immensely informative about how garments one can read about and sometimes even see preserved in the collections of fashion museums were actually intended to be worn. They also show how a trendy Parisienne of the late seventeenth century could put together the various components that made up a high-fashion outfit. Fashion plates are thus indispensable "reading" for anyone interested in this brief but crucial period in the history of fashion. In addition to clothes, they show off at the same time many other new things as well: newly fashionable foods and beverages, trendy new styles in home furnishing and interior decoration, and even new words. In the captions to fashion plates, words are sometimes used a decade or so before dictionaries attest to their official acceptance into the French language.

The invention of a new object or concept is always accompanied by the creation of a new word to designate it. We know that the invention has won acceptance when the word created to describe it is recorded in a dictionary. Happily, a golden age for French lexicography took place during the final decades of the seventeenth century, when three of the greatest French dictionaries of all time were published, by Pierre Richelet (1680), Antoine Furetière (1690), and the Académie Française (1694). The three dictionaries were reedited, sometimes several times, in the course of the eighteenth century. It is therefore possible to trace, for example, the growing presence of champagne on the French scene by noting when the verbs such as *mousser* used to describe its foaming and fizzing properties began to be used to speak of the new type of wine.

All over Europe in the late seventeenth century, French was the universal language of style. When Europeans spoke about luxury goods and high fashion in particular, they used the French words that had been created to designate them, often long after their native languages had invented their own words to refer to the trendy objects. Works published outside of France—the 1690 *Fop Dictionary, an Alphabetical Catalogue of the Hard or Foreign Names and Terms of the Art Cosmetick* (apparently composed by John Evelyn's daughter Mary) is a perfect example—can thus provide as much information about the impact of new styles on the French language as a work published in French.

The publication in France during Louis XIV's reign of treatises on subjects ranging from the making of champagne to the making of mirrors is perhaps the most convincing proof that the Sun King's subjects saw their country as having invented (or at the very least as having reinvented) the wheel in all these fields. In almost every area discussed in this book, at least one significant seventeenth-century publication attempted to present the advances being made in France to a general audience. I often found these works to be the surest guide both to understanding what was truly innovative about seventeenth-century developments in the field and to identifying the contributions that were seen at the time as quintessentially French.

I relied whenever possible on advertising material from the seventeenth century to see how each invention was presented to its original public. Not much of this ephemeral, fragile material has come down to us. Amazingly, a few of the earliest posters, the broadsheets intended to be posted on the walls of seventeenth-century Parisian buildings, have been preserved. The kind of information found, for example, in the announcement of the original system of street lighting would never otherwise be recoverable.

Finally, the compilations produced in the late nineteenth century by several French historians—notably Henry d'Allemagne, Henry Havard, and Jules Quicherat—are indispensable guides to seventeenth-century French styles in fashion and interior decoration. These works proved immensely valuable for more than one chapter of this study, even though I cite them only once in the bibliography that follows. One name, that of Alfred Franklin, could have appeared in the bibliography of almost every chapter. The twenty-three volumes of his *La Vie privée d'autrefois* (Private Life in the Past, 1887–1901) pack an astonishing amount of information into a compact format.

I include whenever possible tracking information such as dates of letters or journal entries. All quotations are taken from either the modern edition considered definitive or, when no standard modern edition exists, from the first edition. In cases when a reliable seventeenth-century English translation exists, I quote from it; otherwise, all translations are my own.

Here is a list of the works that proved most valuable for individual chapters.

Introduction

Bernard, Leon. *The Emerging City: Paris in the Age of Louis XIV.* Durham, N.C.: Duke University Press, 1970.

Chung, C. J., J. Inaba, R. Koolhaas, S. Leong, eds. *The Harvard Design School Guide to Shopping.* Köln and London: Taschen, 2001.

Fauconnet, François, ed. *Les Boutiques à Paris.* Paris: Editions du Pavillon de l'Arsenal, 1997.

Hunter-Stiebel, Penelope, and Odile Nouvel-Kammerer. *Matières de rêves/Stuff of Dreams.* Portland Art Museum, 2002.

Payless Shoes. Barkley Evergreen and Associates.

Postrel, Virginia. *The Substance of Style: How the Rise of Aesthetic Value Is Remaking Commerce, Culture, and Consciousness.* New York: Harper-Collins, 2003.

Roche, Daniel, et al. *La Ville promise: mobilité et accueil à Paris (fin XVIIe–début XIXe siècle).* Paris: Fayard, 2000.

Voltaire [François-Marie Arouet]. *The Age of Louis XIV.* Trans. Martyn Pollack. New York: Dutton, 1966.

Chapter 1

Boucher [first name unknown]. *Champagne le Coiffeur.* In *Les Contemporains de Molière,* ed. Victor Fournel. Vol. 3. Paris, 1863–65.

Lebas, Catherine, and Annie Jacques, eds. *La Coiffure en France du Moyen Age à nos jours.* Paris: Delmas International, 1979.

Tallemant des Réaux, Gédéon. *Historiettes.* Ed. Antoine Adam. 2 vols. Paris: Gallimard, 1961.

Thiers, Abbé Jean-Baptiste. *Histoire des perruques.* Avignon: Louis Chambeau, 1689.

Chapters 2 and 3

Allemagne, Henry d'. *Les Accessoires du costume et du mobilier depuis le treizième siècle jusqu'au milieu du dix-neuvième siècle.* 3 vols. Paris: Schemit, 1928.

Arnold, Janet. *A Handbook of Costume.* London: Macmillan, 1973.

Crowston, Clare. *Fabricating Women: The Seamstresses of Old Regime France, 1675–1791.* Durham and London: Duke University Press, 2001.

Delpierre, Madeleine, ed. *La Mode et les poupées du XVIIIe siècle à nos jours.* Paris: Musée de la Mode et du Costume/Palais Galliéra, 1981.

Grivel, Marianne. *Le Commerce de l'estampe à Paris au dix-septième siècle.* Geneva: Droz, 1986.

Quicherat, Jules. *Histoire du costume en France depuis les temps les plus reculés jusqu'à la fin du dix-huitième siècle.* Paris: Hachette, 1875.

Roche, Daniel. *The Culture of Clothing: Dress and Fashion in the Ancien Régime.* Trans. Jean Birrell. Cambridge: Cambridge University Press, 1994.

Weigert, Roger-Armand. *Bonnart: Personnages de qualité.* Paris: Editions Rombaldi, 1956.

Chapter 4

Lacroix, Paul, Alphonse Duchesne, and Ferdinand Seré. *Histoire des cordonniers et des artisans dont la profession se rattache à la cordonnerie.* Paris: Librairies Historique, Archéologique et Scientifique de Seré, 1852.

McDowell, Colin. *Shoes: Fashion and Fantasy.* London: Thames and Hudson, 1989.

Sejourné, Jean, ed. *Le Présent des bottes sans coûture fait au roi par le sieur Nicolas Lestage, Maître Cordonnier de sa Majesté.* Bordeaux: Jean Sejourné, 1666.

Swan, June. *Shoes.* London: B. T. Batsford, 1982.

Wilson, Eunice. *A History of Shoe Fashions.* London: Pitman Publishing, 1969.

Chapter 5

Coron, Sabine, et al., eds. *Livres en bouche: Cinq siècles d'art culinaire français.* Paris: Bibliothèque Nationale de France/Hermann, 2001.

Flandrin, Jean-Louis, and Massimo Montanari, eds. *Histoire de l'alimentation.* Paris: Fayard, 1996.

Michel, Dominique. *Vatel et la naissance de la gastronomie.* Paris: Fayard, 2000.

Peterson, T. Sarah. *Acquired Taste: The French Origins of Modern Cooking.* Ithaca and London: Cornell University Press, 1994.

Sabban, Françoise, and Silvano Serventi. *La Gastronomie au Grand Siècle.* Paris: Stock, 1998.

Wheaton, Barbara. *Savoring the Past: The French Kitchen and Table from 1300 to 1789.* Philadelphia: University of Pennsylvania Press, 1983.

Chapter 6

Bologne, J.-C. *Histoire des cafés et des cafetiers.* Paris: Larousse, 1993.

La Roque, Jean de. *Voyage de l'Arabie heureuse.* Appendix: "Traité de l'origine et du progrès du café." Paris: André Cailleau, 1716.

Leclant, Jean. "Le Café et les cafés à Paris (1644–1693)." *Annales: Economie. Société. Civilisation* 6 (January-March 1951): 1–14.

Weinberg, Bennett Alan, and Bonnie K. Bealer. *The World of Caffeine: The Science and Culture of the World's Most Popular Drug.* New York and London: Routledge, 2001.

Chapter 7

Bonal, François. "Les Débuts du Champagne." In *Vins de Champagne et d'ailleurs*. (Médiathèque d'Epernay). Paris: Direction du Livre et de la Lecture, 2000: 17–22.

Gandilhon, René. *Naissance du champagne: Dom Pierre Pérignon*. Paris: Hachette, 1968.

Godinot, Jean. *Manière de cultiver la vigne et de faire le vin en Champagne*. 1718. Ed. F. Bonal. Langres: D. Guéniot, 1990.

Manceaux, Jean-Baptiste. *Histoire de l'Abbaye et du village d'Hautvillers*. 3 vols. Epernay: L. Doublat, 1880.

Chapter 8

Balfour, Ian. *Famous Diamonds*. London: Christie, Manson and Woods, 2000.

Landman, Neil, Paula Mikkelsen, Rüdiger Bieler, and Bennet Bronson. *Pearls: A Natural History*. New York: Harry Abrams, 2001.

Morel, Bernard. *Les Joyaux de la Couronne de France*. Paris: Albin Michel, 1988.

A Sparkling Age: 17th-Century Diamond Jewellery. Antwerpen: Diamantmuseum, 1993.

Tavernier, Jean-Baptiste. *Les Six Voyages*. 3 vols. Paris: Gervais Clouzier, 1676–1679.

Chapter 9

Frémy, Elphège. *Histoire de la manufacture royale des glaces de France au XVIIe et au XVIIIe siècle*. Paris: Plon-Nourrit et Cie, 1909.

Hamon, Maurice, and Dominique Perrin. *Au Coeur du XVIIIe siècle industriel: Condition ouvrière et tradition villageoise à Saint-Gobain*. Paris: Editions P.A.U., 1993.

Haudicquer de Blancourt, M. *L'Art de la verrerie, où l'on apprend à faire le verre, le cristal, . . . et les miroirs*. Paris: Claude Jombert, 1718.

Havard, Henry. *Dictionnaire de l'ameublement*. 5 vols. Paris: Librairies-Imprimeurs Réunis, 1894.

Pris, Claude. *La Manufacture royale des glaces de Saint-Gobain: Une grande entreprise sous l'ancien régime*. 3 vols. Lille: Service de Reproduction des Thèses de l'Université de Lille III, 1975.

Chapter 10

Defrance, Eugène. *Histoire de l'éclairage des rues de Paris.* Paris: Imprimerie Nationale, 1904.

Fournier, Edouard. *Les Lanternes.* Paris: Dentu, 1854.

Herlaut, Commandant. "L'Eclairage des rues à Paris." In *Mémoires de la société de l'histoire de Paris et de l'Ile de France,* vol. 43, pp. 129–265. Paris: Honoré Champion, 1916.

Schivelbusch, Wolfgang. *Disenchanted Night: The Industrialization of Light in the Nineteenth Century.* Trans. Angela Davies. Berkeley and London: University of California Press, 1988.

Chapter 11

Crawford, T. S. *A History of the Umbrella.* New York: Taplinger Publishing, 1970.

Fairchilds, Cissie. "The Production and Marketing of Populuxe Goods in Eighteenth-Century Paris." In *Consumption and the World of Goods.* Eds. John Brewer and Roy Porter. London and New York: Routledge, 1993.

Farrell, Jeremy. *Umbrellas and Parasols.* New York: Drama Book Publishers, 1985.

Leloir, Maurice. "Les Accessoires de costume: Parasols et parapluies." *Bulletin de la société de l'histoire du costume,* no. 5 (October 1908): 103–11; no. 6 (January 1909): 129–37.

Chapter 12

Bonnaffé, Edmond. *Le Commerce de la curiosité.* Paris: Champion, 1895.

Dancourt, Florent. *La Foire Saint-Germain.* Paris: T. Guillain, 1696.

Fromageot, Paul. "La Foire Saint-Germain." *Bulletin de la société historique du VIe arrondissement de Paris* IV (1901): 185–248.

Regnard, Jean-François, and Charles Dufresny. *La Foire Saint-Germain.* Grenoble, 1696.

Walford, Edward. *Frost Fairs on the Thames.* London: Wyman, 1882.

Chapter 13

Barbe, Simon. *Le Parfumeur français.* Lyons: Thomas Amaulry, 1693.

———. *Le Parfumeur royal.* Paris: Simon Augustin Brunet, 1699.

Eamon, William. *Science and the Secrets of Nature: Books of Secrets in Medieval and Early Modern Culture.* Princeton: Princeton University Press, 1994.

Le Roi, J.-A., ed. *Journal de la santé du roi Louis XIV de l'année 1647 à l'année 1711 écrit par Vallot, d'Aquin et Fagon, tous trois ses premiers médecins.* Paris: A. Durand, 1862.

Meurdrac, Marie. *La Chymie charitable et facile en faveur des dames.* 1666. Paris: CNRS, 1999.

Morris, Edwin T. *Fragrance: The Story of Perfume from Cleopatra to Chanel.* New York: Charles Scribner's Sons, 1984.

Illustration Credits

Frontispiece

Nicolas Arnoult. *Monsieur et Madame de Bourgogne au rafreschissement des liqueurs*. Engraving by Nicolas Bonnart. Private collection.

Introduction

Figure I: Drawing by Jean Bérain. Engraving by Jean Le Pautre. *Le Mercure galant,* extraordinaire, January 1678. Photograph by Patrick Lorette for Joan DeJean.

Chapter 1

Figure 1.1: *La Coiffeuse.* Engraving by Chiquet, c. 1690. Private collection.

Chapter 2

Figure 2.1: *Femme de qualité en stenkerke et falbala.* Engraving by Jean Dieu de Saint-Jean, 1693. Musée Carnavalet. PMVP. Photograph: Joffre.

Figure 2.2: *Habit d'Hyver.* Drawing by Jean Bérain. Engraving by Jean Le Pautre. *Le Mercure galant,* extraordinaire, January 1678. Photograph by Patrick Lorette for Joan DeJean.

Figure 2.3: *Habit d'Esté.* Drawing by Jean Bérain. Engraving by Jean Le Pautre. *Le Mercure galant,* extraordinaire, April 1678. Photograph by Patrick Lorette for Joan DeJean.

Chapter 3

Figure 3.1: Fashion doll, c. 1760, 66 cm. Copyright: Rijksmuseum, Amsterdam.

Figure 3.2: Fashion doll, late seventeenth century or early eighteenth century, 35 cm. Musée National de Monaco. Collection Galéa. Photograph: J. L. Ravoire.

Figure 3.3: Fashion doll in eighteenth-century outfit. Musée National de Monaco. Collection Galéa. Photograph: J. L. Ravoire.

Figure 3.4: *Dame de qualité sur un canapé lisant le Mercure galant en avril 1688.* Engraving by François Gérard Jollain. Private collection.

Figure 3.5: *Madame la Comtesse de Mailly.* Engraving by Claude-Auguste Berey. Bibliothèque de l'Arsenal. Photograph: Bibliothèque Nationale de France.

Figure 3.6: *Monsieur le Chevalier Jean Bart.* Engraving by Jean Mariette, 1696. Private Collection.

Figure 3.7: *Femme de qualité en deshabillé negligé.* Engraving by Jean Dieu de Saint-Jean, 1693. Musée Carnavalet. PMVP. Photograph: Degraces.

Chapter 4

Figure 4.1: *Louis XIV, roi de France.* Hyacinthe Rigaud, 1701. ClipArt.

Figure 4.2: French mule, c. 1740. Musée International de la Chaussure, Romans-sur-Isère, France. Photograph: Christophe Villard.

Figure 4.3: Detail from *Le Diné du Roy à l'Hôtel de Ville de Paris.* Engraving by Nicolas Langlois. Almanac for 1687. Private collection.

Figure 4.4: *The Swing.* Jean-Honoré Fragonard, c. 1766. ClipArt.

Chapter 5

Figure 5.1: *La Manière de ramolir les os et de faire cuire toutes sortes de viande en fort peu de temps.* Denis Papin. Paris: Etienne Michallet, 1683. Private collection.

Figure 5.2: *Plan du service de viande d'une des deux tables du Roy qui sera servie à Marly lorsque sa Majesté ira demeurer, arresté par Elle le 24 septembre 1699.* Drawing. Private collection.

Figure 5.3: *Le Diné du Roy à l'Hôtel de Ville de Paris.* Engraving by Nicolas Langlois. Almanac for 1687. Private collection.

Chapter 6

Figure 6.1: *Entretiens sur les cafés.* Louis de Mailly. Frontispiece. Trévoux: Etienne Ganeau, 1702. Bibliothèque Historique de la Ville de Paris. Photograph: Gérard Leyris.

Figure 6.2: *Un Cavalier et une dame.* Engraving by Nicolas Bonnart. Private collection.

Chapter 8

Figure 8.1: *Louis le Grand, roi de France.* Engraving by Claude-Auguste Berey. Photograph by Patrick Lorette for Joan DeJean.

Chapter 9

Figure 9.1: Engraving by Nicolas de Larmessin. Almanac for 1687. Musée Carnavalet. PMVP. Photograph: Ladet.

Figure 9.2: *Femme de Qualité en deshabillé.* Engraving by Jean Dieu de Saint-Jean, 1690. Musée Carnavalet. PMVP. Photograph: Degraces.

Figure 9.3: *Dame en habit de ville.* Engraving by Jean Dieu de Saint-Jean. Musée Carnavalet. PMVP. Photograph: Joffre.

Chapter 10

Figure 10.1: *La Sonnette a sonné: Abaisse la lanterne.* Engraving by Nicolas Guérard, fils. Musée Carnavalet. PMVP. Photograph: Habouzit.

Chapter 11

Figure 11.1: Folding umbrella. Jean Marius, c. 1709. Musée Galliéra. PMVP. Photograph: Ladet.

Figure 11.2: Diagram of the folding umbrella's construction. Engraving. In *Machines et inventions approuvées par l'Académie Royale des Sciences.* Tome second, *1702–1712.* Paris: Gabriel Martin, Jean-Baptiste Coignard, fils, and Hippolyte-Louis Guérin, 1735. Photograph by Patrick Lorette for Joan DeJean.

Figure 11.3: Poster advertising Jean Marius's umbrella, June 1715. In Henry d'Allemagne, *Les Accessoires du costume.* Bibliothèque Historique de la Ville de Paris. Photograph: Gérard Leyris.

Chapter 12

Figure 12.1: *Plan de la Foire Saint-Germain.* Late-seventeenth-century engraving. Photograph: Bibliothèque Nationale de France.

Figure 12.2: *La Foire Saint-Germain.* Jean-François Regnard and Charles Dufresnoy. Frontispiece. In *Le Théâtre italien de Gherardi.* Amsterdam: M. Charles, 1721. Bibliothèque Historique de la Ville de Paris. Photograph: Gérard Leyris.

Index

About the Author

JOAN DEJEAN received her Ph.D. from Yale University, has taught at Yale and Princeton, and is currently Trustee Professor of French at the University of Pennsylvania. She is the author of seven books and some seventy articles on seventeenth- and eighteenth-century French literature and culture. She has received fellowships from the Guggenheim Foundation and the National Endowment for the Humanities. She divides her time between Philadelphia and Paris, where she lives in the most fashionable neighborhood of seventeenth-century Paris, the Marais.